Doing Tropology

Doing Tropology

Analysis of Narrative Discourse

James M. Mellard

UNIVERSITY OF ILLINOIS PRESS
Urbana and Chicago

This book is printed on acid-free paper.

Library of Congress Cataloging-in-Publication Data

Mellard, James M.
  Doing tropology.

  Includes index.
  1. Discourse analysis, Narrative. 2. Figures of
speech. 3. Languages—Philosophy. 4. American fiction
—History and criticism. I. Title.
P302.7.M45 1987   808.3   86-11370
ISBN 0-252-01356-5 (alk. paper)

Contents

Preface

━━━━━━━━

A book is not shut in by its contours, is not walled-up as in a fortress. It asks nothing better than to exist outside itself, or to let you exist in it. In short, the extraordinary fact in the case of a book is the falling away of the barriers between you and it. You are inside it; it is inside you; there is no longer either outside or inside.
　　　　　　　　　　—Georges Poulet, "Phenomenology of Reading"

Doing Tropology is meant primarily to be an introduction to "tropology"—the theory and application of tropes—for the scholar of literature who is interested in such disciplines as rhetoric, narratology, psychoanalysis, philosophy, and philosophy of language, as well as the specific narratives and authors I take up. Though the dominant theory I have employed here is that of Hayden V. White, the tropology underlying the psychoanalysis of Jacques Lacan is also included and related to the (I think) broader, tetradic theory of White and his precursors, Kenneth Burke and Giambattista Vico. In addition, *Doing Tropology* attempts to locate tropology in a discipline that in itself is more comprehensive than tropology and capable therefore of giving it an extrinsic grounding. By placing tropic theory within the discipline of philosophy and, there, within the framework of a phenomenology of language, this study attempts to avoid a merely tautological validation of theories of tropes. Though the study is not phenomenological itself, a phenomenological notion of language validates tropology in ways different from those validations that have been attempted through, for example, philology, cultural history, psychoanalytic theory, and Kantian philosophy.

　　The aim of *Doing Tropology*, in a sense, is to domesticate tropological analysis by making it more readily available to scholars of British and American literature. Scholarship on tropology, including both theory and application of theory, has heretofore been concentrated primarily in disciplines outside literature (history; psychoanalysis) and, when in literary analysis, concentrated in literatures other than Anglo-American, particularly the French. I feel that an important subsidiary contribution of *Doing Tropology*, therefore, is the application of a theory of tropes to the reading of familiar texts of American literature; those I have chosen, besides work by Hayden White, are Henry Adams's *The Education of Henry Adams*, William Faulkner's *Absalom, Absalom!*, John Updike's *The Centaur*, and Joseph Heller's *Something Happened*. My hope here is to make illustration of the concepts underlying tropology available to a wider audience than has been the case so far, when the most knowledgeable scholars in, for example, the Modern Language Association have been in romance languages departments, often in French departments.

My aim has been domestication of extant paradigms, not creation of new ones. Neither in my introduction nor in the chapter on White has there been an effort to construct new tropological theory. Current theory is quite adequate, I believe. In addition to White's works, an essay by Kenneth Burke, and Vico's *The New Science*, the germane work on tropes at this moment is by historian Hans Kellner (whom I frequently cite) and French-language scholars Donald Rice and Peter Schofer. Unlike Kellner, who is a proponent of White (and a former student), Rice and Schofer outline in *Rhetorical Poetics* (1983) what they consider a revisionist theory, but the theory is nonetheless quite consistent with that of White, whom they mention once. I do not find the work of others—such as Harold Bloom—as compelling as those named, nor do I find dyadic theories such as those out of Roman Jakobson by Claude Lévi-Strauss and Jacques Lacan generally persuasive, though I do use—fruitfully, I believe—the Lacanian dyad on Heller's novel. The tetradic models seem to me considerably more flexible and instructive for discursive analysis. They are especially attractive tools for literary critics—or certainly should be—because they fit so well into the great variety of other tetrads found in literary theory or adopted from disciplines such as philosophy.

Doing Tropology has as its ultimate aim precisely that: the doing of tropology, the presentation of one reader's tropological readings of several works of modern American narrative—mainly fiction. This aim necessarily involves an effort, as well, to explain a tropology sufficient to achieve the original aim of doing it. The primary purpose of my brief introductory chapter is thus to provide a historical and philosophical context, particularly in the phenomenology of language, for the more concrete discussion that follows. Hayden White's *Metahistory* and, especially, the introduction and several essays in *Tropics of Discourse* have provided my indispensable theoretical and, often, practical models. In chapter 1, which "names" tropology through a detailed exploration of White's tropics, I also show the fundamentally tropological nature of White's own representations of tropology, both in the introduction to *Tropics* (where White discusses, for example, Giambattista Vico, Jean Piaget, and Sigmund Freud) and in the representation of the historical and cultural roots of tropology enunciated by Michel Foucault in *The Order of Things.* By way of responding to critiques of White, finally, I attempt to reestablish what I had suggested in the introduction—namely, the larger phenomenological framework into which White's tropics might be placed.

The tropics of discourse outlined by White—based upon the four-trope set of metaphor, metonymy, synecdoche, and irony—is also based upon the premise that consciousness or understanding and thus discourse proceed through the set in precisely that order. Taking the notion of the *ricorso* from Vico, White also insists that once entropy has settled over the figurative consciousness in the phase of irony, the tropic process returns to metaphor and begins again in the same regenerative cycle. The structure of tropology, then, is narrative, a venturing of thought "out and back," essentially the archetypal journey, shall we say, of departure and initiation, followed by the cyclic return. To suggest this "narrative curriculum," as Hans Kellner has called it, I have organized the chapters of *Doing Tropology* (after the introduction) so as to stress not only the sequential and incremental nature of the tropes as they operate in discourse, but also their potentially cyclic recursiveness in a tropology. The sequence of tropic enfigurations as they occur *in thought* will be diachronic, and the diachronic, as well as recursive, process of discourse can usually be reconstructed, even if the moments of each tropic phase are almost infinitesimal. But in no sense would I claim a diachronic (or historical and evolutionary) relation among the texts used here for illustrative analysis. I have avoided a chronological ordering of exemplary texts, therefore, not only to avoid suggesting a historical development among them, but also in order progressively to escalate the complexity of the readings in the cumulation of the chapters.

The function of chapter 1 is to name a tropology through the work of Hayden White and to begin to show how the tropes, *as a tropology,*

infuse White's own rhetoric and discourse. The second chapter becomes
a bit more complicated by virtue of its "renaming" tropology in a tropological theory developed not in rhetoric or the philosophy of history,
but in the linguistically based psychoanalytic model of Jacques Lacan, who
turns for theory not to Vico or Burke, but to Roman Jakobson and Claude
Lévi-Strauss. The Lacanian dyadic tropology applied in a reading of Joseph
Heller's *Something Happened* is meant to be a closed dialectic, but I do
try briefly to suggest how it might usefully be opened out into a tetradic
theory consistent with that of Hayden White. The third chapter—on *The
Education of Henry Adams*—focuses on a narrative deservedly well known
for its metaphoric figurations, but, significantly, Adams's tropic modality,
which grows out of his eighteenth-century episteme, is more usually metonymic than metaphoric, at the same time that Adams's thought, moreover, is caught up in the search for a synecdochic trope adequate to a
twentieth century whose mode of knowing he foresees in modern, post-
Newtonian science.

The fourth chapter focuses on Faulkner's *Absalom, Absalom!*, a
novel every bit as difficult as Heller's and conveying interests in "history"
as complex as those in Henry Adams. I regard it as the climax to *Doing
Tropology*. In its cumulative force, the chapter—as it takes us back through
each of the tropic moments of metaphor, metonymy, and synecdoche,
and adds to them the considerable difficulties of the ironic, represented
not just once, but twice (as trope and metatrope or overtrope), and adds
to these the problems of emplotments by various narrative voices—un-
questionably will present the severest challenge to readers. As a consciously
ironic discourse on tropes, moreover, it threatens—as irony always threatens—to explode the entire tropics of discourse. Thus, the aim of the fifth
and concluding chapter is no more—and no less—than to restore the cred-
ibility, the "innocence," of tropology by returning to the enfigurations of
metaphor, the concreteness of metaphoric thinking, and the (synecdochic)
inclusiveness of myth and symbol. Of my exemplary text in the chapter,
John Updike's *The Centaur*, all I would claim is that it draws one—as
Updike puts it—into a linguistic world "resonant with metaphor," where
at least momentarily our innocence of vision is restored. Updike is enabled
to do that by drawing his figures within vividly concrete phenomenological
contexts, thus illustrating, I think, that metaphor indeed provides language,
if not life itself, with the means to restoration by its rootedness in lived
experience.

In its structural organization, then, *Doing Tropology* represents something of a tropological "object." The tetradic tropology serving as its base entails a roughly cyclical movement through the "tropic moments," the stages or phases identified by each trope (metaphor, metonymy, synecdoche, and irony). Each of the chapters in *Doing Tropology* is placed in order to show the structural force of the individual tropes, the incremental progression through the tropes, and the cyclic return to metaphor after the entropic loss of creative energy in the "moment" of irony. There is a dominant trope underlying such a structural concept; it is synecdoche, the figurative move wherein the part is represented by and in the whole, as in the relation of microcosm to macrocosm. Any work that pretends to a total structural unity inevitably is erected, at least in consciousness, upon a synecdochic base, but the test of that unity—as any disciple of New Criticism knows—comes in the reader's response to the whole work. If the author's vision and execution are successful, the reader will come away with a consciousness of the whole and the synthesis of the parts within that whole.

The next—and potentially fatal—step of understanding beyond synecdoche is irony, the step that scholarly authors would like to disallow for readers. But (ironically—what else?) we often induce that step ourselves. The self-consciousness that becomes manifest in prefaces too often leads the reader to the awareness that might deconstruct the whole project. Irony persuades readers that the structural rationales and enabling moves all may finally be nothing *but* tropological. Here, I think, is where the regenerative sense of the phenomenological in tropology has to come back into play. In the abstract, in mere tropic consciousness, the structures of *Doing Tropology* (as of any linguistic object) may begin to take on the evanescence of a platonic mist. But *doing* tropology, whether writing or reading, chapter by chapter generates or regenerates in us a good, honest, intellectual sweat. In the doing, tropology begins to fuse again the abstract and the concrete and to validate itself once more as a phenomenological object—at once ideal and material—in our total language experience. Doing tropology is to work at—and through—the tropic enfigurations manifested in discourse, but it is a working through, finally, that needs not just the labors of an author, but a reader's active participation.

Acknowledgments

I acknowledge my debt to editors for permission to reuse material originally published in the following: "*Something Happened*: The Imaginary, the Symbolic, and the Discourse of the Family," in *Critical Essays on Joseph Heller*, ed. James Nagel (Boston: G. K. Hall, 1984), pp. 138–55; and "The Novel as Lyric Elegy: The Mode of Updike's *The Centaur*," *Texas Studies in Literature and Language* 21.1 (Spring 1979):112–27.

This work was carried out and published through two kinds of support from the College of Liberal Arts and Sciences at Northern Illinois University. First, the college provided continuous typing and manuscript service, and I would be greatly remiss if I did not here express my gratitude to the college and to those brave and hearty souls in the Word Processing Service who day in and day out processed my words, words, words: Amber Oldham, Cheryl Fuller, Crystal Swanson, Susan Amaloo, and Karen Blaser. Many thanks. Second, the college has generously provided a subvention toward the publication of this book, and I thank Dean James D. Norris for material assistance indicative of the moral support he has long given to research in the College. Much obliged.

Finally, I express my indebtedness to those who have helped me work my way through this study in ways neither they nor I can always entirely understand, though I do appreciate them fully: to Charles Hagelman, ever a source of inspiration; to Steve Franklin, a useful sounding board and great lender of books; and to the members of my family—"Sudy," T. Alice, Cindy K., and Cat—who daily take me through all the tropic moments and back again, for theirs are the names that enfigure life for me.

Introduction

Tropology and Phenomenology of Language

Language, Signs, and Tropes

> Tropes . . . have become a kind of *lingua franca* bridging linguistics, rhetoric, poetics, philosophy, criticism, and intellectual history; the descriptive power of tropes has extended itself into an explanatory power, and the solvent capability of these dual processes—description and explanation—seems to offer virtually limitless possibilities of analytical power in many different directions.
>
> —Hans Kellner, "The Inflatable Trope"

One of the hotly contested issues of recent critical and rhetorical theory has been what Hayden V. White calls a "tropics," the conceptualization and application of tropes—tropology, in short. In classical rhetoric, the term *trope* might refer to any figure of speech from alliteration and antanaclasis to synecdoche and zeugma, so a list of tropes might include anywhere from twenty to a hundred or more. But tropologies—not mere lists, but theories about the number and arrangement of tropes—provide philosophical reasons for limiting the number and order of primary rhetorical figures. The most common tropologies today are either dyadic or tetradic.[1] Modern dyadic tropologies such as those of Claude Lévi-Strauss and Jacques Lacan are usually based upon the linguistics of Roman Jakobson.[2] Jakobson suggests that only the tropes of metaphor and metonymy are needed to establish the basic rhetorical axes of language. The linguistic "axis of selection" follows metaphor (he says, quite arbitrarily) along a vertical line; the "axis of combination" follows metonymy (again, arbitrarily) along a horizontal line. For Jakobson, the metaphoric axis represents the ability of language to permit substitutions in a functional or grammatical space, while the metonymic axis represents the ability of

1

language to establish connections or syntactical relationships in a linear string.

Tetradic tropologies include those of Peter Ramus (who reduced Quintilian's twelve-trope system), Giambattista Vico, and Kenneth Burke, as well as Hayden White and, more recently, Peter Schofer and Donald Rice.[3] Each of these insists that though the sequence may vary, a complete tropology must include a basic set of four: the common dyad of metaphor and metonymy, but also synecdoche and irony. We might say, as Jakobson suggests, that a system of tropes defines the generative activity of language at the semantic level, but tropological systems, according to White, Kellner, and others, also determine lexical, grammatical, syntactical, and semantic activities in the *discourses* toward which language is drawn. The current battle regarding tropological systems among rhetoricians, literary critics, philosphers, and psychoanalysts is being waged over a momentous prize: namely, the prime source of energy in human consciousness, creativity, and verbal expression. Tropology has become important, in other words, because after the overthrow of the authorities behind religion, history, and the sciences, it has assumed virtually all the authority of a new god-term.

There is a long history behind tropology, however, for the rhetorical power of tropes and problems caused by them have been noted at least as far back as the Greeks. In general, the subject of tropes is involved (though not always explicitly) whenever an issue such as the representational function of language is raised. Tzvetan Todorov, in *Theories of the Symbol*, thus almost inevitably is led to the discussion of tropes in his semiotic consideration of symbolism, wherein he studies the ways in which symbols affect production of meaning in human discourse.[4] Influenced by post-Saussurean linguistics, Todorov suggests that any notion of a figural or symbolic—or, therefore, tropological—function in speech and writing depends not only upon an awareness of the representational authority of *similarity*, but also of the presence of *difference* in language. Difference, whether seen in the sign or the referent, creates language's capability for producing dual, contradictory, and even manifold meanings, from the same set of words. There can be no symbolism—no figures or tropes—where a language (such as the stipulated languages of mathematics and symbolic logic) is totally univocal, thus always producing the same message through a given string of signs. Though it is plain that there can be no conception

2

of difference where there is no conception of identity, the ideal aim of language as a means of pure communication would involve only identity.[5]

The history of semiotics is formed, Todorov suggests, by the various stresses placed upon conceptions of identity and difference as they operate (or are thought to operate) in the signs constituting ordinary language. According to Todorov, classical theory of language and rhetoric valorized identity and thus saw difference as a *deviation* from a presumed norm operating in the sign-system of language. Since classical theory focused more directly upon the ideal of matching signifier and signified, the "turns" that occur in linguistic tropes were generally considered suspect, even when acknowledged as beneficial, because they introduced the likelihood for miscommunication in the disparity between sign and represented content. Authorities writing on figuration or tropes up until about 1830 took this view, including the leading "tropologists" (except for Vico) prior to Kenneth Burke. Among those studied by Todorov are César Du Marsais, *Des tropes* (1730), N. Beauzée, *Grammaire générale* (1767), E. B. de Condillac, *De l'art d'écrire* (c. 1780), and Pierre Fontanier, *Manuel classique pour l'étude des tropes* (4th ed., 1830), who all contribute unwittingly to what Todorov considers "the end of rhetoric" in the traditional fashion. But after the "Romantic crisis" in rhetoric, as Todorov calls it, tropic or figural difference, in a sense, *became* the norm, for every work, perhaps every utterance, was thought to establish its own interpretive code, its own rules for decoding. A universal grammar and logic based upon identity became lost in a multiverse of individual expression, where all language is taken as metaphorical—tropical. Modern Saussurean linguistics seems more in agreement with romantic than classical philosophy of language, for after the work of Ferdinand de Saussure it has been assumed that language is constructed upon principles of difference, is totally arbitrary in structure and semantics, and permits no absolute "norm" for use or analysis. There is, moreover, the principal difference noted by Saussure—the gap existing between *la langue* (which is the ideal language seen as atemporal or synchronic—existing in a timeless space, as it were) and *la parole* (which is the diachronic, historical, particular utterance enacted in speech or writing). Saussurean linguistics, therefore, while it has not eradicated the concept of "the same," has valorized difference over identity and thus, in its way, has valorized the tropic, figural process of language in every form of discourse.

There is a crucial third step in the development of the theory of signs on which modern linguistics rests. Saussure made the distinction between *la langue* and *la parole*, but he also made a distinction between the signifier and the signified—between, that is, the sign or symbol or figure and the content or meaning or signification. Classical linguistics assumed that there was a natural or motivated relationship between the signifier and the signified; with Saussure, modern linguistics assumed, on the contrary, that no such "real" relationships exist: they are all determined by the system within which the signifiers operate. Even with Saussure, however, there was an assumption that the system was only binary—signifier versus signified—and that the object of the signifier was to apprehend the original meaning contained in the signified. What has come to be called postmodern or poststructuralist linguistics, of the sort exemplified by Jacques Derrida, has assumed that the binary system of structural or Saussurean linguistics is based upon a faulty metaphysics of the origin: there is no original signified, or at least there is none that can be recaptured in language. There are only traces, displacements of the original being, object, or signified. Classical linguistics and rhetoric predicated an ultimate, original meaning that was apprehensible in language; postmodern linguistics—and any correlative rhetoric—assumes that there is no origin, there is only a play of meaning observable in the displacements and permutations of the signifiers that constitute language in its existential enactment.[6]

In "The Imagination of the Sign," Roland Barthes initiates a redefinition of the sign that fits both the postmodernist notion of language and the potentiality within language for a tropics, tropology, or figurativity. Barthes's view is ternary rather than binary. A sign has three elements—signifier and signified and, most importantly, the signifying unit formed by combination of the first two; the sign, therefore, exists only in the fusion of the signifier and signified in the actual expression, which for Barthes may be verbal or nonverbal. Barthes discusses his concept of levels of the sign in terms of "relations." "Every sign," he says, "includes or implies three relations. To start with, an interior relation which unites its signifier to its signified; then two exterior relations: a virtual one that unites the sign to a specific reservoir of other signs it may be drawn from in order to be inserted in discourse; and an actual one that unites the sign to other signs in the discourse preceding or succeeding it."[7] As Barthes explains these relations, the first suggests what is known as the *symbol*, which, in conventional usage, entails the assumption of an identity between the sign and the signified. In our tropological terms, though not in Barthes's, we would call this figure *metaphor*. The second relation, Barthes suggests, entails the presence of difference; it "implies the existence, for each sign, of a reservoir or organized 'memory' of forms from which it is distinguished by the smallest difference necessary and sufficient to effect a change of meaning" (p. 212). In tropological terms, we would call this figure *metonymy*. The third relation draws upon the notion of a whole system of signs within which each signifying unit functions. Where the second relation announces the presence of the system in the binary differences that establish the paradigm, the third relation suggests the actual function of the systemic process and defines the syntagm. Between two signifying units, says Barthes, "a temporary but signifying association, analogous to the one uniting the words of a sentence," exists (p. 212). In tropological terms, we would call this relation of part to whole *synecdoche*.

Barthes's view of the sign is important here because not only does it provide a linguistic grounding for the moves or turns determined by the tropes already named (metaphor, metonymy, and synecdoche), but it also provides a concept of plural consciousnesses of the sign—*imaginations* of the sign—that can undergird a tropological theory of discourse. Though postmodernist linguistics would call it a mistake literally to believe in, say, the metaphoric, symbolic relation of sign to meaning, Barthes permits consciousness to rest provisionally in that or the other moments of language. "Now it seems that when we consider the signifying phenomenon," says Barthes, "we are obliged to focus on one of these three relations more than on the other two; sometimes we 'see' the sign in its symbolic aspect, sometimes in its systematic [or paradigmatic] aspect, sometimes in its syntagmatic" (p. 212).

These three relations, Barthes tells us, are forms of consciousness we have in our experience of language, and, what is more, these forms recapitulate (somewhat, we might say, as ontogeny recapitulates phylogeny) the history of the sign. He points out that different schools of linguistics valorize different relations or moments, so while there apparently are different forms of semiological consciousnesses available to us, each form will bring with it an ideology. "Now, on the one hand," Barthes says, "the choice of a dominant relation implies a certain ideology; and, on the other hand, one might say that each consciousness of the sign (symbolic, paradigmatic, and syntagmatic) corresponds to a certain moment of reflection, either individual or collective." Barthes points out, for example, that "structuralism, in particular, can be defined historically as the passage from symbolic consciousness to paradigmatic consciousness."

While Barthes insists that "there is a history of the sign, which is the history of its 'consciousness'" (pp. 212-13), he does not tell us that his own view merely seems situated above history, outside the battles of linguistic schools or even the conflict of the forms of consciousness toward the sign. Clearly, Barthes's view represents a form of semiological consciousness—a fourth, metalinguistic moment marking the passage from the system to the play of the syntagm, a move characterized in the trope of *irony*. Barthes cannot claim to stand above ideology, therefore, and the ideology he expresses—in this essay and elsewhere—is itself the one later to be defined by Michel Foucault and others as the postmodern and by Hayden White as the ironic, the "absurdist," moment.

Tropology and Phenomenology

> I don't believe that anything like perception exists. Perception is precisely a concept, a concept of an intuition or of a given originating from the thing itself, present itself in its meaning, independently from language, from the system of reference.
>
> —Jacques Derrida, "Structure, Sign, and Play"

> There are no metaphors in nature; there are no metaphors in perception. Metaphor can arise only when we try actually to put experience into words.
>
> —James M. Edie, *Speaking and Meaning*

The linguistic grounding for tropes to be found in Barthes has a far-reaching significance for the study of language and literature. It turns all actualized utterance (*parole*) into a play of language and thus a form of rhetoric, whereas classical theory of language held speech to the standard of the more stable, idealized modes of "grammar" and "logic." In that view, rhetoric is seen as an imprecise worldly endeavor that reflects the fallen human condition, which literature was thought to transcend by reapproaching the ideal located in language. In their recent *Rhetorical Poetics*, Donald Rice and Peter Schofer elaborate on the consequences for literature entailed by a post-Saussurean, poststructuralist conception of symbolism, figuration, language in general. The extreme consequence is shown in their study through the position they share with Paul de Man; de Man takes a radical view, expressed in "Semiology and Rhetoric," that literature can be equated with the "rhetorical, figural potentiality of language" itself.[8] Such a premise leaves little space for figural language used in ordinary speech or writing, much less in those "discourses" Barthes sees in clothing, cooking, cinema, and the like. But Rice and Schofer provide room for degrees of figurality. For them, literary texts are simply more insistently figural than ordinary language use, since in literature "language is continually displaced, condensed, twisted, and deformed. In literature [they say] we can see most clearly the effects of figurations and symbolization, where rhetorical language becomes a second sign system working on and against conventional written language" (*RP*, pp. xvi–xvii). Where classical rhetoric is interested in textual construction, their interest is not devoted to the construction of the text (or the given utterance, whatever it might be). In what amounts to a deconstructive turn in their rhetoric, they shift the focus of the tropological process from the text to the reader. "A theory of rhetoric," they say, "means that texts, with the letters present on the page, are incomplete artifacts. They achieve completion only when the reader provides what is absent. The reader carries to the text a knowledge, a psyche, a culture, which fills in the gaps and the incomplete meanings" (*RP*, p. xvii). This shift has considerable significance where the philosophical authorization of figuration, symbolization, tropology is concerned. For, like Barthes in his definition of the sign as existing only in the *combination* of signifier and signified, they suggest that signs in language, in effect, do not exist except in the linguistic performance.

Though Rice and Schofer do not elaborate on the philosophical basis for their rhetoric of reading, significantly, their deconstructive turn (in keeping with Barthes, Derrida, de Man, et al.) suggests very clearly the philosophy of language on which their rhetorical poetics must be based. One assumes that any methodology ought to find an ultimate justification in philosophy, but not all philosophical justifications can be regarded as equally authoritative. The claims of a pure idealism of the sort classical language theory longed for, but could never really have—are generally denied; "Platonic"—to the materialists—is an epithet today for sheer emptiness or nonsense, as often as not. But, similarly, the claims of a pure materialism are equally denied; "hardheaded empiricist," for example, is an epithet for another sort of emptiness or nonsense. Traditional philosophy of language was interested in the construction of texts, utterances, messages, shall we say, but it—no less than contemporary reader-oriented deconstruction—was forced to recognize the creative power of tropes, figures, symbols, turns of speech, words, phrases. But traditional philosophy of language simply is not adequate to explain the relation between *la langue* and *la parole*, the ideal constructive rules of language and their concrete expression in speech and writing. Whether viewed constructively or deconstructively, the figurative power of language—embraced in tropology—seems ultimately responsible to or authorized by what we would now call a phenomenological philosophy of language.

Phenomenology has seized hold of so much of the best of modern—or modernist—thought primarily because it can validate—in the way of any philosophical "realism"—both the ideality and the materiality constituting human thought and experience. James M. Edie, in *Speaking and Meaning: The Phenomenology of Language*, has put the matter plainly in his analysis of Edmund Husserl's linguistic phenomenology. Husserl's phenomenology of language invalidates the claims of both the Platonic "metaphysical hypostatization" of universals and the "psychological hypostatization" of objects as existing *in* the mind. Says Edie, "Husserl's phenomenological analysis of meaning escapes the Scylla of idealism on the one side and the Charybdis of empiricism on the other." It can do so because Husserl focuses on meaning: "*Meaning* clearly involves the mind and arises as the structure of the world only for psychological subjects." Meaning is thus always personal, always in part subjective and experiential, "as it clearly refers to real (or possible) objects of experience" (p. 29). But meaning is also objective, for "in analyzing 'the meant' as such, not only what 'I mean' but what 'is meant' by such an experience or such an expression, we are led from our subjective, private, inner psychological states toward the 'objective sense,' or *Sinn*, which has an *eidetic structure*" (pp. 29–30). For Husserl, no eidetic or essential or ideal structures exist in things. These putative essences, Husserl says, "exist only for the mind; they are, in a sense, what the mind adds to nature; but neither are they individual acts of individual consciousness, since any description of the content of experience must recognize the *objectivity of the ideal*, of the typical, of the structural, in our experience of the world" (p. 30). This is perhaps the most vital contribution of phenomenology to modern philosophy and literary criticism—the reconciliation of idealism and materialism. And, for rhetorical theory, this reconciliation means that we can authorize tropology in a phenomenology of language derived from both classical and modern theory of language.

Edie has outlined for us what a phenomenology of language ought to entail, even though he would contend that such does not yet exist, not

8

even in Husserl—or Paul Ricoeur or Maurice Merleau-Ponty, the two other major phenomenological philosophers of language. Edie's "complete" phenomenology of language, based as it must be upon a pursuit of meaning in utterance, would include three stages. First, it "would begin with an analysis of the intentionality of consciousness and the phenomenology of the life-world, based on the fundamental primacy of perceiving consciousness over language-using consciousness." Second, "it would then move on to a consideration of the relation of *the experience of meaning* in perceptual and linguistic psychological acts of consciousness (*noeses*), and in other subjective acts, to objects of reference in the real world, to meant ideal 'contents,' and to the various levels of meaning in experience and in language." Third, and finally, "it would discuss the relation of the structures of language to speech-acts, the ideality of language to its historical employment and evolution, the *structures* of usage as opposed to *actual acts* of usage" (p. ix).

But even if a completed phenomenology of language is beyond our grasp at the present time, as Edie says (p. ix), the phases outlined here provide a curriculum and foundation for study. In the set, one can see that there are critical activities in which one can engage that will demonstrate the authority of a phenomenological grounding of language. In the analysis of the enacted language of specific literary works, one can show, for example, "the experience of meaning in language." Literary texts express concretely our human experience as "signifying, speaking, communicating beings within different contexts of our common intersubjectively constituted life-world" (p. x). Moreover, if one rigorously investigates the apprehension of meaning in language, one will at the same time demonstrate the indissoluble relationship of human experience to the verbal expression of meaning. Following Edie's curriculum, even though my analyses are not phenomenological in any strict sense, I end by validating tropology through the view of language espoused by phenomenology.

Edie's entire study in *Speaking and Meaning* moves toward the reconciliation of identity and difference, mimetic representation and tropic deviation, though Edie's terms are neither trope nor tropology, but metaphor and polysemy. His thesis, Edie says, "is that while language as a structure, as an ideal entity, is ontologically dependent on historical acts of usage, of speech-acts, which in each actual occurrence mean something new and different from anything which has ever previously been uttered, these same speech-acts logically presuppose the already ideally and objectively established formal laws *according* to which acts of linguistic meaning can take place." The major claim that unifies the five chapters of his book, Edie says, "culminates in the concluding chapter on metaphorical expression" (p. x).

For Edie, a phenomenology of language will rest upon the analysis of the relationship between concrete acts of speech and ideal structural laws, but it is precisely in this phenomenological relationship that tropology—metaphor (in a generic sense) or polysemy—exists. Tropology thus can only manifest itself as an objective "phenomenon" created in the gap between speech act and linguistic structure. "It is in the study of metaphor or polysemy," says Edie, "that the true understanding of the relationship of language as a 'structure' (*la langue*) to acts of speaking (*la parole*) can be set forth" (p. x). Thus, it would appear that given Edie's argument, we may validate the metaphoric or tropic aspect of language through the premises of phenomenological analysis. Doing that, we end by validating a tropics of discourse. Doing tropology, in a real sense, validates itself in its concrete involvements with meaning derived from human experience and verbal expression. Although other bases exist on which one might situate tropology besides phenomenology, all those other grounds may ultimately be subsumed in the phenomenological. I shall outline some of them in a discussion of a specific tropology—Hayden White's tetradic "tropics of discourse."

NOTES

1. The best essay on the historical development of tropologies involving systems of fewer than the twelve tropes posited by Quintilian is a "response" to Hans Kellner's "The Inflatable Trope": see Wallace Martin, "Floating an Issue of Tropes," *Diacritics* 12 (Spring 1982):75–83. Martin is not an exponent of a four-trope system, it should be pointed out, and he is especially critical of the way in which some of the systems—such as Burke's, White's, and Kellner's defense of these—interpret the necessity of a tropological *sequence*. Martin argues, for example, that the historical basis for the sequence of metaphor, metonymy, synecdoche, and irony when it is rooted in Vico is probably a misinterpretation of Vico. If one is not predisposed to accept a theory of tropes, Martin's essay is likely to settle the question in the negative, but one ought to see in its turn Hans Kellner's rebuttal: "The Issue in the Bullrushes: A Reply to Wallace Martin," ibid., 84–88. Whether one sides with Martin or Kellner, clearly they articulate most of the problems associated with theories of tropes.

2. Jakobson works out his dyadic theory of tropes in several places, but the main sources are "Two Aspects of Language and Two Types of Aphasic Disturbances," in Roman Jakobson and Morris Halle, *Fundamentals of Language* (The Hague: Mouton, 1956), pp. 53–82, and "Closing Statement: Linguistics and Poetics," in *Style in Language*, ed. Thomas A. Sebeok (Cambridge, Mass.: M.I.T. Press, 1960), pp. 350–77; for other sources, see Willard Bohn, "Roman Jakobson's Theory of Metaphor and Metonymy: An Annotated Bibliography," *Style* 18.4 (Fall 1984):534–50. White discusses dyadic tropologies (in Lévi-Strauss, Jakobson, and Lacan) in *Metahistory: The Historical Imagination in Nineteenth-Century Europe* (Baltimore: Johns Hopkins University Press, 1973), p. 13, n. 13 (a note that runs in fine print for more than two full pages).

3. See Giambattista Vico, *The New Science*, trans. Thomas G. Bergin and Max H. Fisch (Ithaca, N.Y.: Cornell University Press, 1968); the major source for Kenneth Burke's tropology is "Appendix D: Four Master Tropes," in his *A Grammar of Motives* (Berkeley: University of California Press, 1969), pp. 503–17; Donald Rice and Peter Schofer, *Rhetorical Poetics: Theory and Practice of Figural and Symbolic Reading in Modern French Literature* (Madison: University of Wisconsin Press, 1983), abbreviated RP hereafter in the text. Rice and Schofer provide a useful definition of the trope that includes the basic principles of each of the four tropes: "*A trope is a semantic transposition from a sign in* praesentia *to a sign or signs in* absentia *and (1) based on the perception of a relationship between one or more semantic features of each signified, (2) marked by the semantic incompatibility of microcontext and the macrocontext, (3) motivated by a referential relationship of resemblance* [metaphor] *or causality* [metonymy] *or inclusion* [synecdoche] *or opposition* [irony]" (p. 19).

4. Tzvetan Todorov, *Theories of the Symbol*, trans. Catherine Porter (Ithaca, N.Y.: Cornell University Press, 1982; orig. pub. 1977 in French).

5. Indeed, one may claim that identity is a fiction, though patently a necessary fiction in human existence; see J. Hillis Miller, "The Fiction of Realism: *Sketches by Boz, Oliver Twist*, and Cruikshank's Illustrations," in *Charles Dickens and George Cruikshank*, ed. J. Hillis Miller and David Borowitz (Los Angeles: Clark Memorial Library, 1971), pp. 1–69; see especially pp. 8–9, 39–40. Miller's view—like that of Rice and Schofer—is that all language is a figurative displacement, and so both metaphor and metonymy (the tropes he considers) are versions of the "fiction of identity," which is the underlying epistemological presupposition of "realism" and of the novel as a genre.

6. See Jacques Derrida, *Speech and Phenomena and Other Essays on Husserl's Theory of Signs*, trans. David B. Allison (Evanston, Ill.: Northwestern University Press, 1973).

7. Roland Barthes, "The Imagination of the Sign," in *A Barthes Reader*, ed. by Susan Sontag (New York: Hill and Wang, 1982), p. 211.

8. *Diacritics* 3 (1973):30. In the essay "Language and Literature," Tzvetan Todorov suggests, somewhat as de Man does, but more in the manner of the structuralists, that the techniques and structures of literature are first found in the figures (or tropes) of language, but Todorov does not formulate a tropology that might systematize the claim: see his *The Poetics of Prose*, trans. Richard Howard (Ithaca, N.Y.: Cornell University Press, 1977; orig. pub. in French, 1971), pp. 19–28.

Chapter One

Naming Tropology: The Tropics of Hayden White

Genesis and Structure

> One of the most striking and least examined aspects of the four-trope series—the "master tropes" of Vico and Kenneth Burke—is [its] inherent movement through a fixed course: from metaphor, the preliminary naming operation, to metonymy, the process of reductive manipulation and formalization, to the integrative, macrocosm/microcosm relationships of synecdoche, to the final awareness within the series that all its processes have been relativizing turns, the whole process ironic.
>
> —Hans Kellner, "The Inflatable Trope"

The work of Hayden White almost inevitably generates immense interest these days because of his wide-ranging reconceptualization and applications of a more or less traditional tetradic tropology, particularly as it relates to narrative discourse.[1] White's interests lie in history and nonfiction, but his tropology—he makes plain—can also relate to fiction such as the traditional realistic novel. It is important to understand two dimensions of White's tropological work. First, we need to know how his tropics has grown from past theories, and, second, how it is related to and frequently finds a grounding in contemporary thought in the human sciences. The genesis of White's tropics lies in the mythopoesis Vico believed inherent in language. It is grounded in more recent psychoanalytic and psychological models of cognition—specifically, Freud's and Piaget's—that White can use to describe language's mechanisms and structures. It is grounded, moreover, in a postmodernist, structuralist conception of thought and language seen in the earlier writings of the late Michel Foucault. And there is yet a fourth, generally unacknowledged philosophical basis, one that is extremely valuable in answering the best critiques of White's tropology and, thus, of tropology in general. I shall show, in conclusion, not only

13

how White has identified his tropics with models in various traditions of social science (cultural history, genetic psychology, psychoanalysis), but also how he too might have validated it in that philosophy of language revealed by contemporary phenomenology. By showing, moreover, that White himself deploys tropological strategies in his appropriation of other tetradic systems (Vico's, Piaget's, Freud's, and Foucault's), I shall also begin to illustrate by example—by *doing* tropology—the essentiality of a tropology for the literary study of narrative discourse.

White extrapolates his tetradic tropology most completely in the analyses of histories and theories of history in *Metahistory* (1973), but his most accessible arguments in behalf of the theory appear in the essays collected in *Tropics of Discourse* (1978). His emerging understanding of the tropological nature of discourse is founded in part upon the model of Vico's *The New Science*.[2] White suggests in "The Tropics of History: The Deep Structure of *The New Science*," an essay reprinted in *Tropics* (pp. 197–217), that Vico's metaphysics and logic both originated in a philosophy of language that contrasted the "poetic" uses or functions of language to the "reflective." Primitive humans employ language poetically, Vico says, and, to begin with, that use rests upon metaphor. "The origins of human knowledge," White summarizes, "and *a fortiori* of human society and culture, are to be found in the onomathetic powers of primitive men, the power of 'naming' objects, of distinguishing them from other objects, and, in the process, endowing them with specific attributes." That function, says White, explains why Vico conflates the meaning of the Greek words for "word" and "logic" with the word *logos*. The "logic of primitive men," White suggests, "was nothing but the operation by which they 'named' and thereby 'comprehended' the objects and processes of the world around and within themselves" (T, p. 204).

According to White, the original naming process by which Vico's alleged primitive humans identified "the unfamiliar and threatening world of natural things with the familiar attributes of human nature, and especially of the senses and passions" provides "the true contents and meanings of the myths and fables handed down by primitive peoples to our own times" (T, p. 204). Thus, the "original" function of metaphor, like that of language in general, was to name, and it did so out of one's intuited grasp of the relationship between one's senses and the external world. That function, though Vico could not have so named it and White does not either, has been identified by James Edie as phenomenological,[3] and whenever language is to regain its "innocence" it will do so by returning to a metaphorical sense of a phenomenal world.

For Vico, whose views are paralleled in Edie's discussion of intentionality and our use of language, the function of metaphor has its place in what might be called the "logic of the figures of speech or tropes, the 'sensory topics' of primitive man" (see *The New Science*, pars. 495–98). This "logic," at the same time that it undergirds Edie's phenomenology of language, becomes White's "tropology." It rests upon the notion of a natural or logical or chronological sequence of enfigurations. The sequence begins in metaphor and turns then to metonymy, synecdoche, and, finally, to irony. Vico, says White, regards metaphor as a primal or generic trope. Thus, Vico sees synecdoche and metonymy as "refinements" of metaphor, while he sees irony as metaphor's opposite. Consequently, metaphor will comprise the heart of every story, fable, or myth, but "the escape from metaphorical language and the transition into the use of a consciously figurative language (and thus into literal and denotative, or prose, discourse) are made possible by the emergence of an ironic sensibility" (T, pp. 204–5).

Once the phase of metaphor has been established, thereby creating a "tension between things and the words used to characterize them," the movement of the tropes demands a further refinement or extension or precision. Vico suggests this tropic movement in the way he imagines primitives naming a natural phenomenon such as thunder. "Once thunder is particularized as anger," for example, "it becomes the subject of further specification by two kinds of tropological reduction: metonymy and synecdoche" (T, p. 206). The trope of metonymy identifies the anger of the thunder with a personified cause or agent, thus creating in the tropic process a "god" associated with dramatic expressions manifested in the weather.

Next, the tropic process of synecdoche generalizes the existence of the concrete god of thunder into the abstract concept of "gods." Finally, however, there comes a point when the tropic process of irony begins to call attention to the disparity between words and things, and thereby causes thought to recoil upon itself. "Irony," says White, "represents a stage in the evolution of consciousness in which language itself has become an object of reflection, and the sensed inadequacy of language to the full representation of its object has become perceived as a problem" (T, p. 207). Presumably beyond irony, then, would be the return of consciousness to the original phenomenon and, inevitably, a return to the naming function—once more to metaphor.

In the long essay on Vico, White's major premise is that Vico builds not only his theory of language, but also his conception of all human cultural history upon the sequences embedded in the tropology. "It will be recalled," White says, "that Vico postulates three stages through which all cultures pass in their cycles from primitivism to high civilization—religious, poetic and prosaic—each with its own distinctive form of human nature (religious, heroic, and human) and a reprise of the cycle with the return of barbarism when those cultures have reached their terms" (T, p. 208). But the crucial point for White is that Vico uses the theory of tropes as both a method of analysis and a model for description of human cultures. The originality of Vico, White insists, lies in the dialectic he perceives between language and reality, consciousness and society. The originality inheres in "Vico's belief that the mode of social organization of a given stage of cultural development is analogous to the modes of relating the unknown or problematical aspects of human experience to the known or cognitively secured aspects of it characteristic of the four master tropes" (T, p. 209). The importance of Vico for White, in short, lies in the reciprocal relationship between the process of thought and the process of language, the development of human consciousness and of culture, and the very modalities of human understanding and tropological expression. "It is thus," as White says earlier in the essay, "that the dialectic of figurative (tropological) speech itself becomes conceivable as the model by which the evolution of man from bestiality to humanity can be explained" (T, p. 205).

But we must recognize that White roots his analysis of Vico within a tropology, too. Vico's myth or fable plotting the growth of language has "named," metaphorically, for Hayden White a theory of tropes he shall pursue, metonymically, into related areas of the human sciences beyond those Vico had identified. Vico grounded his fable in a theory of language and history, but White, seeing the reflexiveness of Vico's argument and thus turning in other directions for his own validations of tropology, argues instead for a foundation to all *understanding* or cognition rooted not in language or history, but in human psychogenesis. Where Vico had claimed that the tropes defined the pattern of human linguistic and cultural development, White shows in the introduction to *Tropics*—"Tropology, Discourse, and the Modes of Human Consciousness"—that there may well be, prior to the cultural, an ontogenetic basis for our tropological ways of thinking and their relations to all discourse. White therefore takes another phenomenological turn in the extrapolation of his tropology. He argues, for example, that "an archetypal plot of discursive formations" exists that virtually mandates the precise sequence of metaphor turning to metonymy, synecdoche, and irony. In this plot, says White, "the narrative 'I' of the discourse [must] move from an original metaphorical characterization of a domain of experience, through metonymic deconstructions of its elements, to synecdochic representations of the relations between its superficial attributes and its presumed essence, to, finally, a representation of whatever contrasts or oppositions can legitimately be discerned in the totalities identified in the third phase of discursive representations" (T, p. 5).

White's next move—following the naming found in metaphor—is a more precise metonymical renaming of the phenomenon identified by Vico. For a more "objective," "empirical" modeling of the whole archetypal plot of tropology, White turns to Jean Piaget's representation of the development of cognitive powers in children.[4] White once again specifies the basic shifts of thought as it moves from (1) the "metaphorical apprehension of a 'strange' and 'threatening' reality to (2) a metonymic dispersion of its elements into the contiguities of the series," then (3) toward the integration of the previously dispersed elements "by assigning them to different orders, classes, genera, species, and so on," and, finally, (4) "to a consideration of the extent to which this taxonomic operation fails" of description or fails "to determine the extent to which my own taxonomic system is as much a product of my own need to organize reality in this way rather than in some other as it is of the objective reality of the elements previously identified" (T, p. 6). Since all these turns are consistent with the research findings of Piaget (as well as, I must here suggest, with some theories of Jacques Lacan), White is enabled to argue that whatever else tropology might be rooted in, it certainly is closely related to human psychogenesis.

White offers a more detailed discussion of Piaget than I have space to do, but it may suffice as illustration to follow the shift in Piaget's model from what White regards as the metaphorical to the metonymical stage. Piaget calls the shift from the "sensorimotor" to the "representational" stage a "veritable 'Copernican Revolution' " in the cognitive powers of the child. In the sensorimotor or metaphoric stage the infant apparently fails to distinguish its own physical being and space from those of others. In the representational or metonymic phase, the infant begins to grasp "a notion of a general space" that encompasses "individual varieties" of personal and other spaces. Those spaces include separate objects that "have become solid and permanent," along *"with the body itself as an object among others,"* yet separate from them. But this sense of space also includes a recognition of the range of *"displacements* coordinated and capable of being deduced and anticipated in relation" to any actual displacements that may occur (T, p. 8; Piaget, pp. 15–16). The phenomenon occurring here, White suggests, is the discovery of contiguity and the relationship of the self to objects outside the self. With this discovery come the logic of cause and effect and the inference based on act and agent. This stage, in Piagetian terms, represents a moment Jacques Lacan would call the discovery of the Other in the "mirror stage" of psychogenesis. Like Lacan (whose notion of the mirror stage as preliminary to symbolization lurks in the background of White's thought), White suggests that this metonymic turn or displacement through a decentering of the body encompasses the "radical transformation . . . without which the 'group of displacements' necessary for symbolization, speech, and thought would be impossible" (T, p. 8; Piaget, p. 16).

White's own turn of mind, it seems clear, is synecdochic. Since he tries to draw "parts" into larger "wholes," he is not content with just the one metonymic turn to Piaget for a renaming. He takes another turn—again into a phenomenological realm—that reveals the synecdochic relations among the parts displayed by various disciplines. He does not merely show that the tropological phases of cognition (apparently) are rooted in human ontogenetic development. He suggests that the phases can be renamed once more within a Freudian model of psychic process, insistently phenomenological, that fits neatly within the model of Piaget. The four tropes are closely, if not genetically, related to the phases of that "form of poiesis called dreaming."[5] Since Freud "provides the basis for belief in the operation of tropological schemata of figuration on the level of the Unconscious," White says a Freudian theory "may be taken as complementary to that of Piaget, whose primary concern was to analyze the process by which conscious and self-conscious troping is achieved" (T, p. 13).

White suggests, though in much briefer compass than he had with Piaget, that the stages of metaphor, metonymy, synecdoche, and irony are

18

insistently parallel to the processes Freud called "condensation," "displacement," "representation," and "secondary revision." White says he will not "spell out" the parallels between the process of dream-work and the tropes, and he reminds us that Todorov has already shown in an essay in *Theories of the Symbol* that the match is not perfect. But he insists that the congruences are close enough to make his point—that indeed there are deep psychological reasons for the continual return or reinvention of the tropes. The analogy is close enough, he says, "to permit us to view Freud's analysis of the mediations between the dream thoughts and the dream contents as a key to the understanding of the mechanisms which, in waking consciousness, permit us to move ... from poetic figurations of reality to poetic comprehensions of it" (T, p. 13).

Putting Freud's analysis in the context of a theory of discourse, White thus argues, synecdochically, rather than metonymically, that the psychoanalytic "notion of the mechanisms of the dreamwork" are "psychological equivalents" of what Vico's tropes would be in language and what the transformational patterns described by Piaget would be in conceptual thought (T, p. 14). Once we recognize these interlocking, even monadic relationships, says White, we have a way of relating the two elements—mimetic and diegetic—found in every discursive or diatactical "representation of reality, whether of the sleeping or the waking consciousness" (T, p. 15). Thus White will next turn his attention to the relation of tropology to discourse and, since he is a historian by profession, to narrative as a discourse whose form—mediating between concrete events and structural laws—is inevitably phenomenological and tropological.

Tropology and Narrative Discourse

> The tropes become "moments" of the tropology itself, which is not seen so much as a set of forms or categories, as a system, indeed *the* system, by which mind comes to grasp the world conceptually in language. The order in which the tropes present themselves in this system is strictly and logically entailed. That is, to speak of the "four master tropes" as a tropology necessarily invokes the sequence of the series, which thus represents a narrative curriculum with its own propulsive forces.
> —Hans Kellner, "The Inflatable Trope"

Though White suggests through his own tropological analysis of Piaget and Freud that there is a deep onto- and psychogenetic basis for the workings of tropology, it is not the genesis of the tropological pattern that mainly interests him. It is, rather, the structural function of tropes in discourse, especially the narrative discourse associated with the writing of history. White is persuaded that the major feature of any discourse is the way in which enfiguration or poiesis or imagination works through it. Even logic, White insists, has its enabling tropic moment, the necessity within the syllogism entailing a given "fact" that itself cannot be proved within the syllogism. At the outset of the essay introducing *Tropics of Discourse*, White had explained his view regarding the "levels" of discourse he calls "mimetic," "diegetic," and "diatactic." "Considered as a genre," he says, "discourse must be analyzed on three levels: that of the description (mimesis) of the 'data' found in the field of inquiry being invested or marked out for analysis; that of the argument or narrative (diegesis), running alongside of or interspersed with the descriptive materials; and that on which the combination of these previous two levels is effected (diataxis)" (T, p. 4). These levels of discourse ultimately return us to what White considers the most important roles of the tropes, their power of determining the process of thought as it works itself out discursively.

Tropology's constructive stages, prior to the onset of the deconstructive effects of irony, can also be seen, though White does not so argue, in the series he calls mimesis, diegesis, and diataxis, for each level is parallel to the first three phases of the tropology: mimesis parallel to metaphor, diegesis to metonymy, and diataxis to synecdoche, with synecdoche also permitting the emergence of a fourth, metatropal or ironic phase. Since the level of diataxis is more or less identical to the level of discourse as a whole, it seems legitimate to claim that for White discourse *is* tropology, or at least that *the* discursive is tropological. Thus, having turned metaphorically and metonymically, he next turns toward synecdoche in his validations of tropology. Synecdoche insists upon parts in relation to wholes, upon rules of combination. White's explanation of diataxis suggests this synecdochic turn: "The rules which crystallize on this last, or diatactical, level of discourse determine possible objects of discourse, the ways in which description and argument are to be combined, the phases through which the discourse must pass in the process of earning its right of closure, and the modality of the metalogic used to link up the conclusion of the discourse with its inaugurating gestures" (T, p. 4–5). All these steps (including the potentially deconstructive irony of that metalogic) are embraced in the four phases of White's tropology, whether it is rooted in Vico, Piaget, or Freud—or, more generally, in the curriculum of discursiveness inherent in language itself.

In various essays in *Tropics of Discourse* White examines and reexamines the synecdochic and constructive relations among thought, discourse, and tropology. The principles he educes for discourse, in, for example, "Historicism, History, and the Figurative Imagination" (T, pp. 101–20), are clearly tropological. First, he says, every discourse has a mimetic level that must be drawn into a diegetic level, the former, "a set of events it purports to describe"; the latter, a "generic story form to which it tacitly likens the set in order to disclose its formal coherence considered as either a structure or a process" (T, p. 106). White points out that in writing history and in theory of history, "the two levels conventionally distinguished are those of the *facts* (data or information) on the one side and the *interpretation* (explanation or story told about the facts) on the other" (T, p. 107). But White is at pains to show that the two are really only notionally separate, for the one cannot really exist in the discourse without the other. Moreover, what melds the two indissolubly together is the tropal imagination, for the historian's act of prefiguration generates the discursive enfiguration in the narrative. The constructed result is diatactical, White suggests, rather than merely dialectical, and though the diatactical in some sense is only a third level, it may in fact be regarded as the whole discourse itself. "The point is this," White says:

> even in the simplest prose discourse, and even in one in which the object of representation is intended to be nothing but fact, the use of language itself projects a level of secondary meaning below or behind the phenomena being "described." This secondary meaning exists quite apart from both the "facts" themselves and any explicit argument that might be offered in the extradescriptive, more purely analytical or interpretative, level of the text. This figurative level is produced by a constructive process, poetic in nature, which prepares the reader of the text more or less subconsciously to receive *both* the description of the facts and their explanation as plausible, on the one side, and as adequate to one another, on the other. (T, p. 110)

The synecdochic, monadic relations of tropology and discourse, the virtual identity of the two terms, can be seen in any one of White's analyses in either *Metahistory* or *Tropics*. In order briefly to illustrate the functions of the tropes, I shall turn to the introduction to *Tropics*, where White provides an incisive, paradigmatic analysis of E. P. Thompson's *The Mak-*

ing of the English Working Class.[6] Thompson's monumental history is especially useful to White because it would be seen by most readers as so fundamentally materialistic in its methodology as to be impervious to such a linguistic or apparently formalist critique as tropology provides. White remarks that Thompson's book has been "praised by scholars of many different ideological orientations for its mastery of factual detail, general openness of plan, and explicit rejection of methodology and abstract theory." And yet, inevitably, it falls neatly into the net of White's tropology in its study of the "development of working-class consciousness." The first part of the book, called "The Liberty Tree," shows a "working-class consciousness awakening to itself," says White, "grasping its particularity only in general terms, the kind of consciousness we would call metaphorical, in which working people apprehend their differences from the wealthy and sense their similarity to one another, but are unable to organize themselves except in terms of the general desire for the elusive 'liberty' " (T, p. 15).

The second part of Thompson's study, according to White, begins to define the different types of work and the modes of existence determined by industrial organization for the working class. But these, White says, are "nothing more than the elements of a series," lacking a firm sense of overall unity of purpose apart from the series defined by differences from the upper classes. This mode of class consciousness, White says, is described in metonymic terms. Thompson's third section treats the formation of a coherent class consciousness, one seen in "the actual crystallization of a distinctively 'working class' spirit among the laborers," and that spirit, says White, manifests itself in "a new sense of unity or identity of the parts with the whole—what we would call a synecdochic consciousness" (T, p. 17). The fourth stage of this class consciousness, as Thompson treats it, represents an almost inevitable decline from the euphoria of the third. The disintegration of the group spirit occurs. "The account of the fourth phase," White says, "is shot through with melancholy." It is a "product of a perception of an ironic situation, since it marks not only the ascent of *class* consciousness to *self*-consciousness but also and at the same time the fatal fracturing of the working-class movement itself" (T, p. 18). Thus, the four parts of Thompson's book, as White describes it, move through the phases of the tropes and in sequence: from metaphor, to metonymy, to synecdoche, to irony. White's premise is simply that however much Thompson might have tried to stress the factual "data" in order to avoid the merely "factitious" literary or formulaic history, the shape of his narrative discourse emerges from out of the tropological being of his language.

Tropology, Epistemology, and Foucault's The Order of Things

> Now, I want to make clear that I am using these terms [metaphor, metonymy, synecdoche, irony] as metaphors for the different ways we construe fields or sets of phenomena in order to "work them up" into *possible objects of narrative representation and discursive analysis.*
> —Hayden White, *Tropics of Discourse*

In *Tropics of Discourse* White has "read" other specific works besides Thompson's through the prism of his tropology. In *Metahistory*, moreover, White analyzes the tropological strategies underlying the theories of history propounded by Hegel, Marx, Nietzsche, and Croce, as well as the tropologies implicit in the historical narratives of Michelet, Ranke, Tocqueville, and Burckhardt. But of all the analyses White has performed upon histories and theories of history, the two on Foucault—called "Foucault Decoded" and "Michel Foucault"—seem both the most accessible and (apart from the one on Vico) the most authoritative for White's tropics.[7] The reason is clear: Foucault's project in *The Order of Things*— the unearthing of what he calls the epistemes (*épistèmes*) of successive historical epochs—bears a striking similarity to White's enterprise as seen in both *Metahistory* and *Tropics*. In the preface of *The Order of Things*, Foucault says, "I am not concerned . . . to describe the progress of knowledge towards an objectivity in which today's science can finally be recognized; what I am attempting to bring to light is the epistemological field, the episteme in which knowledge, envisaged apart from all criteria having reference to its rational value or to its objective forms, grounds its positivity and thereby manifests a history which is not that of its growing perfection, but rather that of its conditions of possibility; in this account, what should appear are those configurations within the *space* of knowledge which have given rise to the diverse forms of empirical science."[8] Employing what he calls an "archaeological," rather than a historical, method, Foucault addresses the shifting configurations of "knowledge" in relation to the specific discourses on life, labor, and language across three entire epochs—which he names the Renaissance, the Classical, and the Modern—

and at the end gives hints of the appearance of yet a fourth epoch, the Post-Modern or Contemporary.

Both the analysis and the content of *The Order of Things* are thus important to White's conception of tropology. Thompson's study illustrates the way in which tropology can be used to show a narrative development even where such narrative is deemphasized. But Foucault's book not only shows the range available to tropological analysis; it also provides White a history of Western epistemology that fulfills his own tropology. Foucault's notion of the episteme provides White an ultimate cultural synecdoche, shall we say, to embrace all the parts of his theory of tropes. But Foucault himself, White claims, did not apprehend its massive importance. According to White, Foucault's "archaeology" really conceals a tropology of which Foucault is unaware:

> At the center of his thought is a theory of discourse based upon a rather conventional conception of the relation between language and experience, a theory originating in the now discredited discipline of rhetoric. Foucault uses rhetorical notions of language to project a conception of culture as magical, spectral, delusory. Strangely enough, this idea of language remains unexamined by him. In fact, although his thought is based primarily on a theory of language, he has not elaborated such a theory systematically. And as long as he fails to elaborate it, his thought remains captive to that very power which it has been his aim to dissipate. (MF, p. 114)

White's project in his analysis of *The Order of Things*, thus, is the elucidation of the unrecognized tropological system that underlies Foucault's epistemes. To achieve this aim, White turns Foucault's insight against him, for he shows that within the epistemes, as in Foucault's discourse, there is a fundamental blindness (as Paul de Man might have said) to the role of language. "The human sciences, as they unfold between the sixteenth and twentieth century," says White, "can be characterized in terms of their failure to recognize the extent to which they are captive of language itself, their failure to see language as a problem" (FD, p. 45; T, p. 251). That failure, White insists, "had the effect of concealing to the practitioners of the human sciences the extent to which the very constitution of their field of study was a *poetic* act" (FD, p. 45; T, p. 252). White will show us, therefore, the relationship between Foucault's four epistemes and the four tropes that comprise White's tropology. In the process, White

24

will thus suggest that Foucault's epistemes provide historical determinations for the verbal styles typical of discourse in a given epoch.

In his analysis, White shows that Foucault's epistemes are based upon a tropological development in two reciprocal ways. First, Foucault's description of the sequence of epistemes from the sixteenth to the twentieth century is dependent upon the tropes. Each episteme is dominated by the habit of thought enfigured in a single trope. The dominant trope, says White, "of a given community of discourse determines both 'what can be seen' in the world and 'what can be known' about it. Tropology thus constitutes the basis of what Foucault calls the *épistème* of an age in the history of thought and expression. It also provides him a way of characterizing the sequence of *épistèmes* that makes up the 'history' of thought about the topics he has analysed in his major books" (MF, p. 94). Second, Foucault's analysis of the *style* of discourse within an historical episteme will be influenced by the trope that dominates the episteme. "Typically," says White, "in Foucault's schema, every 'discursive' formation undergoes a finite number of such [tropic] shifts before reaching the limits of the *épistème* that sanctions its operations. This number corresponds to the fundamental modes of figuration identified by the theory of tropology: metaphor, metonymy, synecdoche, and irony (which is here understood as *self-conscious* catachresis)" (MF, p. 95). The historical progression of the epistemes, then, is linked to the succession of metaphor, metonymy, synecdoche, and irony, but so is the development of the styles of discourses within the epistemes themselves.

For my purposes in elucidating White's tropics of discourse and despite Foucault's studying the discourses of "life," "labor," *and* "language," it is necessary to consider the different epistemes only in terms of the latter, their philosophies of language. "Foucault's characterization of sixteenth-century human sciences," says White, "represents nothing more than his ascription to those sciences of *the mode of metaphor* as the method used by them to enmap or encode the world of experience at that time" (FD, pp. 45–46; T, p. 252). Most readers will probably see that what Foucault calls the Renaissance episteme is for White just another term for Vico's idea of "the primitive," for its language seems caught up in the phenomenological web of nature, becomes a part of nature itself, can only be read as nature is read. Words are things, here. "In its raw, historical sixteenth-century being," Foucault says, "language is not an arbitrary system" as it is for linguists today; "it has been set down in the world and forms a part of it, both because things themselves hide and manifest their own enigma like a language and because words offer themselves to men as things to be deciphered" (OT, p. 35).

Language is thus as mysterious as nature and, in this epoch, must be studied in the same ways—that is, in terms of a system of similitudes. Words are probed for their intrinsic properties, and syntax analyzed in order to show how words could be built by means of their properties. "Language is not what it is because it has a meaning," Foucault says; "Its representative content . . . has no role to play here. Words group syllables together, and syllables letters, because there are virtues placed in individual letters that draw them towards each other or keep them apart, exactly as the marks found in nature also repel or attract one another" (OT, p. 35). Ultimately, such views of language and nature rest upon the myths of Adam and of Babel, for these myths of the Fall account for the failure of interpretation in a world "resonant with metaphor," as John Updike calls the mythic world of *The Centaur*, a universe presumably characterized by total similitude or self-identity. The Fall is evident in both language and nature, word and thing. Each possesses a fragmented being, each is "divided against itself and deprived of its original transparency by admixture." Each holds "a secret that carries within itself, though near the surface, the decipherable signs of what it is trying to say." Like nature, however, language is in the process of redemption in both mythic contexts, each "at the same time a buried revelation," but "a revelation that is gradually being restored to ever greater clarity" (OT, p. 35–36).

In Foucault's description of the next episteme, that of the eighteenth century, the human sciences, says White, "represent little more than epistemological projections of the trope of metonymy" (FD, p. 46; T, p. 253). In this episteme, which Foucault calls the *âge classique*, the Classical, language is no longer thought to function through similitude, resemblance, identity; rather, it functions through representation. Language becomes a *sign* of things, but is no longer either a thing in itself or a mark upon things. For this reason, Foucault says, "the written word ceases to be included among the signs and forms of truth; language is no longer one of the figurations of the world, or a signature stamped upon things since the beginning of time." Words have become separated from things, but also from essences, truth. "The manifestation and sign of truth are to be found in evident and distinct perception," says Foucault. "It is the task

26

of words to translate that truth if they can; but they no longer have the right to be considered a mark of it. Language has withdrawn from the midst of beings themselves and has entered a period of transparency and neutrality" (OT, p. 56). Such a view of language, inevitably, is part and parcel of a Classical epistemology based upon analysis, itself based upon the recognition of both identity and difference, not just similitude as before.

The major activity of the mind in the *âge classique* becomes the metonymical effort to discriminate, to establish the identities of things apart from all other things, and then to proceed to their connections as observed in the "successive degrees of a series" (OT, p. 55). As a sign of things, rather than a thing itself, language becomes "co-extensive with representation," with the act of thought, with knowledge. "Analysis of representation and the theory of signs interpenetrate one another absolutely," Foucault says, but within the episteme there can be no separation of sign and representation. When idea and sign no longer are felt to interpenetrate, we are on the verge of the next episteme. Indeed, says Foucault, "the day came, at the end of the eighteenth century, [when] Ideology . . . raise[d] the question of whether the idea or the sign should be accorded primacy." And that very questioning meant, says Foucault, "that their immediate link was already becoming confused." Thus, "idea and sign would soon cease to be perfectly transparent to one another" (OT, p. 65). That failure of representation's transparency is what leads to the next episteme.

In his Modern episteme, which seems concurrent with the nineteenth century, Foucault argues that language no longer exists "only by virtue of the [transparent] representative power" (OT, p. 280) that it possessed as a function of the grid of order assumed to underlie all Classical knowledge. The shift, White suggests, is from metonymy to synecdoche, for "as metonymic language is to synecdochic language, so the human sciences of the eighteenth century are to the human sciences of the nineteenth century" (FD, p. 47; T, p. 254). In the Modern age, Foucault suggests, "if the word is able to figure in a discourse in which it means something," it will be because "in its very form, in the sounds that compose it, in the changes it undergoes in accordance with the grammatical function it is performing, and finally in the modifications to which it finds itself subject in the course of time, it obeys a certain number of strict laws which regulate, in a similar way, all the other elements of the same language; so that the word is no longer attached to a representation except in so far as it is previously a part of the grammatical organization by means of which the language defines and guarantees its own coherence" (OT, pp. 280–81). In short, words in the Modern episteme depended for their power of representation not upon some presumed isomorphism between word and idea, but upon the specific roles they played in a larger synecdochic system. "For the word to be able to say what it says," according to Foucault, "it must belong to a grammatical totality which, in relation to the word, is primary, fundamental, and determining" (OT, p. 281).

The Post-Modern or Contemporary episteme is not defined by Foucault as fully as the other three. But it too has a distinct tropological orientation. According to White, "for Foucault, the human sciences of the twentieth century are characterizable precisely by the *Ironic* relationship which they sustain with their objects" (FD, p. 49; T, p. 255). This episteme, of course, is the one in which we ourselves dwell, and as such it cannot be as plainly visible to us as the others. But Foucault does give us some clues bearing on the role language will play. He suggests that for us language will *become* reality. Language, not the content of the human sciences, will become the object of our study. As the object of knowledge, language will replace "man," a concept Foucault insists was merely an invention of the nineteenth century anyway. But language no longer will have the unity that it had in Renaissance and Classical discourse, nor even that it had in the heroic subjectivity associated with nineteenth-century romanticism.

Language in the Post-Modern age is perhaps irretrievably distanced from us. "And now," says Foucault, "in this philosophical-philological space opened up for us by Nietzsche, language wells up in an enigmatic multiplicity that must be mastered." The nineteenth century had given the mastery of language, of utterance, to man, the almost god-like subject. But the Post-Modern, in a distinctly phenomenological move, gives that mastery only to language itself. "To the Nietzschean question: 'Who is speaking?,'" Foucault asserts that Mallarmé, his paradigm-figure of the artist, would reply, "What is speaking is . . . the word itself." Our human *being*, in short, is mastered by the word: "in its solitude, in its fragile vibration, in its nothingness," the word speaks us (OT, p. 305). So man disappears into a verbal universe, not so much dispersed as absorbed once more, as Ernst Cassirer, Edmund Husserl, Maurice Merleau-Ponty, and Paul Ricoeur might say, into his and her myths, ideologies, and symbols—

to say nothing of those tropological formations of which we are largely unaware unless we have ourselves consciously reached the fourth tropic phase, the metatropological phase of irony.

Phenomenology and the Return to Metaphor

> The return to Metaphorical consciousness would be a rebirth of innocence.
>
> —Hayden White, *Metahistory*

> The relations of metaphor to ambiguity, to figurative language, to simile and parable, and even to symbol and myth, interesting and important as these questions are . . . , presuppose something more fundamental, namely, *the primordial attempt to articulate in language the structure and meaning of the personal life-world.*
>
> —James M. Edie, *Speaking and Meaning*

As we follow Hayden White from Vico through Freud, Piaget, and Thompson, to Foucault, it is easy—but, in White's terms, predictable—for one to lose faith in the hypertrophic symmetries of his tropics. The problem one faces upon seeing that Vico's tropological history of culture is congruent with the ontogenesis of human thought as described by Piaget, that both of these are congruent with Freud's psychoanalytic notions of condensation, displacement, representation, and secondary revision, and that all three are consistent with Foucault's description of the sequence of four historical epistemes (and so on) suggests that a tropology is just *de trop*. Precisely the same impression is the one noted by many reviewers of *Metahistory* when they see White align Northrop Frye's four-fold modes of emplotment, Stephen Pepper's four-fold modes of argument, Karl Mannheim's four-fold modes of ideological implication, and White's own contemporary version of the four-fold tropology. It all begins to seem too much. But while the extraordinary symmetry of alignment among these systems may represent a valid ground for objecting to White's tropics or any such tropology, there are more serious philosophic objections to tropology that are indeed raised in particular against White's. We must therefore see if they can be met on grounds outside those White himself has prepared. White's tropological system has been critiqued rather widely,[9] but it seems that the way beyond the ironic, or what White (in an essay in *Tropics* on contemporary literary theory) calls the Absurdist, moment, ironically lies through the most rigorous of these critiques. This way beyond irony, recursively, will take us back to our beginning.

29

The major charges leveled against White's tropology seem, finally, to develop out of questions raised by the last—the absurdly ironic—tropical moment. Though it is the one to which we ourselves belong, as must also Foucault and White, the ironic moment calls into question the entire tropological sequence and, thus, any systematic tropics. Irony does so because of its deliberate self-reflexiveness. By calling attention to itself as a trope it suggests that each of the other tropes is only a trope, too, and so the objective "truth value" of each tropical moment of thought, just as of each historical episteme, seems radically depressed. David Carroll[10] has put the matter succinctly: "Irony not only undermines the epistemological foundations of history but also the substantiality and specificity (the properness) of the other three tropes. In fact, the existence of a metatrope [irony] puts into question the whole taxonomy" (DC, p. 61). Fredric Jameson[11] has put the matter another way, but it too leads to the same recognition that there is a potentially short-circuiting tautology implicit in the tropology: "We must first observe that the meaning of the individual tropes . . . derives from the relationship of each one to the other three: each trope is read *through* its position in the fourfold scheme, and it should be clear . . . that that scheme is a diachronic one, or in other words, that each trope is understood as a moment within the intelligibility of some larger ongoing process in which it is subsumed" (FJ, p. 8).

The major difficulty here for Jameson is the "refusal of genuinely historical thinking" that such a system of tropic convection seems to entail. That refusal, Jameson suggests, brings its own "retribution" in the form of the mythic/cyclic thinking he sees in White (and, perforce, in Foucault): "The cyclical pattern becomes unavoidable. It was already in the tropes themselves, whose movement from the naive freshness of metaphor to the disabused skepticism of the Ironic mode foretells a return to origins, and a reinvention of the tropological cycle" (FJ, p. 8). Jameson's critique rests upon the notion that the cyclicality of the tropes, which also appears to determine a cyclicality in Foucault's series of epistemes, leaves no possible material grounding in history. Commenting on the relation of the tropes to White's thesis about how history comes to be written, as exposited in *Metahistory*, Jameson says that "we must refuse to admit that history repeats itself and we must patiently insist that the cyclical vision of *Metahistory* as a whole is an optical illusion generated by the autonomization of a set of phenomena—historiography and theories of history—which is not complete in itself and is intelligible concretely only at the price of its reintegration into the social history of culture as a whole" (FJ, p. 9).

Carroll offers the argument, however, that would counter Jameson's simpler linear view of history and of the cycle of tropes and epistemes. Also commenting on *Metahistory*, Carroll says, "The return to Irony which White finds at the end of the nineteenth century in spite of or even because of the struggle against it, is not simply cyclical in the Viconian sense but also dialectical in the Hegelian, for we do not return to exactly the same Irony, nor do we return in exactly the same way." Carroll reminds us that the tropes, like the epistemes in Foucault, are modes of consciousness, and the mode represented by irony—whether of consciousness or of an episteme—permits a tropological self-consciousness that will not allow the return, unchanged, of the other modes in their simpler earlier forms. "White claims that a definitive transcendence of Irony is possible in our time," Carroll says, "because Irony (to use Hegelian terminology) is now aware of itself, for, in, and by itself" (DC, p. 61). Still, Carroll does not entirely accept White's claims in behalf of the transcendent power of irony.

Though Carroll, in defense of White, rejects Jameson's somewhat doctrinaire materialism, he rejects at the same time White's apparent idealism of form on grounds other than a simple materialism or nominalism. "White himself is at least implicitly aware," Carroll concedes, "that to proclaim that language (form) functions as the metahistorical level of history and to give it absolute priority is to determine arbitrarily a process which cannot have its ultimate source in form alone." He says, however, that because "White's recourse to a metahistorical level is idealistic ... it closes off the interpretive-historical process by giving it a simple origin and end *telos* in form, outside of the contradictions of history." Though Carroll here sounds like Jameson, he does not deny that a metahistorical level of analysis is always available in the interpretations of material historical events. Beyond that, "a meta-metahistory is always possible and necessary if one does not want to enclose history within an area defined by a formalist idealism of the nature of White's," Carroll claims, "or within that of a traditional metaphysical Platonic idealism" (DC, p. 62). For Carroll, however, the major failure of White's apparent Platonic idealism is none of these. It is White's failure to recognize the role of ideology, for ideology—including, of course, his own—operates within White's tropology and *in his own terms*. "White's mistake," Carroll suggests, "is in never raising in a serious manner the problem of form in general and in too quickly and uncritically accepting certain formal categories as universal ones, in pretending that the categories he uses are not themselves open to challenge and do not limit, preform, and determine the sense and scope of his own work" (DC, p. 63).

There are several ways to respond to the critique of White's tropics by Jameson and Carroll. One way is to show that much of what they claim is simply not in accord with White's own arguments. Part of the problem—unavoidable, historically—is that Jameson and Carroll are responding to *Metahistory* without recourse to all the essays White gathered together in *Tropics of Discourse* (though, clearly, some of the essays were in print in journals and collections at the time Jameson and Carroll attacked *Metahistory*). While *Metahistory* may often lead one toward Jameson's and Carroll's conclusion about White's formal or even Platonic idealism, the essays in *Tropics of Discourse* simply will not permit such a conclusion. Neither White's tropology nor the tropics of discourse it opens to us is idealistic in any naive way. Nor does White claim, as Jameson says, that "history repeats itself," any more than White "uncritically [accepts] certain formal categories as universal ones" or pretends "that the categories he uses are not themselves open to challenge," as Jameson insists. What White would—and does—contend is that the ways in which history, apart from its events, gets *written* will repeat themselves, and that those ways (governed by the tropes) have an objectively ideal status in our experience of the world. The system of tropes, as White outlines it in essay after essay in *Tropics of Discourse*, especially, is as open and indeterminate—however predictable within concrete contexts—as our use of language itself.

The best answer to both Jameson and Carroll, I suggest, returning to my initial understanding, lies in the philosophical claims of phenomenology. Phenomenology—as seen in Husserl and in Edie's extrapolation—seems to split the difference between the materialism of both Jameson and Carroll and the simple idealism they claim to see in White. The problem for White is similar to the problem faced by all who create formal systems, either of logic or of language itself, for those systems can always be viewed as if they were only ideal structural objects, with no objective existence. The problem where language is concerned is simply that the *syntax* of the mimetic or representational system cannot make the shift to the *semantics* necessary for determining the meaning generated by concrete exercise within the rules of the system. An intuitive leap or turn or troping is always necessary to bridge the gap between the logic of the items in the atemporal series and the significations of those items generated in the logical or linguistic, temporal and historical performance. At some point, then, for a tropological system to be validated, we must descend from the abstract idea of tropes to concrete tropological utterances rooted in our experience within what the phenomenologists call the "life-world." In linguistic terms, we must have recourse to actual writing or speech, as opposed to abstract language—*la parole*, rather than *la langue*.

Our recourse, therefore, as I have already suggested, is to a phenomenology of language. A phenomenology of language means, first, that we cannot or "are not obliged to draw a sharp distinction between language conceived as a pre-given entity and speech, the actual use made of language," in the words of John C. Sallis.[12] In addition, it means that speech, particularly in the exercise of its figurative, tropological energies, will be constructive, providing a way in which human beings can creatively give meaning to themselves and their world (JCS, p. 500). Third, it means— and Carroll is correct on this point, as is White's tropology—that there will always be an ideological element in our speech, for by virtue of its positioning in concrete human experience, our use of language inevitably will involve not only "a fundamental value commitment," but also "a fundamental responsibility" (JCS, p. 502). But finally and above all, it means that at its origin speech is figurative, metaphoric—or, more generally, tropological—and is thus "poetic," for it expresses phenomenologically our "dialogue of existence with the world" (JCS, p. 506). New knowledge is always phenomenological and, finally, "poetic." Thus, our ultimate recourse to expressiveness, phenomenologists claim, is to poetry, taken in its broadest sense as verbal art. In poetry, the objective life-world and our subjective experience are most intensely expressed. Mikel Dufrenne, in *Language and Philosophy*, has gone so far as to suggest that a phenomenological apprehension of languages seems to reverse our relation to the world through language: "This is the essential point: the world speaks to us; it comes and lets itself be caught in the snare of words; the words that [the world's] grand images wrench from us are full of its presence. And here perhaps we are at the very source that we sought to regain, at that point where the world reveals itself to us, where what is spoken is itself speaking" (p. 96).

The philosophic advantage that a phenomenology of language brings to tropology—especially a tropology in our current ironic moment—is its permitting us once more to believe that we can engage in a reciprocal relation to the world through language, instead of—in the terms of irony— its merely, absurdly, speaking us or our speaking phenomenally empty words. In the terms of John Updike's *The Centaur*, which attempts to regain such a phenomenological and linguistic innocence in the midst of an ironic literary and entropic physical universe, this indeed would be a world "resonant with metaphor." In White's terms, that would be again to see the world as metaphorical—with all the implications for one's epistemology such a troping would bring.

I suspect Hayden White would agree with a phenomenological view of language *and* tropology *and* narrative discourse. He would not deny the relationship between one's responsible choices of tropes and one's lived experience, nor would he deny the creative dialectic between tropology and one's existential freedom. Sallis reminds us that "man's freedom is a situational freedom" (JCS, p. 501), so while it may be fair of Carroll to imply that our freedom of choice among the tropes is no more meaningful than our choices of goods within a consumer society (DC, p. 64), still that may well be the actual "situation" within which our freedom exists. White has many ideas available to him, but he recognizes that his existence in a historical epoch will make some more desirable than others. In his case, it seems plain that White's tropology is situated, as he says of Foucault's work, in the metalinguistics of postmodernist psychology, philosophy, and literature. It thus provides the basis for his intellectual freedom; at the same time it binds him to a historical—indeed, a tropical— moment.

NOTES

1. See *Metahistory: The Historical Imagination in Nineteenth-Century Europe* (Baltimore: Johns Hopkins University Press, 1973), and *Tropics of Discourse: Essays in Cultural Criticism* (Baltimore: Johns Hopkins University Press, 1978), abbreviated M and T, respectively, with page numbers in parentheses in my text whenever practicable hereafter. The best essays of which I am aware that both explain and extrapolate White's "tropology" are by Hans Kellner: "A Bedrock of Order: Hayden White's Linguistic Humanism," *History and Theory* 19: *Beiheft* 19 (1980):1–29, and "The Inflatable Trope as Narrative Theory: Structure or Allegory?" *Diacritics* 11 (Mar. 1981):14–28.

2. See the translation by Thomas G. Bergin and Max H. Fisch (Ithaca, N.Y.: Cornell University Press, 1968).

3. James M. Edie, *Speaking and Meaning: The Phenomenology of Language* (Bloomington: Indiana University Press, 1976), pp. 166–71.

4. See Jean Piaget, *The Child and Reality: Problems of Genetic Psychology*, trans. Arnold Rosin (New York: Grossman Publishers, 1973).

5. See Sigmund Freud, *The Interpretation of Dreams*, trans. James Strachey (New York: Norton, 1965).

6. See E. P. Thompson, *The Making of the English Working Class* (New York: Pantheon, 1963).

7. See Hayden V. White, "Foucault Decoded: Notes from Underground," *History and Theory* 12.1 (1973):23–54, abbreviated FD with page numbers in parentheses in my text hereafter; since this essay also appears in *Tropics of Discourse*, pp. 230–60, I will give the citations there too. See also White's "Michel Foucault," in *Structuralism and Since: From Lévi-Strauss to Derrida*, ed. John Sturrock (Oxford: Oxford University Press, 1979), pp. 81–115, abbreviated MF with page numbers in parentheses in my text hereafter.

8. Michel Foucault, *The Order of Things: An Archaeology of the Human Sciences* (New York: Pantheon, 1970), p. xxii, abbreviated OT with page numbers in parentheses in my text hereafter. Foucault's later work changes the line of thought initiated with *The Order of Things* and extended in *The Archaeology of Knowledge* and "The Discourse of Language," but those later, more sociologically oriented studies are not germane to my interests here. I should point out that I have frequently turned to specific passages in *The Order of Things* in order to flesh out White's tropological analysis: these passages are not always acknowledged by White, though I assume they lie within his purview.

9. See *History and Theory* 19: *Beiheft* 19 (1980), for example, which is entirely devoted to review, criticism, and extrapolation of *Metahistory*.

10. "On Tropology: The Forms of History," *Diacritics* 6 (Fall 1976):58–64, abbreviated DC with page numbers in parentheses in my text hereafter. For some reason, Carroll makes the statement that "for White no age can be characterized by one trope alone" (DC, p. 61, n. 5). In general, neither *Metahistory* nor "Foucault Decoded" would support that claim; what White does indicate is that an age will not be limited to use of just one trope, though it can be characterized by one alone.

11. "Figural Relativism, or the Poetics of Historiography," *Diacritics* 6 (Spring 1976):2–9, abbreviated FJ with page numbers in parentheses in my text hereafter.

12. "Phenomenology and Language," *The Personalist* 48.4 (Autumn 1967):496, abbreviated JCS with page numbers in parentheses in my text hereafter. Along with James M. Edie (see 3), Sallis is a major contributor to studies in the phenomenology of language, and his essay is at the same time an overview of the relation of phenomenology and language and a review of three important, relatively early books on the topic: Mikel Dufrenne, *Language and Philosophy*, trans. Henry

B. Veatch (Bloomington: Indiana University Press, 1963); Georges Gusdorf, *Speaking*, trans. Paul T. Brockelman (Evanston, Ill.: Northwestern University Press, 1965); and Remy C. Kwant, *Phenomenology of Language* (Pittsburgh: Duquesne University Press, 1965). In my concluding chapter, on *The Centaur*, in addition to using ideas from these scholars (Dufrenne and Gusdorf, in particular), I will employ ideas of Ernst Cassirer, who, though not regarded as a phenomenologist, has a view of language (as a "symbolic form") that sits well with the avowed phenomenologists. See, for example, Cassirer's *Language and Myth*, trans. Susanne K. Langer (New York: Dover, 1953; orig. pub. 1925), and his *An Essay on Man* (New Haven: Yale University Press, 1944), in addition to *The Philosophy of Symbolic Forms*, trans. Ralph Manheim, 3 vols. (New Haven: Yale University Press, 1953, 1955, 1957).

Chapter Two

Metaphor, Metonymy, and Lacanian Discourse in Heller's *Something Happened*

Lacan's Dyadic Tropology

> The effects not only of the elements of the horizontal signifying chain, but also of its vertical dependencies in the signified, [are] divided into two fundamental structures called metonymy and metaphor.
>
> —Jacques Lacan, *Écrits: A Selection*

Joseph Heller took a tremendous risk in *Something Happened*. He has spoken of the risks in his technique, the manner in which the "first and third person," he says, "are fused in a way I've never seen before, and time is compressed into almost a solid substance."[1] But one may suggest that the greater risk lies in the novel's psychological subtlety of content, structure, and theme. Though the psychological dimensions of *Something Happened* are evident from the outset, readers are perhaps thrown off the track by an overt invocation of the Oedipus complex as an explanation of those psychological disturbances suggested in narrator Bob Slocum's fear of closed doors and in other features of behavior. Slocum seems to imply that since he actually invokes an outmoded Freudian etiology, one must look elsewhere for the "real" causes of his neurotic behavior. In truth, though it is possible to assimilate Freudian structures to a tetradic system of tropes,[2] one does well by the novel by merely shifting toward a post-Freudian, dyadic tropology propounded by Lévi-Strauss and Jakobson and adapted in the psychoanalytic theory of Jacques Lacan, who, disregarding synecdoche and irony, like the anthropologist and the linguist, builds his analysis upon the tropes of metaphor and metonymy.

Lacan's version of Freudian psychoanalysis entails what one commentator calls a "classic narrative" pattern operating through the discourse of the family. Its stages or phases begin with birth and then move "in turn through the territorialization of the body, the mirror stage, access to language, and the Oedipus complex. The last two of these events belong to what Lacan calls the symbolic order, and they mark the subject's coming of age within culture."[3] These stages in turn operate within a system Lacan calls the Imaginary and the Symbolic. The mirror stage, initiating the movement into language, is essentially egocentric and thus may develop into the secondary narcissism of the Imaginary. Ordinary psychological growth, culminating in the cultural "coming of age," involves one's moving from the Imaginary to the Symbolic. Caught up in the Imaginary, the neurotic is defined by the belief that one can permanently recapture an initial plenitude or fullness of meaning and being. All neurosis, in Lacanian theory, is therefore dominated by the terms of the Oedipal complex—castration, desire, the forbidden, sacrifice, the father. Fredric Jameson has said that "neurosis for Lacan is essentially a failure to accept castration, a failure to accept the primal lack which is at the center of life itself: a vain and impossible nostalgia for that first essential plenitude, a belief that one really can in one form or another repossess the phallus."[4] For Lacan, genuine—rather than neurotic or nostalgic—forms of desire entail a recognition that one's very human fate is incompleteness and that one's desires, unless one comes to terms with them, will inevitably be repeated endlessly. There is no "ultimate satisfaction" (p. 172) of desire available to us in reality, and neurosis itself is manifested for Lacan in one's attempts "to achieve ultimate certainty" (pp. 172–73).

Plenitude belongs to a symbolic order, and within that order it is identified as the Phallus. The Phallus exists as a function, not as a thing (least of all an actual penis). Thus it will always be known through a signifier—through something that stands for it, rather than through the "thing" itself. Phallic plenitude thus really belongs to language. It will find its place in the order of signification where the denominator stands in Lacan's formula: S/s. Because the virgule here represents a bar, forever impassable, between signifier (S) and signified (s), it also defines the structure of desire: just as the signifier represents the effort to recapture the signified, so the objects of desire represent the subject's efforts to recapture the original fullness of being that underlies desire. Thus the structure of desire is observed in the structure of language; it operates in the two main axes found in language: the paradigmatic (or axis of similarity) and the syntagmatic (or axis of contiguity). These two axes of language, according to Lévi-Strauss and Jakobson, provide the two tropological modes—metaphor and metonymy—by which literary texts are ordinarily expanded or developed, but they are also related, Lacan suggests, to Freudian psychoanalytic concepts of condensation and displacement, as well as to the linguistic concepts of the synchronic and the diachronic. According to Kaja Silverman, "Metaphor and metonymy respond to similarity and contiguity as the basis for the *temporary replacement* of one signifying element by another. . . . Within metaphor and metonymy the primary and secondary processes find a kind of equilibrium, one which permits profound affinities and adjacencies to be discovered without differences being lost."[5]

In Lacanian terms, one can make two important points about technique and narrative structure in *Something Happened*. First, Heller's text is largely the representation of the many linguistic displacements of desire in Bob Slocum as he searches the labyrinth of memory for the ultimate signifier (the Phallus)—that representation of the source, origin, essence of his primal self, being, identity. Second, *histoire* or story in the novel is almost swallowed up in the massive volume of those displacements, but it finally produces a narrative structure displaying Slocum's movement from a desire to achieve ultimate completeness, certainty, plenitude to a mature, if ironic, realization that these can never be achieved. At the novel's end, following Slocum's resigned acquiescence to the terms of the Oedipus complex, Heller shows his subject coming of age within culture by his moving out of the narcissism of the Imaginary into the objectivity and indeterminacy of the Symbolic.

Metaphor and Metonymy

> Lacan [says] that the unconscious is structured like a language. The repressed is of the order of the signifier and the unconscious signifiers are organized in a network governed by various relationships of association, above all metaphoric and metonymic associations.
>
> —Anika Lemaire, *Jacques Lacan*

If readers are to grasp the unconscious underlying the signifiers of Slocum's consciousness, that consciousness will have to be read as a language. Lacan suggests that the unconscious, like language, operates largely through the processes of metaphor and metonymy, forms of distancing through substitutions based on similarity or on displacement toward other objects associated within a context. The "profound affinities and adjacencies" of metaphoric and metonymic displacement characteristic of the entire novel are bountifully illustrated in the first chapter. They become visible in the very first sentence: "I get the willies when I see closed doors."[6] Heller's protagonist, like any reader, wonders why he dreads "that something horrible is happening behind" closed doors. He says that "something must have happened to me sometime" (p. 3), and he even offers potential explanations developed in a combination of metonymic and metaphoric displacements that ordinarily would gladden the heart of any Freudian analyst. "Maybe it was the day I came home unexpectedly with a fever and a sore throat and caught my father in bed with my mother." This metonymic association, however, is just the beginning of a series of other associations closed by a metaphoric substitution for that primal scene. He offers, for example, four alternative explanations for his fear of closed doors. [1] "Or maybe it was the knowledge that we were poor. . . . [2] Or the day my father died and left me feeling guilty and ashamed. . . . [3] Or maybe it was the realization . . . that I would never have broad shoulders and huge biceps. . . . [4] Or maybe it was the day I did open another door and saw my big sister standing naked" (pp. 3–4).

Any one of these might have been sufficient as an explanation for Slocum's fear, but he offers them less to explain, it seems, than to mask its real cause or causes. Lacan suggests that the unconscious operates through the same means of signification as language, but language can never fully recover the signified through the agency of the signifier. Thus, the subject-consciousness (Slocum's here), in his discourse about himself, will be "caught up in an order of symbols" and therefore will move "progressively away from the truth of his essence."[7] Such progressive distancing from the Oedipal "truth" is precisely what one confronts in Slocum's narration. After the series of alternative causes for his fear of closed doors, he launches into the first dramatized scene of the novel. That scene is simply a metaphoric substitution, with greater metonymic detail, for the parental primal scene mentioned first. "I remember also," he says, "with amusement now, because it happened so long ago, the hot summer day I wandered into the old wooden coal shed behind our red-brick apartment building and found my big brother lying on the floor with Billy Foster's skinny kid sister." Slocum is never able or willing to provide details of what he observed in his parents' bedroom, but he does give readers considerable information about the substitute "primal" scene in which his older brother is involved. The language he uses suggests he had stepped upon a snake, or perhaps a mouse. When he had first "heard a faint, frantic stirring" upon entering "the dark place," he felt as though he "had stepped on something live." Thus, he was momentarily relieved to discover it was only his "brother lying on the floor with someone." But after his brother yelled at him and threw a lump of coal, the pre-pubescent Slocum "bolted outside," feeling "too guilty to escape," he says, "and almost too frightened to stay and take the punishment I knew I deserved—though I didn't know for what" (p. 4). Slocum's question, upon the couple's exit from "the yawning blackness behind" the "enor-mous wooden door," will be the one that haunts the novel: "What was happening in there, Eddie? Did something happen?" (p. 5).

Slocum's ambivalent desire to know what "happened," his gener-alized pursuit of knowledge, sexual and otherwise, thus, by a process of displacement, becomes associated with doors. The closed door is thus the bar between exterior and interior, known and unknown, signifier and signified (S/s) in Slocum's personal "language" of images. Inevitably, the signified is readily transferred to other large gaps in Slocum's knowledge where desire and fear are mingled. It is rather abruptly shifted in Slocum's discourse from the domain of sex toward the domain of death as a result of metonymic associations with his brother. He is reminded that his big brother is now dead, as is his father, so Slocum cannot ever ask what he was "never bold enough to ask" while Eddie was alive. Thus, he admits, "Today, there are so many things I *don't* want to find out." He does not want to visit hospitalized friends, he says, because "I might open the door of the private or semiprivate room and come upon some awful sight for which I could not have prepared myself." And he will not phone hospitals to inquire after his friends "because there's always the danger I might find out they are dead" (p. 6). But he is never satisfied with any stance he takes. Thus he admits to a ghoulish episode when he did phone a hospital after he knew of someone's death, but he says he wanted merely to know how the hospital would handle the issue. The question, for Slocum, thus had been shifted, metonymically, from one of death to one of "technique": "Would they decide he had died, passed away, succumbed, was deceased, or perhaps even had expired?" What he really wanted to know were the words by which the death would be signified. He was surprised when the woman on the phone said that the person was "no longer listed as a patient." But the reader is surprised at Slocum's reaction to the episode, for it generates the same emotional effect in Slocum as his sexual inquiries: "Certainly, my heart was pounding with great joy and excitement at my narrow escape," he says, as if the approach to knowledge of sex and death is of the same order as his escape from *discovery* of what he is actually doing—as if escape from the embarrassment of being found out in one's morbid or erotic inquiries is tantamount to escaping one's mortality or sexuality (p. 7).

One final representation of Slocum's psychosexual concerns makes up the bulk of the brief first chapter's remaining two pages. If it were not for the fact, as Lacan sees it, that metaphor and metonymy are the primary means to knowledge of the subject, one would surmise that Slocum has strayed totally away from "the truth of his essence" in his recounting the episode of the mice. The mice would seem to function, in the language of the unconscious, in the place of the signified, and thus in the place of the Phallus, for they are quite as unapproachable as the "s" is beyond the bar separating it from the "S": (S/s). "I didn't know what to do about those mice," he says. "I never saw them. Only the cleaning lady did, or said she did, and one time my wife thought she did, and one time my wife's mother was almost sure she did. After a while the mice just disappeared" (pp. 8–9). Slocum admits that he is not certain they were ever really there, but like any unknown yet somehow desired object, they nonetheless made his life miserable for a time. They inevitably brought back the other significances represented in doors. "I never knew what I would find when I opened the doors to inspect my traps" (p. 9), he says, not sure whether he most feared catching or not catching the mice. He is sure, however, that he dreaded he might "open a door in the kitchen and find a live mouse crouching in a dark corner" (pp. 9–10), and he would have to kill it. "The possibility of finding a live mouse behind every door I opened each morning filled me with nausea and made me tremble. It was not that I was afraid of the mouse itself (I'm not that silly), but if I ever did find one, I knew I would have to do something about it" (p. 10).

Clearly, the live mouse has come to have a powerful symbolic function in Slocum's imagination. As a metaphor, it will have (Lacan would say) significance as a symptom of what ails Slocum. What ails Slocum is his inability to come to terms with the duality of the Oedipus complex: desire to possess the phallic plenitude forever lost at the separation from the mother, and fear of the consequences of possessing that which will represent the plenitude. Thus, by way of the processes of metaphor and metonymy operating through the first chapter, one is led back to the concerns expressed in the novel's initial sentence, which has produced the metonymical image representing the duality of Slocum's major theme: *eros* and *thanatos*. In its positive aspect, this theme is the Phallus; in its negative, it is castration. "Lacan will say," according to Anika Lemaire, "that what corresponds in the unconscious to any possible imaginable form of sexual relation is an individual 'lack,' an original and chronic state of self-insufficiency. He will say that it is in this that the universality of the castration complex lies."[8] The closed door thus becomes the object in Slocum's imagination representing the absence or lack that defines his life, as well as the bar separating him from the fulfillment he seeks.

The Discourse of the Family

> In the Oedipus, the child moves from an immediate, non-distanced relationship with its mother to a mediate relationship thanks to its insertions into the symbolic order of the Family.
>
> —Anika Lemaire, *Jacques Lacan*

Robert Slocum is a man caught in the grip of a neurosis, and it is expressed in the facility with which he fills the void through those metonymic and metaphoric expansions. These tropological moves project into the world his own contradictory fears, thus creating an environment in his own image. On the one hand, for example, every door in Slocum's life will be identified with every other; on the other hand, his every experience or feeling contradicts itself: "I've always been afraid I was about to be fired. Actually, I have never been fired from a job" (p. 15); "When I grow up I want to be a little boy. . . . When I grow up, I want to be someone dignified, tasteful, and important" (pp. 340–41). His world may indeed be just exactly as he says it is, but there is no perspective upon it except his. The "reality" of the world Slocum projects is inconsequential to any analysis of *Something Happened*, however, for readers are forced to regard all his utterances as symptoms of his ailment. In Lacan's terms, Slocum has become fixed at the stage of the Imaginary, precisely the stage that works through principles of identification seen in metaphor and of duality seen in metonymy. Slocum's "confession" thus rather clearly illustrates the functioning of the Imaginary: "Lacan defines the essence of the imaginary as a dual relationship, a reduplication in the mirror, an immediate opposition between consciousness and its other in which each term becomes its opposite and is lost in the play of the reflection. In its quest for itself, consciousness thus believes that it has found itself in the mirror of its creatures and loses itself in something which is not consciousness."[9]

The etiology for his fears concerning doors that Slocum provides in the first few paragraphs of the novel focuses largely upon the "classical narrative," *récit*, or story underlying the family romance, the Oedipal drama structuring the discourse of the family. If, that is, the Oedipus complex is the "cause" of Slocum's problems, then it seems likely it will be displayed repeatedly in those displacements of metonymy and substitutions of metaphor produced within his discourse. What Slocum will not do, presumably, is talk directly about his father and mother as sexual beings. What he might well do, however, is push them aside for others who can replace them as less threatening objects. He seems clearly to do such substituting in his recollections concerning his brother and Billy Foster's kid sister and in other rather clearly sexual memories. A few others occur occasionally. Several are brought together, symptomatically, in one passage in the chapter entitled "It is not true." He relates all the images to his reasons for self-hatred. "I can even hate myself—me—generous, tolerant, lovable old Bob Slocum . . . for staying married to the same wife so long when I've had such doubts that I wanted to, molesting my little girl cousin once in the summertime when no mothers were looking" (p. 360). The memory here of the "molesting" of the girl cousin is paired with another passage relating the same incident. In the earlier recollection he recounts that "once in my early teens, I paid a younger cousin of mine, a girl, a dime to pull it for me and was terrified afterward that she would tell my mother or my brother or someone in her own family" (p. 339). In the later account he says, "I can still recall her vacant, oblivious little girl's stare. I didn't hurt or frighten her. I only touched her underpants a moment between the legs, and then I touched her there again. I gave her a dime and was sorry afterward when I realized she might mention that. Nobody said anything. I still keep thinking they will" (p. 360). In the first account, he says, "She made me happy. For only a dime" (p. 339); in the second, "I didn't get my dime's worth" (p. 360).

The other recollections that float up during this second passage involve the same frustrations and self-accusations. They clearly manifest Slocum's entrapment at the stage of the Imaginary, with its identifications and oppositions. He says, "I can kick myself for fumbling all those priceless chances I had with Virginia at the office for more than half a year, and with a couple of Girl Scout sisters I knew from high school earlier." He can even hate himself, he says, for "seeing my big brother with his fly open on the floor of that shadowy coal shed beside our brick apartment house with a kid named Billy Foster's skinny kid sister." And he can feel self-disgust at his lack of sexual knowledge or experience in comparison to that of the girl, Geraldine Foster: even though she was not "as smart" as he, she "was going all the way already with guys as old and big as my big brother. While *I* wasn't even jerking off yet!" (p. 360). He can feel disgust, moreover, for his cravenly reactions to all those powerful, domineering women in his life who evoke those fears of interdiction, discovery, and rebuke associated with sexuality: his mother-in-law, his sister-in-law, his retarded son Derek's nurses, and "broad and overbearing unforgettable Mrs. Yerger in the automobile casualty insurance company, who towered over me then, it seemed . . . , when she hove into view like a smirking battleship" (p. 361).

Slocum's adult behavior suggests the obsession with sex and sexual fulfillment associated with neurotic desire. His behavior reflects the anxieties that emerged in his childhood and youth. Though any of the varied memories may locate the site of his "problem," the one memory that most insistently returns and is most strikingly elaborated is the one concerning Virginia—"Virgin for short, but not for long" (p. 14). Since Mrs. Yerger evokes all those figures of authority who preside over Slocum's feelings of sexual guilt, frustration, and hostility, the usual conjunction of Mrs. Yerger and Virginia in Slocum's mind suggests something of the nature of his problem: "I remember Mrs. Yerger, and I remember Virginia. . . . What a feeble-minded idiot: I could have had her then. She was hot. I was petrified. What in hell was inhibiting me so long, strangulating me? No wonder when I finally tore free it was with a vengeance" (pp. 336–37). What readers confront here (though it is not clear that Slocum himself understands) is the classic castration complex. In its unresolved form, according to Lacan, it will remain fixed in the Imaginary phase, whereas a "cure" would involve translation into the phase of the Symbolic. "In the castration complex," writes Anika Lemaire, "the Imaginary is the insatiability with which roles and modes of being are sought to compensate, together with sex, for the profound ill of human incompleteness. It is also the uninterrupted rotation of reflex adaptations to styles and functions of being which prove themselves by experiment to be adequate to the unconscious wish which produces them. In short, the Imaginary is everything in the human mind and its reflexive life which is in a state of flux before the fixation is effected by the symbol, a fixation which, at the very least, tempers the incessant sliding of the mutations of being and of desire."[10]

45

Dyadic Tropology and Discursive Structure

> The three sets of signifying clusters—condensation and displacement, paradigm and syntagm, and metaphor and metonymy—coexist in complex ways. Not only is each already the product of a certain facilitation between the primary and secondary processes, but they form additional accommodations and imbrications within discourse.
>
> —Kaja Silverman, *The Subject of Semiotics*

Slocum's memories of his relationship with Virginia in the office of the automobile casualty insurance company are both metaphoric and metonymic in relation to the material they displace. The structure of the memory is metaphoric because it imitates the basic pattern of the other sexual memories, beginning with the primal parental scene (A observes B engaged sexually with C). Its structure can thus substitute for all the others, especially for the more threatening primal scene. But the structure also allows movement from point to point around the triangle of signification formed by the S, the s, and the bar between: S/s. The memory in its metonymic power provides syntax, a syntagmatic chain of signifiers that begins to take the form of a discursive structure. If one follows out the chain, in other words, one can begin to understand the statement Slocum is making to readers—and perhaps to himself as well.

Paradigmatically, the office situation replaces the family situation because it can produce substitutes for the authority of the father (here it is the figure of authority, the commanding presence of Mrs. Yerger, who in Slocum's mind represents all authority), the mother (represented by Virginia, an "older woman," who is both innocent and seductive, nurturing and threatening), and of course the "child" (seventeen-year-old Bobby Slocum). The office also provides substitutes for the sibling relationship and the representation of the violation of the interdiction against incest. Slocum's "brother" is twenty-one-year-old Tom Johnson and another "mother/lover" is twenty-eight-year-old Marie Jencks; "tall, blond, buxom," "striking and attractive," Marie Jencks "was humping" Slocum's friend "whenever she wanted to," and the relationship amazed him, Slocum says, more "than I'd been to find my big brother on the floor of that wooden coal shed with Billy Foster's skinny kid sister" (p. 80). Syntagmatically, the office situation also provides a connected plot, a story that eventually puts young Slocum inside a room, on the other side of a closed door, with an apparent opportunity to engage Virginia sexually. Slocum crosses the bar, moves to the side of the other, replaces father-brother-friend in the embrace of the desired object, only to find he cannot possess that which he seeks. Each day, often several times a day, Slocum and Virginia would sneak off to a file storage room for "swift, incredible trysts," but they always ended, their desires unconsummated, with Virginia's invariable, transparent lie, "Someone's coming" (p. 370), a cry that represents, ambiguously, both a fear of discovery and a desire for sexual consummation.

Ultimately, Slocum has his chance to ravish Virginia in that storage room and discovers that she is no more possessable through seizure than seduction. In the company of two older boys, teased into going there with Virginia, Slocum is more daunted than ever, no more able to consummate the act than before. He is fearful of exposure, fearful of being displayed as sexually lacking, fearful of the potential violence of the whole scene. So, seeing Virginia's taunts turn to terror, he changes from would-be rapist to would-be hero, and, despite a tumult of contradictory sexual feelings, manages to drive the other boys away. Until this episode of the near-rape, the scenes Slocum performs with Virginia are essentially rehearsals for both—for young Slocum, an opportunity to work through his adolescent Oedipal conflicts; for Virginia, an opportunity to break out of her own Oedipal entrapment (she had once been gang raped, she claims, by the Duke University football squad; her father had committed suicide while she was in college; and she seduces fifty-five-year-old Len Lewis, a married coworker). Virginia has given Slocum the chance to act out his Oedipal fantasies, but, he feels fortunate to admit, he never had to act *on* them with her in any conclusive way. Thus, never having had her, he can forever dream of her as the object that would provide complete satisfaction to his desires.

Just as the casualty company office formed a structure that could substitute, metaphorically, for the family, the company for which Slocum works in the present also forms a family structure. Slocum's adventures at the casualty company seemed to focus upon incest through the maternal/female aspect of the forbidden in the Oedipal triangle; his work nowadays seems more clearly focused upon the paternal/male aspects of the interdiction of incest. The twelve directors at the top of the company represent a paternal force that seems to reside in the realm of Lacan's Symbolic, the locus of the Dead Father. "In the domain of social symbolism," says Lemaire, "the third term which mediates between the living will be the Ancestor, the Dead, God, the Sacred Cause, the Institution,

Ideology, etc."[11] The directors, Slocum says, "seem friendly, slow, and content when I come upon them in the halls (they seem dead) and are always courteous and mute when they ride with others in the public elevators" (p. 13). Slocum has little contact with them, but he does have contact with their apostle, Arthur Baron, "who is boss of us all in this division" (p. 37). Arthur Baron serves in their stead as the Symbolic father, the Absent Father whose power to reward and punish mediates Slocum's relationship with his horde of rivals, his primitive "brothers." Those rivals, potentially innumerable in the company, are reduced to just one: Jack Green. Green serves as the chief competitor for a job Baron holds out to Slocum, though Slocum fears others, too, including Ed Phelps, Red Parker, and Johnny Brown—whom everyone fears.

The new job becomes the object that replaces the mother in the yet further displaced Oedipal family structure. Andy Kagle, who already is wedded to that job, becomes the figure in the realm of the Imaginary who most readily substitutes for the father against whom Slocum must struggle. Slocum is as ambivalent about Kagle and his job as he would have been over replacing his real father. After Arthur Baron has told Slocum to begin preparing in secret to take it over, Slocum even warns Kagle to shape up in order to save his job: "Grow up, Andy," he says. "You're a middle-aged man with two kids and a big job in a pretty big company. There's a lot that's expected of you. It's time to mature. It's time to take it seriously and start doing all the things you should be doing. You know what they are. You keep telling me what they are" (p. 65). But Kagle is unable or unwilling to "grow up," and Slocum realizes that, despite all, he wants that "better job" himself (p. 67). That job thus becomes the virtually sexual "object" Slocum seeks—as he sought after women—in order to appease his desire.

Slocum clearly stands in relation to Kagle as the male child to the father. But Kagle resides in the Imaginary for Slocum, not in the Symbolic where Baron stands, for he is an other who merely reduplicates Slocum. Like Kagle, Slocum has two (normal) children and a responsible job in a big company. The two are "comfortable" (p. 49) with each other, as a father and son might be, and Slocum admits that Kagle "has been good to me from the day I came to work here. . . . He makes my job easier. He relies on my judgment, takes my word, and backs me up in disputes I have with his salesmen. Many of his salesmen . . . hold me in some kind of awe because they sense I operate under his protection" (p. 50). But in addition to the identifications associated with the Imaginary realm, there are also oppositions, for contradictions in Slocum's feelings toward Kagle will also mark the Oedipal relation. Slocum knows that "Kagle trusts me and knows he is safe with me," but Slocum translates Kagle's feelings into weakness and thus no longer fears Kagle. "In fact," Slocum says, "I feel that I could scare him whenever I chose to, that he is weak in relation to me and that I am strong in relation to him." Worse yet, Slocum acknowledges a "hideous urge every now and then while he is confiding in me to shock him suddenly . . . or to kick his crippled leg. It's a weird mixture of injured rage and cruel loathing that starts to rise within me and has to be suppressed" (p. 49).

Slocum says he does not know where this urge comes from or whether he will be able to control it, but it will seem clear to readers that the source of the urge is distinctly Oedipal. Heller makes no mistake about this source, for that limp he gives Kagle is the metonymic connection to Oedipus one might most readily expect in this context. Moreover, on days that Slocum has been with Kagle, he too takes on the Oedipus impediment: "If I'm with Andy Kagle, I will limp" (p. 75). But if Slocum is to be "cured," he must transcend such merely immediate, mirror relationships. As much as he may like Kagle, Kagle cannot be the father figure to Slocum who will signify the place of the father in the Symbolic or perform the role of the symbolic law that effectively prohibits the child's union with the figure of the mother in the Oedipal configuration. Kagle, in short, does not have the power of interdiction where Slocum's relation to the position of the mother (that is, the job) is concerned.

The company for which Slocum works may substitute for the family structure, but there is also the actual nuclear family within which Slocum must play his role. One may assume that the biological family—at least in a novel—is never just a family. It will reveal important aspects of the character of the main subject, too. "Psychoanalysis has shown the family, like language," writes Kaja Silverman, "to be a vital relay between the various territories that make up subjectivity and the larger cultural field."[12] With his actual family, however, Slocum remains just as much within the mirror stage of the Imaginary as he does with the company. He feels just as contradictory toward his wife as he does toward Kagle and others at work. "We are no longer close enough for honest conversation," Slocum says, but adds, parenthetically, "we *are* close enough for frequent sexual intercourse." When they were young their sexual endeavors were largely

replays of Slocum's relationship with Virginia, with the significant excep-
tion that he did make it with his wife, whose frightened response, back
then, was as skittish as Virginia's. "I think we liked each other once," he
says. "I think we used to have fun; at least it seems that way now, although
we were always struggling about one thing or another. I was always struggling to get her clothes off, and she was always struggling to keep them
on" (p. 119).

Nowadays, Slocum says, "I lay girls . . . that are as young as she was
then, and much more nimble, profligate, and responsive but it isn't as rich
with impulse and excitement and generally not as satisfying afterward"
(pp. 120–21). Moreover, now, his wife is just as nimble, profligate, and
responsive as the young women, but, Slocum laments, "I'm not sure I like
her this way, although I would have liked it back then, but I'm not sure
about that, either. I'm really not sure I *want* my wife to be as lustful and
compliant as one of Kagle's whores or my girl friends, although I know
I am dissatisfied with her when she isn't" (p. 125). What neither Slocum
nor his wife knows is that they are simply caught up in the syntax of
Slocum's desire, she being just one more element in a chain that includes
countless unnamed sexual partners of Slocum, as well as many who *are*
named: Penny, Jill, Rosemary, young coeds, various prostitutes. If Slocum
is to overcome his problem, he will have to demonstrate that he can break
this chain of apparently unappeasable desire anchoring him in the Imaginary.

Slocum also manifests his entrapment at the realm of the Imaginary
in his relations with the other members of his family—the three children.
Each of the children seems to represent for Slocum a stage along the way
to the development of a normal "self." Derek, the mentally retarded child
and the only family member other than Bob ever named, seems associated
in Slocum's mind with himself as a linguistic or sexual or social "idiot."
He also represents Slocum's fear of the absence of love, for he feels that
no one in his family (except perhaps the other son) really cares for Derek.
And Derek also represents Slocum's speechlessness in the face of authority.
By a process of metonymic linkages, Derek comes to stand in relation to
his nurses as Slocum had stood to Mrs. Yerger, back in the casualty
company office. He says of the nurse they have now, "She reminds me of
Mrs. Yerger. I want to yell dirty things at this nurse now for the debasement
Mrs. Yerger made me suffer then" (p. 129). But, then, one of the problems
the idiot child brings with him is that he evokes the Oedipal range of

Slocum's anxieties concerning himself through the metonymic sequences he initiates: "Every older woman I find myself afraid of reminds me of Mrs. Yerger. Every feeble old woman I see reminds me of my mother. Every young girl who attacks my pride reminds me of my daughter. No one reminds me of my father, which is okay with me, I guess, since I don't remember a father for anyone to remind me of. Except Arthur Baron. I think I may feel a little bit about Arthur Baron the way I might have felt about my father if he had lived a little longer and been nice to me" (pp. 129–30). Derek represents for Slocum the double-sidedness of his problem, for on the one hand, he wants much of the time to return to the condition of somatic, speechless immediacy vis à vis "reality" that Derek represents, but on the other, that condition of idiocy is precisely the image of human vacancy most contrary to the plenitude Slocum seeks. Thus Derek's existence is a physical plenitude marked by mental vacancy, just as Slocum's life is a material largess marked by spiritual emptiness.

Slocum's daughter represents a stage of development much closer to psychosocial maturity than that attained by either Derek or the other son. She of course invokes the threat of Oedipus from a second side, the side opposite that of the maternal relations (mother, Virginia, Marie Jencks, Mrs. Yerger). The relationship of father and daughter is marked by the expected pattern of love/hate. Their favorite game is what psychologist Eric Berne calls "Uproar," in which the two engage in verbal sparring and the daughter ends by stalking into her room and slamming the door after her. "She still has power to wound me," he says; "I have power to wound her (so maybe we have not really written each other off entirely yet. Maybe that's why we want to, we are dangerous to each other. My wife can't hurt me. My daughter can)" (p. 187).

But trapped with him in the Imaginary, his daughter reminds Slocum invariably of his relation to himself. His reflections on her turn into reflections upon his own past. "I also think I may have been *more* unhappy than my daughter when I was young, and felt even more entrapped than she does in my own sense of pathless isolation," he says, upon shifting toward a long passage concerning his childhood and youth that culminates in a description suggesting the extent of his dissociation from a coherent self:

> There must have been a second person who grew up alongside me (or *inside* me) and filled in for me on occasions to experience things of which I did not wish to become a part. And there was even a third person of whom I

am aware only dimly and about whom I know almost nothing, only that he is there. And I am aware of still one more person whom I am not even aware of; and this one watches everything shrewdly, even me, from some secure hideout in my mind in which he remains invisible and anonymous, and makes stern, censorious judgments, about everything, even me. (P. 135)

The passage had begun with the lament that "there are long gaps in my past that remain obscure and give no clue" (p. 134); it ends, equally lamentably, "I am lacking in sequence for everything but my succession of jobs, love affairs, and fornications; and these are not important; none matters more than any of the others; except that they do give me some sense of a connected past" (pp. 135–36). But, obviously, all these do matter, for they are all he has, so long as he is locked in the Imaginary phase of psychological development.

Slocum's normal son is the one who stands in the most problematical relation to Slocum. Slocum suspects that his daughter has already escaped him for her own personality beyond his, and he knows his idiot son will never ascend to the level of personality, consciousness, language, that is, to the Symbolic. But he still has hope for "my boy." His son is good, kind, thoughtful, generous, loving. One hopes he will retain all his good qualities even after absorption into his culture, but they are precisely everything that is almost inevitably to be lost. This son is involved in his own rite of passage, the conflict with his own father substitute—Forgione—at school, a passage into that heart of darkness known as civilized life. But at the outset he is clearly that *puer aeternus* Slocum feels must reside deep down inside himself somewhere. He is Slocum's pre-Oedipal self: "He is probably the only person in the world for whom I would do almost anything I could to shield from all torment and harm. Yet I fail continually; I can't seem to help him, I do seem to harm him. . . . In my dreams sometimes he is in mortal danger, and I cannot move quickly enough to save him. . . . He perishes, but the tragedy, in my dreams, is always mine" (p. 159). The son is representative of that self Slocum longs to regain, but which Slocum is perhaps also responsible for having destroyed. "I am still a little boy," he says. "I am a deserted little boy I know who will never grow older and never change, who goes away and then comes back. . . . He never goes far away and always comes back." But as between his son and that self Slocum once had been, "between us now there is a cavernous void" (p. 158). That void becomes infinite when, just as Slocum had feared, his son does die—and not just in his arms, but also, finally, and accidentally, at Slocum's hands.

The Symbolic Father

> The Oedipus complex will not only determine the subject's future rela-
> tions with itself, but those it entertains with others. Desire will therefore
> always be impossible, whether it pertains to the self or to an other.
> —Kaja Silverman, *The Subject of Semiotics*

Something Happened is a novel that moves forward so glacially it hardly seems to move at all. But there is forward progress in its plot: Slocum does change, there is growing intensity of emotional effect, and several complications are resolved or goals achieved (as in any well-made plot). The plot kernel embedded within Slocum's work focuses on Kagle's job. Slocum gets it. Slocum is not entirely happy that he "won" it, and his wife gives him a hard time about it, for which he seems to assume Kagle's limp (see p. 540). Slocum also gets to make his speech at the company convention; he heads the convention, but the speech, "at Arthur Baron's suggestion, was kept short" (p. 565), while Kagle and Green both get to speak at great length, much to Slocum's chagrin. With Kagle's job come other problems that Slocum has to solve: he retires those friends who are thought to be detrimental to his job or the company's success, including Ed Phelps, Red Parker, and Kagle; he transfers the feared Johnny Brown to another company and deals with Martha the typist (who has slowly been going crazy) when she has her expected breakdown, but he feels that Jack Green still has "the whammy" on him, though Slocum now is his superior. Within his family, Slocum manages to settle several complications. "I have told my wife I love her," he says; he had been unable to do so since he had found out about the possibility of his getting Kagle's job. He and his wife have "decided to keep Derek longer (he may get better. They may be wrong. They're finding new things out every day)," he says. And finally, he reports, "I have given my daughter a car of her own," and he has given his wife a new convertible ("We are now a three-car family," he says [p. 566]) and permission to shop for the new house they want because of his promotion.

If Slocum's problem, the cause of his neurosis, were material, it would surely be resolved along with these other complications. His success at the company certainly has brought material plenitude. But the plenitude he has sought has been more primal than that. It has been the plenitude Lacan associates with the symbolic role of the Phallus, the really androgynous signifier that locates the original fullness of being that one found first at the breast of the mother, and secondarily in the authority of the father. But the lesson of psychoanalysis is that such primal undifferentiated being is lost at the accession to language and cannot be regained. Slocum, toward the end of the novel, begins to recognize that fact, and the emotional intensity of the narrative escalates rapidly. All the elements in the discourse of the family begin to coalesce. Toward the end, following a description of his own birth trauma, Slocum says, "Fear. Loss of love, loss of the loved one, loss of love of the loved one. Separation. We don't want to go, we don't want them to go, we can't wait for them to leave, we wish they'd return. There seem to be conflicts" (p. 559).

The items, the contradictions, the feelings are precisely those associated with the Oedipal theme of castration and the fixation at Lacan's Imaginary stage. Slocum realizes that the apparent solution for the lack he suffers lies in his past: "I was in need of whatever nipple succored me," he says, "and whatever arms lifted me. I didn't know names. I loved the food that fed me—that's all I knew—and the arms that held and hugged and turned me and gave me to understand, at least for those periods, that I was not alone and someone else knew I was there" (p. 559). But the plain fact is, and Slocum has begun to realize it, that he will never regain that place virtually inside the mother, she who has, he believes, reinforced his fears of inadequacy to replace the father in her dying words, "You're no good. . . . You're just no good" (p. 545). Nor will he ever regain the father who died when Slocum was very young, the father who, Slocum's dreams tell him, is missed as desperately as the brother, Eddie, who also died young, and the son who has begun to slip away from Slocum and who, like the father and brother, dies young too.

> Oh, my father—why have you done this to me?
> I want him back.
> I want my little boy back too.
> I don't want to lose him.
> I do.
> "Something happened!" . . . (P. 561)

If there were any doubt that the death of Slocum's boy is the most important event in this novel, the congruence of the novel's title and the exclamation announcing the accident leading to the death surely would inform readers. The death of Slocum's son is the climactic event that causes those critical changes in Slocum suggesting he has moved, belatedly, from the Imaginary into the Symbolic. Lacan has written that the moment in which the mirror stage, embraced within the Imaginary, comes to an end is the moment in which the *I* becomes linked, within the Symbolic, to "socially elaborated situations." "It is this moment," Lacan says, "that decisively tips the whole of human knowledge into mediatization through the desire of the other, constitutes its objects in an abstract equivalence by the co-operation of others, and turns the *I* into that apparatus for which every instinctual thrust constitutes a danger, even though it should correspond to a natural maturation—the very normalization of this maturation being henceforth dependent, in man, on a cultural mediation as exemplified, in the case of the sexual object, by the Oedipus complex."[13] His psychological victory is ironic, however, not to say Pyrrhic. Since the Symbolic, as Lacan tells us, is very closely tied to a specific culture, if one does not appreciate the values of that culture, one may not particularly like what Slocum has become after his "cure." Anika Lemaire has summarized the problem as Lacan sees it:

> If symbolism [that is, the Symbolic phase] is . . . a human dimension or even a positive human condition in that it socializes and organizes man, it also presents the disadvantage of formalizing the vital individual experience. What is more, symbolization is human, it is the work of human minds, which implies from the start: imperfection, reduction, arbitrariness, submission to external constraints and a partial failure to recognize its own mechanisms. The impossible task of symbolization in the broadest sense of the word is to organize at its own level the multiplicity of 'vital human conditions.' Each type of social organization has only been able to respond to these necessities in a partial way, accentuating certain aspects of life at the expense of others and therefore effecting repression.[14]

One is free not to like what Slocum has become at the end, but it seems evident he has at last internalized the values of his culture, as it has taken him into itself. In this exchange Slocum has assumed his place in the Oedipal structure not as the child but as the father. His boy had represented for Slocum the desire to remain in the place of the child. Slocum had felt a powerful identification with the boy, and through him had hoped to cling to the pre-Oedipal innocence of the child. It would seem that the boy, rather than Derek, should have been described as "a product of [his] imagination." "I never think of Derek in danger," he says; "I only think of my boy or myself" (p. 533). The boy represents the innocence (vis à vis the ambiguities of the Symbolic) that Slocum wishes to protect forever. Thus, it seems, finally, that the death—the killing, really, since apparently Slocum accidentally smothers the boy while trying to comfort him after the accident, which would not, the doctor says, have been fatal—is almost more a figurative or allegorical sacrifice than a real death.[15] The boy's death *had* to happen. It was the something that had to happen if Slocum was to come to terms with his life—that is, the Oedipus structure—within his culture.

Joseph Heller has assumed a very difficult technical risk in *Something Happened*. Given the limitations of the first-person confessional narration, he has to find some way to suggest that Slocum has indeed changed as a result of the great mental rift the boy's death causes. For better or worse, Heller has to show that Slocum is wedded to the values his culture associates with the Symbolic role of the father. He does that in the final, very brief chapter in several ways. First, he reduces the amount of parenthetical qualification in which Slocum engages and, along with that, almost totally eliminates the metaphoric identifications and metonymic contradictions associated with the stage of the Imaginary. Second, he shows that Slocum's focus has shifted entirely to the external complications in his business and family life, demonstrating that he is "putting [his] affairs in order" (p. 566). Third, he gives Slocum new "voices" to hear, voices of approbation representing the Symbolic authority of the father, which of course is now the company:

> "You're a good administrator, Slocum."
> "You've done a good job, Slocum."
> "I liked the way you stepped right in and took over."
> "You've got the department really humming, Slocum."
> "You got Kagle out pretty smoothly, didn't you, Slocum? Ha, ha." (P. 568)

Fourth, he shows that Slocum has taken up golf—the company game—and meets a "much higher class of executives at Arthur Baron's now when he has us to dinner" (p. 568). And, finally, Heller dramatizes Slocum's taking "command" in the handling of Martha the typist's breakdown. Martha has been mentioned occasionally throughout the narrative, and she comes to stand, one suspects, for the psychological catastrophe Slocum himself becomes aware he is facing, but cannot acknowledge publicly:

56

"The company takes a strong view against psychotherapy for executives because it denotes unhappiness, and unhappiness is a disgraceful social disease for which there is no excuse or forgiveness" (p. 534). Martha's psychological problem is also no doubt associated with those Slocum finally realizes he had not recognized in Virginia, whose sexual teasing and quirky behavior masked the deep emotional troubles that led her to suicide by the same method her father had used. Martha's problem thus has almost incalculable range for Slocum, so that when she "went crazy for [him] finally at just the right time in a way he was able to handle suavely," taking "charge like a ballet master" (p. 568), she provides Slocum with the means to display his "coming of age" within the company, his accession to the role of authority, the law, the place of the father. In the final analysis, he is enabled to say, "Everyone seems pleased with the way I've taken command" (p. 569).

The question of what it is that has taken Slocum unto itself raises a final issue related to tropological analysis as represented in Lacan (as well as, of course, in Lévi-Strauss and Jakobson). The analysis here of *Something Happened* suggests that Lacan's dyadic theory conceivably would be more intelligible as a tetradic system. The addition of synecdoche and irony would provide more adequate conceptual space for the four-stage narrative the discourse of the family outlines in the move from Imaginary to Symbolic levels. In this view, which would be consistent with Todorov's analysis of the tropic basis of Freud's dream-work and Hayden White's accounts of both Freud and Piaget,[16] the onset of the mirror stage would be metaphoric, a stage of simple, one-for-one correspondence or total identity. The onset of language would initiate a metonymic stage, one partaking of features of the mirror phase in the constant reduplication in language of the objects of desire. The entry into the Symbolic would involve the trope of synecdoche (in White's terms) at the point where the individual arrives at an identification (*pars pro toto*) with the law or the father in the Oedipal complex. When the identification is secure, the fitting of the part into the whole will be entirely synecdochic, but when the sense of unity or completion or satisfaction wanes, then the Oedipus stage will bring with it the ambivalences assigned to the trope of irony.

It seems fairly plain that Bob Slocum has settled, ambiguously, into a place oscillating between the synecdochic and the ironic. The novel's trope for the whole—his company, his culture—may be an entity sufficient to encompass him, but it is not sufficient to purge him of his son's memory, tropic or otherwise. Though he still misses his boy, he seems to know what his mature social place must be. Slocum himself may be no more than a small part of a larger whole now, but he can "fit in" only because he has lost a part of himself, that son who stood for all he loved most. It is in this context that the Hebrew story of the father and son, Abraham and Isaac, and the Christian tale of the Father and the Son begin to have special meaning in *Something Happened*. They are our major cultural parables of the synecdochic message of *pars pro toto*, a message that adumbrates the almost inevitable—and ironic—alienation of our being in the world.

NOTES

1. "An interview with Joseph Heller," *Playboy* 22.6 (June 1975):74.

2. See Hayden V. White, "Introduction: Tropology, Discourse, and the Modes of Human Consciousness," in *Tropics of Discourse: Essays in Cultural Criticism* (Baltimore: Johns Hopkins University Press, 1978), pp. 13–15, as well as Tzvetan Todorov, "Freud's Rhetoric and Symbolics," in *Theories of the Symbol*, trans. Catherine Porter (Ithaca, N.Y.: Cornell University Press, 1982), pp. 246–54, where Todorov assimilates Freud's basic terms for the dream-work to a series of tropes, though he does not suggest as White does that a tropology underlies the sequence.

3. Kaja Silverman, *The Subject of Semiotics* (New York: Oxford University Press, 1983), p. 150. Silverman's chapter on Lacan and Freud (pp. 126–93) is excellent. See also Jacques Lacan's *Speech and Language in Psychoanalysis*, trans. Anthony Wilden (Baltimore: Johns Hopkins University Press, 1981), and Lacan's *The Four Fundamental Concepts of Psycho-Analysis*, ed. Jacques-Alain Miller and trans. Alan Sheridan (New York: Norton, 1978). Lacan is an especially difficult writer, so one is likely to find the commentators very helpful, particularly some of those who attempt to show Lacan's place within the structuralist, poststructuralist, and deconstructionist movements. For Lacan's relation to Freudian concepts, one will find useful J. Laplanche and J.-B. Pontalis, *The Language of Psycho-Analysis*, trans. Donald Nicholson-Smith (New York: Norton, 1973). For those interested in other uses of Lacan for literary interpretation, see also two books edited by Robert Con Davis: *The Fictional Father: Lacanian Readings of the Text* (Amherst: University of Massachusetts Press, 1981) and *Lacan and Narration: The Psychoanalytic Difference in Narrative Theory* (Baltimore: Johns Hopkins University Press, 1983). The best synthesis of Lacan's thought now available is Ellie Ragland-Sullivan, *Jacques Lacan and the Philosophy of Psychoanalysis* (Urbana, Ill.: University of Illinois Press, 1985).

4. Fredric Jameson, *The Prison-House of Language: A Critical Account of Structuralism and Russian Formalism* (Princeton: Princeton University Press, 1972), p. 172. The quotations following are also from this text, for which page references are given within parentheses.

5. *The Subject of Semiotics*, p. 109.

6. Joseph Heller, *Something Happened* (New York: Knopf, 1974), p. 3. All further quotations from the novel will be cited parenthetically within the text. There are several interesting essays on the novel that one might want to see in conjunction with the present essay: the best lengthy analysis available is Thomas LeClair, "Joseph Heller, *Something Happened*, and the Art of Excess," *Studies in American Fiction* 9 (1981):245–60; other good essays include Walker Percy, "The State of the Novel: Dying Art or New Science?" *Michigan Quarterly Review* 16 (1977):359–73; George J. Searles, "*Something Happened*: A New Direction for Joseph Heller," *Critique* 18.3 (1977):74–82; Nicholas Canaday, "Joseph Heller: Something Happened to the American Dream," *CEA Critic* 40.1 (1977):34–38; Susan Strehle Klemtner, " 'A Permanent Game of Excuses': Determinism in Heller's *Something Happened*," *Modern Fiction Studies* 24 (1978–79):550–56; and George Sebouhian, "From Abraham and Isaac to Bob Slocum and My Boy: Why Fathers Kill Their Sons," *Twentieth Century Literature* 27 (Spring 1981):43–52.

7. Anika Lemaire, *Jacques Lacan*, trans. David Macey (London: Routledge and Kegan Paul, 1977), pp. 6–7. Lemaire's is an excellent study.

8. Ibid., p. 59.

9. Ibid., p. 60.

10. Ibid., p. 61.

11. Ibid., p. 60.

12. Silverman, *Subject of Semiotics*, p. 130.

13. *Écrits: A Selection*, trans. Alan Sheridan (New York: Norton, 1977), pp. 5–6.

14. Lemaire, *Jacques Lacan*, p. 58.

15. One should note that the way in which Slocum's son is run down by a car in a shopping center is foreshadowed in the imagination of Chaplain Tappman of *Catch-22*, where the Chaplain's "wife's trim and fragile body [is] crushed to a viscous pulp against the brick wall of a market building by a half-witted drunken automobile driver." See Joseph Heller, *Catch-22* (New York: Simon & Schuster, 1961), p. 266.

16. See n. 3 above for the references to Todorov and White.

Chapter Three

Metaphor, Metonymy, Synecdoche: Tropology, Epistemology, and Historiography in *The Education of Henry Adams*

> The theory of tropes provides a way of characterizing the dominant modes of historical thinking which took shape . . . in the nineteenth century. . . . For each of the modes can be regarded as a phase, or moment, within a tradition of discourse which evolves from Metaphorical, through Metonymical and Synecdochic comprehensions of the historical world, into an Ironic apprehension of the irreducible relativism of all knowledge.
>
> —Hayden White, *Metahistory*

The Education of Henry Adams is widely recognized as one of the most prescient texts of the late nineteenth or early twentieth century.[1] It is so regarded because it can still speak to us today in a variety of ways. It provides all the fascination that autobiography at its best can claim. It reads very much as might a novel in the third-person point of view, and thus finds a place in the highly intellectualized genre brought to a fine point by Adams's friend Henry James. And it contains as well a history of the main currents of nineteenth-century thought as they flow into the larger stream of the twentieth. Perhaps the main appeal of *The Education*, however, is the style that Adams developed in it. Adams's style is marked by elements now highly valorized—its pervasive irony, for one, and, for another, its densely packed verbal enfigurations. The first element always makes one aware of the authorial persona; at the same time it makes one question the meaning of everything that is written. The second element exacerbates the first, for the highly figurative verbal medium breaks down one's ordinary fusion of the word and the thing, utterance and meaning, style and content. Adams's style, in short, makes one aware of the tropological nature of any discourse, particularly any narrative discourse, and most especially any narrative discourse canted toward a modernist irony.

60

A tropological analysis of *The Education* in terms set out by Hayden White in *Metahistory*, on the one hand, and in two essays on Foucault, on the other, can help to make sense of some of the problems that haunt the book.[2] One of these is its somewhat disjunct structure—its distinct division into two parts that do not always seem tightly related.[3] The division we notice is that between the first twenty chapters and the final fifteen, the two parts somewhat tenuously linked by a chapter called "Failure (1871)." The next chapter is called "Twenty Years After (1892)," leading us to believe that the main plot has ended and we are now to get a neat epilogue—as in many novels—only to find another entire plot movement drawn out through more than 200 pages. To many readers, presumably, the explanation of Adams's failure in 1871 is not always very clear, nor is the basis for the new departure after a twenty-year gap. It is not always apparent what Adams wants from his education, so it cannot be clear why it—or he—is a failure after the first movement, or what it is that he then expects to achieve in the second. Hayden White's new tropological analysis can answer both questions: Adams's tropic vision fails him in the first movement, and he must discover a new tropic vision in the second.

Both tropic visions are linked to the different epochal epistemological perspectives that Michel Foucault calls an "episteme," and both form the basis of conflict with yet two other epistemes. The character "Henry Adams"—to be distinguished from the author of the same name—begins *The Education* by assuming the validity of the episteme of the eighteenth century and its dominant tropic bent toward the cause-effect relations of metonymy. By the end of the first six chapters, "Adams" has discovered that the episteme of the *âge classique* simply does not match up with the reality he begins to perceive. But as he shifts toward the episteme of the nineteenth century, which according to Hayden White is dominated by the trope of synecdoche and a synthesizing historicism in all intellectual fields, Adams (I shall drop the quotation marks now) continues to think in dominantly metonymical terms. So his "nineteenth-century education" is destined to fail as badly as the other. Thus, the second movement of *The Education* forms around the development of a new trope—which, now, *is* synecdoche—and the projection of a new episteme—one for the twentieth century—consistent with yet a fourth episteme Adams enfigures in the metaphor of the Virgin and locates in the magical, mystical, medieval thirteenth-century past.

Metonymy and "The Eighteenth Century"

> Eighteenth-century historical reflection originated in an attempt to apply Metonymical strategies of reduction to the data of history in such a way as to justify belief in the possibility of a human community conceived in the Synecdochic mode. To put it another way, the Enlightenment attempted to justify an Organicist conception of the ideal human community on the basis of an analysis of social process which was essentially Mechanistic in nature. It thus criticized society in the light of an ideal that was moral and valuative, but it pretended to base that criticism on a purely causal analysis of historical processes.
>
> —Hayden White, *Metahistory*

Henry Adams begins *The Education* with the suggestion that as a boy he merely assumed the validity of the eighteenth-century way of knowledge. The epistemology Adams was born into was a product of the Enlightenment, itself a result of the Christian humanism Adams associates not only with St. Augustine and St. Thomas Aquinas, but also with members of his own illustrious family. In *The Education*, the episteme of Adams's birthright is usually identified abstractly as "the eighteenth century." Adams frequently remarks that he is a product of the epoch that produced his two most distinguished forebears, John Adams (America's second president) and John Quincy Adams (its sixth president), Henry Adams's great-grandfather and grandfather, respectively. "A boy who began his education in these surroundings," Adams says, "ought rightly to have felt at home in the eighteenth century and should, in proper self-respect, have rebelled against the standards of the nineteenth."[4] Indeed, Adams says, the "eighteenth century ruled society long after 1850" (pp. 19–20), and ruled his own life well beyond 1848, when appropriately it might have ended its rule over him. That was the year in which his grandfather, John Quincy Adams, "the old President," died and "took with him" the eighteenth century, at least "as an actual and living companion" (p. 20).

An episteme rules, however, largely because its assumptions are virtually invisible to those who live with it. The ways in which one thinks are determined, as Foucault, White, and others would argue, by the normative enfigurations of the age. "Once men have culturally organized their experience in a distinctive manner," says James M. Edie, "and chosen their metaphors, they tend to think within the cultural-linguistic bounds that they have unwittingly set up for themselves. They no longer think as they *will* but as they can,"[5] a phenomenon also noted by Alfred North White-head. As John Conder points out, Whitehead commented that the fundamental assumptions presupposed by people who adhere to diverse systems within an epistemological framework or epoch "appear so obvious that people do not know what they are assuming because no other way of putting things has ever occurred to them."[6] And, in truth, the conceptual entity called "the eighteenth century" in *The Education* is mainly a set of unstated assumptions built upon the trope of metonymy, the explanatory mode of cause-effect, the linguistic principle of difference and opposition, and the dominant metaphor of the universe as a machine, a cosmic mechanism. When the assumptions of an episteme become widely evident, they usually are already departing as an article of implicit faith. Thus Adams's essential problem in the first three decades of his life is simply to uncover and then understand his epistemological assumptions, to name the boundaries delimiting the field within which his knowledge of being has been constituted, and, finally, in the utmost consciousness, to consider the potentialities for another episteme, one he might somehow absorb into the being of thought and utterance.

The general process of understanding at first is inevitably metaphorical, and it happens that in the names of the three cities that dominate Adams's youth—Quincy, Boston, and Washington—we can see the trajectory of the growth of his understanding. Quincy becomes Adams's trope for the purest, most naive condition of eighteenth-century social life and thought. But the trope, while loosely called metaphorical, is really a metonymy, rather than a metaphor, since the city does not display a *similarity* to eighteenth-century principles; instead, it harbors a wealth of *associations* for Adams that are linked in his experience to values and intellectual responses one would call eighteenth century or characteristic of the *âge classique*. This distinction between the tropes is important here, for a metaphor would suggest that it was the essence of Quincy to be such and such—in this case, the repository of eighteenth-century values. But a metonymy suggests only that those values are associated by Adams's mind with the place. In this context, moreover, it is important to note the distinction between Adams, the subject of *The Education*, and Adams, the author of the book. Noting this distinction, we can then see that the problem of the character Adams is to learn the difference between metaphorical thinking and metonymical thinking—the difference between a

Quincy taken as the real embodiment of a mode of life and thought, and a Quincy taken as merely a place where experiences occurred that one can associate with that mode.

Although the epistemological assumptions of Adams's eighteenth century are indeed largely matters left unstated, it is clear enough in Adams's recounting what some of the assumed values are. Most of these values are associated—metonymically, of course—with another name, that of John Locke. Many social and political assumptions underlying Adams's eighteenth century are founded upon metonymical principles enunciated by Locke (1632–1704). One principle, from Locke's *Of Civil Government: The Second Treatise* (1690), which had a very direct impact upon America's Declaration of Independence, held that all men are free and equal because "by nature" no one should have sovereignty over another. Thus, Adams's eighteenth century is permeated by the concepts of "nature" and the "state of nature." Locke argued that in humanity's ideal condition a state of harmony existed, just as it existed among the smoothly working parts of a fine machine and among the various spheres or levels of the universe. At the lower level, these principles held that reason permitted an individual to perceive an innate order, a natural law, in the universe. The law of nature determined that individuals should be free and equal, for the same law held that the identity of each person was derived from a higher level, the law of God—or, simply, God. Nature and the state of nature are governed by the law of nature, but the law of nature is derived from God, with human reason the bridge enabling the individual to pass from the lower, natural level to the higher, divine level. Thus, when the individual acted according to his nature, behaving toward others according to the God-given laws perceived through reason, the natural functioning of society was harmonious, as was that of nature itself. The social state was founded upon a contract or compact by which each individual gave up certain rights in order to form a civil society. But even within the civil society, the nature of an individual was to be free, equal, and independent, so long as one did no harm to another's "life, health, liberty, or possessions"—the Lockean values that prompted Thomas Jefferson's terms "life, liberty, and the pursuit of happiness."

In *The Education* perhaps the most appealing evocation of Locke's mechanistic principles regarding individual freedom and the social compact is the episode in chapter 1, "Quincy (1838–1848)," in which the "old President" politely quells young Henry's rebellion against going to

64

school by taking him in tow like some manifestation of divine law. The anecdote can serve as an exemplum of Adams's eighteenth-century mode of thought because its two antagonists—the boy Adams and the old president—represent nature's two aspects: will and reason, individual impulse and universal rationality. The account occurs immediately following Adams's famous remark that "running order through chaos" was humanity's biggest problem from "the cradle to the grave" (p. 12). The "boy" is Adams's figure of the potential disorder found in one's natural state, just as the "savage" is the term opposite the "civilized" in the eighteenth-century dialectic between nature and culture. He says since "a boy's will is his life," the "boy" dies when the primitive will is broken. In the process, which entails gaining culture and becoming civilized, the boy does not evolve; instead he becomes a new being, just "as the colt dies in harness, taking a new nature in becoming tame." Neoclassical thought is founded on such principles of opposition, and Adams suggests that a state of war, like that between colt and trainer, exists between the boy and his master. "Henry Adams never knew a boy of his generation to like a master," yet the grandfather made so compelling the rule of civility—in taking the boy's hand and walking the mile or more to school with him—that, Adams says, what should have left "a lifelong sting, left rather an impression of as fair treatment as could be expected from a natural enemy" (p. 12).

But the fact is, the boy-colt never has a chance, for the old president appears here in all the potency of the eighteenth-century God himself, silently descending the staircase leading from his library, meeting the boy at the bottom, and taking him in hand like some irresistible manifestation of universal law. Adams says, ironically, that this act "ought to have made him dislike his grandfather for life" (p. 13). But the old man's great tact turns the social rebellion into the beginning of "a moral education" (p. 14). "He had shown no temper, no irritation, no personal feeling, and had made no display of force. . . . He had uttered no syllable of revolting cant about the duty of obedience and the wickedness of resistance to law; he had shown no concern in the matter; hardly even a consciousness of the boy's existence" (p. 13). Plainly, the old president effectively represents the eighteenth-century because he acts, rather than speaks, because he embodies, rather than utters, the words of the law. In a mechanistic universe of discrete objects acted upon by rationally comprehensible force, that is as it should be.

In the rhythmic development of Adams's early education, a turning point is identified (again, metonymically) with the city of Washington, D.C. The boy soon recognizes the differences between Quincy and Boston, which naturally is opposed to Adams's primal, epochal home. For him, all life seems caught up in politics, and while both Quincy and Boston represent a political philosophy, that of Boston is much more complex than that of Quincy, and that of Washington is yet more complex than either. "Within Boston, a boy was first an eighteenth-century politician, and afterwards only a possibility; beyond Boston the first step led only further into politics." The journey from Boston to Washington is intellectually immense. "The journey was meant as education, as education it served the purpose of fixing in memory the stage of a boy's thought in 1850," Adams says (p. 43). Washington and the surrounding Maryland countryside introduce a novel raggedness to the boy's thought that contradicts the tidiness of his eighteenth-century worldview. He comes to associate the disorder with the evils of slavery. Typically, he assumes a metonymical, mechanistic, cause-and-effect relationship between the conditions of life and the premises on which they must rest: "The railway, about the size and character of a modern tram, rambled through unfenced fields and woods, or through village streets, among a haphazard variety of pigs, cows, and negro babies, who might all have used the cabins for pens and styes, had the Southern pig required styes, but who never showed a sign of care. This was the boy's impression of what slavery caused, and, for him, was all it taught" (p. 44).

The city of Washington, for the boy, is an extension of the figure of George Washington. Just as Quincy is enfigured in the old president, so the national capital becomes an image of the way of the American reality for Adams. It is marked not by harmony, but by contradictions, and, he says, "Luckily boys accept contradictions as readily as their elders do, or this boy might have become prematurely wise" (p. 47). Premature wisdom, in this instance, would be to understand the full implications of the mechanistic modality of eighteenth-century thinking: parts are linked to other parts in a rational, causal relation, and contradiction (not opposition) becomes the height of irrationality. If Adams the boy were thinking entirely in his eighteenth-century modality, he would see immediately that his nation's most peculiar contradiction and irrational feature is the apparent fact that the institution of slavery might somehow be derived from—or lead to—the American form of government that George Washington and the city named for him symbolize for Adams. He says that "he never thought to ask himself or his father how to deal with the moral problem that deduced George Washington from the sum of all wickedness" (p. 48). Nonetheless, he does perceive that something is wrong with the works when he suggests that his journey to Washington made him "dimly conscious that he might meet some personal difficulties in trying to reconcile sixteenth-century principles and eighteenth-century statesmanship with late nineteenth-century party organization" such as he saw carrying on the fight over slavery in the nation's capital. And of the end of his Washington sojourn with his father, Adams the author concludes (from the perspective of 1904) that up to that point, "the education he had received bore little relation to the education he needed. Speaking as an American of 1900, he had as yet no education at all. He knew not even where or how to begin" (p. 53).

Synecdoche and "The Nineteenth Century"

> From the nineteenth century, History was to deploy, in a temporal series, the analogies that connect distinct organic structures to one another. . . . History gives place to analogical organic structures, just as Order opened the way to successive identities and differences [in the *âge classique*].
> —Michel Foucault, *The Order of Things*

The names Quincy, Boston, and Washington locate the rhythmic series of points marking Adams's growing disillusionment with the episteme of the eighteenth century, a disillusionment taken up and extended through many other sites—Harvard College, Berlin, Rome—where education becomes "accidental," rather than rationally purposeful. All the episodes in the boy's life, as Adams represents them, seem to point to a similar, faith-shattering contradiction and irrationality at the heart of existence, whether observed through philosophy, politics, or science. Locke and eighteenth-century philosophical principles cannot account for all that Adams even at age fifteen begins to perceive, for man does not seem entirely what he is claimed to be in the natural law, but then neither does that "nature" from which man derives rights, identity, and even government. The Civil War, to which, proleptically, Adams alludes in his celebrated evocation of a Boston snowball fight between "North-enders" and "South-enders," is the most important political challenge to Adams's belief in the natural goodness of humanity and the perfection of human society, moral themes

67

that Locke and the eighteenth century had built into their metaphysical assumptions.[7]

Those eighteenth-century ethical and metaphysical assumptions might even have withstood the social and political cataclysm of the Civil War but for those factors at work destroying Adams's faith in eighteenth-century science. Ethics might be separated from metaphysics, and thus politics eliminated along with it, but metaphysics had to be connected to knowledge of the physical universe known by science. A whole host of new developments challenged neoclassical, metonymical, mechanistic science, predicated on the possibility of reason's discovering the unifying laws of nature. "The atomic theory; the correlation and conservation of energy; the mechanical theory of the universe; the kinetic theory of gases, and Darwin's Law of Natural Selection, were examples of what a young man had to take on trust," not rationality, Adams says. All but Newton's mechanical theory of the universe were theories built on "such narrow foundations as to shock the conservative" (p. 224). Of these, Darwinism was the most problematic development acting upon Adams as he attempted to replace his eighteenth-century education with one fit for the nineteenth.

Adams might have been able to cling to his eighteenth-century episteme had not his faith in the orderly physical nature adduced by the eighteenth-century episteme been shattered by Darwinism and its new conception of nature and natural law. A central premise of the eighteenth-century assumptions Adams had inherited was the principle that uniformity reigned from society and natural law through science and scientific law and on through theology and divine law. The epistemology of John Locke—the philosophical source of the empiricism that ever since has dominated science—was developed in *An Essay Concerning Human Understanding* (1690) largely to coincide with rapidly accumulating scientific discoveries. Among these, the invention and development of calculus by Sir Isaac Newton and his application to the problems of motion and gravitation in 1665–66 apparently demonstrated that the mathematical principles upon which the universe was constructed gave it the orderliness, consistency, and uniformity of a vast, finely tuned machine. The universe operated on principles of force and acceleration, motion, gravitation, and inertia, and—by virtue of the clockwork regularity of the solar system that Newton had explained—it seemed entirely predictable. Thus, the universe opened itself to depiction through the orderly analytic procedures of human reason.

Locke's empiricism in epistemology, moreover, gained entry to theology by way of the faculty of reason. Human reason seemed an analogue to the uniformity found in God's Nature or Creation, and even Christianity was given a rationalistic basis in William Paley's *A View of the Evidence of Christianity* (1794). Paley's rationalist explanation of Christian religion was based upon "reasonable" conclusions drawn from an examination of evidence provided by both "natural" and "revealed" religion, and by the duties reason infers from them. Paley's theology—not influenced by Hume or Kant, it is important to note—reduces the purpose of the universe, and therefore the purpose of moral principles, to human happiness. His theology seems quite of a piece, therefore, with Locke's empiricism and theory of government. In addition, Paley's *Natural Theology or Evidences of the Existence and Attributes of the Deity Collected from the Appearances of Nature* (1802) gave the age its dominant image of God as a watchmaker whose creation was a clock. The mechanical metaphor neatly fit Locke's sense of order, regularity, and uniformity in nature. But for Adams this eighteenth-century image of an orderly universe based on cause and effect is shattered when it confronts a new universe founded on chance, mutation, accident—on irrational, teleologically directed life forces, all features metonymically identified in the name "Darwinism."

The chapter called "Darwinism (1867–1868)" provides Adams's main account of the struggle of his eighteenth-century creationist epistemology to survive the nineteenth-century Darwinian theory of evolution. Adams for a time sees fit to disregard the implications Darwinism cast up. But he takes a critical look at Darwinism when he agrees to write a review of Sir Charles Lyell's new edition of *Principles of Geology*, an earlier edition of which had influenced Darwin himself in 1831 at the outset of the voyage of the *Beagle*. Lyell's new edition, Adams says, increases the stature of "Darwinian doctrine" and makes possible the acceptance of it in place not only of older science, but also of older religion. "Natural Selection led back to Natural Evolution, and at last to Natural Uniformity," says Adams, summarizing the doctrine. "Unbroken Evolution under uniform conditions pleased everyone—except curates and bishops," Adams says. But that was all right, too, for evolution "was the very best substitute for religion; a safe, conservative, practical, thoroughly Common-Law deity"

(p. 225). But when Adams gives a hard look at the *Principles* for his review, he begins to feel that he must ask questions that Sir Charles could not easily answer. He says that he "undertook the task chiefly to educate . . . himself, and if Sir Isaac Newton had, like Sir Charles Lyell, asked him to explain for Americans his last edition of the 'Principia,' Adams would have jumped at the chance" (p. 226). But since "ignorance must begin at the beginning," Adams says he "must inevitably have begun by asking Sir Isaac for an intelligible reason why the apple fell to the ground. He did not know enough to be satisfied with the fact. The Law of Gravitation was so-and-so, but what was Gravitation? and he would have been thrown quite off his base if Sir Isaac had answered that he did not know" (pp. 226–27).

Essentially, as far as Adams is concerned, Lyell answered the basic question of evolution's relation to findings in geology with "I don't know." Though Adams says he feels "an instinctive belief in Evolution" (p. 225), he is troubled that the geologist's uniformitarian theory did not account for what Adams perceived as almost certain discontinuities because of catastrophes such as the glacial epochs.[8] Adams begins to find gaps in the relation between theory and fact, just as he had with his eighteenth-century social theory. "To him," Adams says, "the two or three labored guesses that Sir Charles suggested or borrowed to explain glaciation were proof of nothing, and were quite unsolid as support for so immense a super-structure as geological uniformity." Adams is thus led to wonder what the difference is between the rules of the scientist and those of the theologian. "If one were at liberty to be as lax in science as in theology, and to assume unity from the start, one might better say so, as the Church did, and not invite attack by appearing weak in evidence" (p. 227). Consequently, when Lyell tells Adams that there are certain forms, like *Terebratula*, more or less identical "from the beginning to the end of geological time," Adams decides that this fact suggests "too much uniformity and much too little selection" (p. 228). Evolution, as a common-law deity, begins to look about as suspect as God-the-watchmaker of eighteenth-century Deism.

Giving up on finding first causes or origins, Adams then decides to begin at the end of evolution, with the effects of evolution—with himself and the vertebrates, with the *Pteraspis*, the oldest known vertebrate. But his move, far from salvaging his eighteenth-century baggage, or leading him to his nineteenth-century destination, leads him deeper into contradiction and inconsistency. For the *Pteraspis*, found at Wenlock Edge in Shropshire, where Adams visits often in these years, leaves no trace that would lead upward toward the human. "When the vertebrate vanished in Siluria," Adams says, "it disappeared instantly and forever. Neither vertebra nor scale nor print reappeared, nor any trace of ascent or descent to a lower type." As far as Adams can tell, geology has not yet proven Lyell's and Darwin's thesis. "Ponder over it as he might, Adams could see nothing in the theory of Sir Charles but pure inference, precisely like the inference of [William] Paley, that, if one found a watch, one inferred a maker" (p. 230). Thus, concludes Adams, "behind the lesson of the day, he was conscious that, in geology as in theology, he could prove only Evolution that did not evolve; Uniformity that was not uniform; and Selection that did not select" (p. 231). But for him it all matters little at this time, for he decides that he "was the first in an infinite series to discover and to admit to himself that he really did not care whether truth was, or was not, true. He did not even care that it should be proved true, unless the process were new and amusing. He was a Darwinian for fun" (pp. 231–32).

Ultimately, not "Darwinism" but "chaos" is the name—and perhaps the site as well—of Adams's total disillusionment with the education his eighteenth-century episteme had brought him and with the theory of evolution, which might have been an adequate nineteenth-century epistemological substitute. For Adams, order gives way to chaos when his sister dies in convulsions from tetanus at the Bagni di Lucca, in Tuscany, Italy. Adams had said already that it was as "though Nature were playing tricks on her spoiled child" (p. 286) when an article he had written on the Gold Conspiracy and cockily submitted was refused by the *Edinburgh Review*. Heretofore, he had "lost sight of education" and had been basking in the enjoyment of London, Cheapside, Oxford Street, May Fair, the Royal Exchange, the St. James Club, and the Legation. The "first shock," the quarterly's surprising rejection, "came lightly" (p. 286), Adams says, but the shock of his sister's death is absolutely numbing, for it constitutes a total loss of the moral innocence the eighteenth century had given him, and it does nothing to confirm the metaphysical implications of the doctrine of evolution.

Nothing in his thirty or so years had ever had such impact upon him. "He had never seen Nature—only her surface—the sugar-coating that she shows to youth," he says. "Flung suddenly in his face, with the harsh brutality of chance, the terror of the blow stayed by him thenceforth for life, until repetition made it more than the will could struggle with; more than he could call on himself to bear" (p. 287). It is as if for the first time Adams has really seen death, and the meaning death has within nature. Death is chaos, not unity, and nature glories in it. "Death," Adams says, "took features altogether new to him in these rich and sensuous surroundings. Nature enjoyed it, played with it, the horror added to her charm, she liked the torture, and smothered her victim with caresses." The violent contrast between his own feelings of loss and the rampant, irrational beauty of the Tuscany countryside finally destroys for Adams any conviction of a classical world of reason, order, and balance, at the same time it destroys any vestige of belief in the ordained future promised by the trinity of the church of Darwinism—evolution, uniformity, selection—and its common-law deity. He admits that his impressions "are not reasoned or catalogued in the mind," as would be proper for an eighteenth-century gentleman's; "they are felt as part of violent emotion; and the mind that feels them is a different one from that which reasons; it is thought of a different power and a different person" (p. 288).

These impressions change Adams's awareness of—and, inevitably, his trope for—the motivations within the mind, nature, society, and religion. As virtually material realms, each of these explodes into disunity, multiplicity, chaos. They belong now to a kinetic universe of energy, force, power. "For the first time, the stage-scenery of the senses collapsed; the human mind felt itself stripped naked, vibrating in a void of shapeless energies, with resistless mass, colliding, crushing, wasting, and destroying what these same energies had created and labored from eternity to perfect." For the first time, nature "took form . . . as a phantasm, a nightmare, an insanity of force." Likewise, "society became fantastic, a vision of pantomime with a mechanical motion; and its so-called thought merged in the mere sense of life, and pleasure in the sense" (p. 288). Finally, the God of the old theology vanishes as a material being: "the idea that any personal deity could find pleasure or profit in torturing a poor woman, by accident, with a fiendish cruelty known to man only in perverted and insane temperaments, could not be held for a moment. For pure blasphemy, it made pure atheism a comfort. God might be, as the Church said, a Substance, but he could not be a Person." Then, as if these blows were insufficient to destroy Adams's eighteenth-century innocence and nineteenth-century education, war breaks out between France and Ger-

many, "and before the illusions of Nature were wholly restored, the illusions of Europe vanished, leaving a new world to learn" (p. 289). The
new world Adams must learn, ironically, is precisely that observed in
Foucault's Modern episteme—which *is* the nineteenth century's; and it is
a world to be constructed around a new trope, synecdoche and its vitalistic,
organic figures of force, power, energy, rather than metonymy's figures of
substance, contiguity, cause-effect. Unwittingly, Adams—at last—has become a citizen of the century in which he was born and lived most of his
life.

Metaphoric Consciousness and the Search for a Post-Modern Episteme

> Against the categories of Measurement and Order, which had dominated
> thought in the *âge classique*, we now witness the rise of the categories of
> Analogy and Succession as the presiding modalities of analysis in the new
> age. This advent signalled the growing consciousness of the significance
> of Time for the understanding of life, labor, and language, and attests to
> the historicization of the human sciences.
> —Hayden White, *Tropics of Discourse*

Perhaps we have now reached the point at which further comprehension
of Adams's tropological shifts from one epochal episteme to another entails review of backgrounds in Hayden White and Michel Foucault. Foucault's *The Order of Things* provides us with the concept of the episteme,
though of course, mutatis mutandis, such a concept inheres in other, more
familiar terms, too, such as worldview, frame of reference, Weltan-
schauung, and the like. But Foucault's epistemes are conceived a bit dif-
ferently in that an epoch is subjected to its epochal way of knowledge; a
culture does not consciously form it, thereby making the episteme subject
to cultural control; nor does the individual consciously choose an epochal
episteme. But it is possible to become aware of one's episteme, to understand its features, the ways in which it determines or delimits knowledge, and its potentialities for transformation into another episteme. White
is helpful on this latter point. His two major works pertaining to tropology—*Metahistory* and *Tropics of Discourse*—are especially useful for
their insights into the dominant epistemes of the last four centuries and
for their demonstration of how tropological analysis can get at the core
of those epistemes that Foucault outlines in greater detail, but often with
less clarity. Where Foucault and White converge is on the shifting relations

between epochal epistemes and specific tropic modalities. This set of relations is what advances our understanding of *The Education*.

According to White, the episteme Foucault describes as the *âge classique*—Adams's "the eighteenth century"—operates, linguistically, through the trope of metonymy and explains operations through analogies to mechanisms. The objects of our knowledge, that is, are regarded as parts of larger wholes, the parts existing in relations of cause and effect or agent and act, all belonging to a spatial dimension in which time is dependent upon the sequential, orderly, measurable effect of part acting directly upon contiguous part, whether in the analytic procedures of reason or in the putative machine of nature, the clockwork universe of Newtonian physics. "Metonymy," White says, "is the poetic strategy by which contiguous entities can be *reduced* to the status of functions of one another"; furthermore, "the study of things under the aspect of their existence as wholes made up of discrete parts . . . is the true basis of the *mechanistic* nature of thought" in the *âge classique* (T, p. 253). But as Henry Adams discovers in his sequentially ordered analysis of the places of his education (Quincy, Boston, Washington, Harvard, Berlin, Rome, et cetera), the search for a single part that can represent the essence of the whole—whether an epoch, a nation, or a national "character"—forces one, eventually, into the recognition not of unity, but a mind-boggling multiplicity. Thus the "blindness" of an episteme leads to its replacement by another that is strong where it is weak. The spatial, mechanistic orientation of the *âge classique*, White says, calls up the temporal, organismic orientation of the nineteenth century, whose trope is synecdoche and whose favored analogies are vitalistic or kinetic. In the nineteenth century, time becomes the medium within which beings exist, evolution becomes the modality for change, and history becomes the favored genre of explanation.

History, for Adams, thus becomes the focal point for all epistemological discourse. The career of the historian was the one most appropriate—even symptomatic—for the citizen of the nineteenth century (if one could not be a scientist, especially a geologist),[9] for the premises of its episteme enabled the creation of history as we know it today. But the profession of history in America was then still only forming along the "realist" lines already well advanced in Europe (see *Metahistory* for White's full discussion of nineteenth-century historiography), and while he had rejected antiquarian and romantic histories out of hand, the earliest efforts Adams had made in the profession he regards as a failure. This part of

Adams's story is well known. Adams had returned to America following the outbreak of the Franco-Prussian War, having accepted from President Charles W. Eliot an offer of an assistant professorship in medieval history at Harvard. Adams holds the position for seven years, but he leaves it convinced that the discipline of history is "a hundred years behind the experimental sciences" (p. 301), whose rigorous method it ought to emulate. "Historical method," he says, is a "rather pretentious name" (p. 302) for something that can be easily and quickly taught to any students. But, Adams says, "their teacher knew from his own experience that his wonderful method led nowhere" (p. 303). The purported "science" he teaches has no system, he begins to believe, so, "content neither with what he had taught nor with the way he had taught it" (p. 304), he leaves Harvard to become a practicing historian. Adams insists that the seven years in teaching seem "lost" to him. But those years give him a goal he will pursue to the end of his life. That goal is to be a theory of history adequate to the episteme of his epoch—whichever epoch he should choose.

It turns out that his search will require two theories—one for an old and one for a new episteme, both of which have to conform to appropriate models of science. The first theory of history is developed hardly at all in *The Education*, but it is visible in Adams's practice of history during those twenty years that form the gaping narrative hole in the book.[10] Like European historians such as Ranke, Adams employs a historiography based upon good eighteenth-century, metonymic, mechanistic principles of "realism," precisely the principles informing the four major modes White identifies in nineteenth-century historicism.[11] But whether history proper or novel of manners, the works of these years—*The Life of Albert Gallatin* (1879), *Democracy, an American Novel* (1880), *John Randolph* (1882), *Esther, a Novel* (1884), and the nine volumes of *The History of the United States during the Administrations of Jefferson and Madison* (1889–91)—fail to give him the satisfaction he needs and, worse, fail to produce a theory of history capable of meeting the needs of a twentieth-century education. Of his career as a realist historian and the calamities that afflicted his life in the twenty-year gap from 1871 to 1890, Adams says almost nothing at all in *The Education*: "Education had ended in 1871; his life was complete in 1890; the rest mattered so little!" (p. 316). Adams then turns himself out to pasture, he says, leaving his education and his career as a historian behind. But at the Chicago Exposition of 1893, Adams is initiated into startling aspects of an emerging new science. In Chicago, he claims, his interest in "education" is suddenly rekindled by a new force—electricity—expressed in a new symbol—the dynamo—which when paired with that other symbol, the Virgin, catapults Adams into "the practice of his final profession," a "methodical survey—a triangulation— of the twelfth century" and the twentieth, founded upon the fragmenting episteme of the nineteenth, itself resting on the ruins of the eighteenth (p. 369).

Concepts positing absolute, monistic grounds for knowledge explode during the latter part of the nineteenth century, producing profound shocks to Adams's thinking. He undertakes to study the thought of the Middle Ages, therefore, largely because he feels that the period, in its worship of the Virgin and its attendant philosophy/theology, provides a standard against which an imminent twentieth-century epistemology may be judged. The twelfth century represents unity, the twentieth, multiplicity. Unity and multiplicity—the major dialectical polarities between which Adams's mind constantly shuttles—are the key terms in his epistemology. John Conder has said, "As Adams employed these terms, they took on a variety of colors and values, but always they had reference to the central problems of existence—for the individual, for humanity as a whole. It was the eternal problem of the one and the many. Unity is coherence which provides man with an explanation of his place in the universe; multiplicity is either meaninglessness or partial meaning, the explanation of man in relation to individual facets of experience, not in relation to an absolute" (*A Formula of His Own*, p. 57).

Adams was to continue throughout his life to believe that unity is a necessary principle underlying reality and our knowledge of it. As it is represented in *The Education*, Adams's view through about the age of thirty-two had been that though multiplicity is illusory and unity is real, comprehensive, and permanent, the object of education—the achievement of knowledge—involves mediating both principles. Early in *The Education*, he remarks on the interrelationship: "From cradle to grave this problem of running order through chaos, direction through space, discipline through freedom, unity through multiplicity, has always been and must always be, the task of education, as it is the moral of religion, philosophy, science, art, politics, and economy" (p. 12). Adams apparently went to his grave (he was born in 1838; he died in 1918) believing that this problem is humanity's most serious concern, one made egregiously difficult in the nineteenth century because the eighteenth-century frame of reference provided Adams had become outmoded with advances in science that altered epistemological bases.

The issues that come into focus for Adams during this period of his education, 1892–98, are pinpointed, of course, on the perceptual grid provided by the subjects of the histories he had written—politics, society, economics, art, science. Having concluded that "whatever was right, all he had ever taught was wrong" (p. 376), Adams focuses upon the kind of knowledge a historian—or anyone—might produce. His career as a historian becomes, in effect, an experiment to salvage his eighteenth-century episteme, just as—according to White—nineteenth-century European historiography attempts to salvage that of the *âge classique*, but without its debilitating irony. So just before committing himself to the triangulation of the epochs represented by the Virgin and the dynamo, he despairs that it must have been the subjects of his previous work, not the method, that had been ill chosen: "The law had proved as futile as politics or religion, or any other single thread spun by the human spider; it offered no more continuity than architecture or coinage, and no more force of its own. St. Francis expressed supreme contempt for them all, and solved the whole problem by rejecting it altogether" (p. 368). Perhaps he should have emulated the method of St. Francis, he thinks, but he continues to operate on the premise that historical, like scientific, understanding depends upon unity and continuity. "History," he says, "had no use for multiplicity; it needed unity; it could study only motion, direction, attraction, relation" (pp. 377–78).

As a historian, he had engaged himself experimentally in a multitude of studies of law, politics, and the careers of statesmen, hoping that these would lead to a unified understanding through the narrative continuities he constructed. But now he comes to the pessimistic conclusion—his pessimism exacerbated in the personal tribulations of financial turmoil (the crashes of 1873 and 1893), his wife's suicide (1885), and various wars (the Civil War, 1861–65, and the Franco-Prussian War, 1870)—that all his carefully articulated experiments had failed in the battle against multiplicity. He says he "had toiled in vain to find out what he meant. He had even published a dozen volumes of American history for no other purpose than to satisfy himself whether, by the severest process of stating, with the least possible comment, such facts as seemed rigorously consequent, he could fix for a familiar moment a necessary sequence of human movement" (p. 382). But every sequence he had arranged, he realizes, has become not necessary, but quite relative, determined by his particular point of view. Other points of view would just as rigorously determine other sequences. Yet, still insisting upon seeing relations as sequences "called stories, or histories," he resolves to discover another method, one consonant with the new universe he sees in the dynamo, but one that he sees as well in the medieval Virgin of Chartres. He finds it in the study of the concept of force, rather than in the actions of men: "Satisfied that the sequence of men led to nothing and that the sequence of their society could lead no further, while the mere sequence of time was artificial, and the sequence of thought was chaos, he turned at last to the sequence of force; and thus it happened that, after ten years' pursuit, he found himself lying in the Gallery of Machines at the Great [Paris] Exposition of 1900, with his historical neck broken by the sudden irruption of forces totally new" (p. 382).

He discovers, in effect, that the epistemological basis for his study of history—his first "real" profession—is no longer adequate for modern science and technology and so cannot be adequate for history either. Adams's metaphor here is ironic, of course, but his sense of "his historical neck broken"—meaning that his previously held knowledge is left with no connection to a substantial body—is profoundly, if not fatally, painful. The new forces for which Adams must now account—X-rays and electricity, for example—seem to have no place in his old positivist epistemology, but then neither do they have a place in the old science, the mechanistic science of Newton. Adams's friend Samuel Langley, a scientist of the old episteme and Adams's guide through the Paris Exposition, has been left as epistemologically bereft as the historian. Adams tells us that his friend "constantly repeated that the new forces were anarchical," and especially that his mode of science "was not responsible for the new rays, [which] were little short of parricidal in their wicked spirit towards science." Adams says that while he himself can worship the dynamo as a new symbol of knowledge, the creatures expressed in the new forces were not so charitable to their progenitors. As Adams puts it, "Radium denied its God—or, what was to Langley the same thing, denied the truths of his Science" (p. 381). The cognitive result of these recognitions is to catapult Adams into "a new universe which had no common scale of measurement with the old. He had entered a supersensual world, in which he could measure nothing except by chance collisions of movements imperceptible to his senses." These forces might be "perceptible to each other, and so

78

to some known ray at the end of the scale" (pp. 381–82), but they are not, alas, perceptible to any human observer in the way of objects in the old mechanical science.

As a historian "reduced to his last resources," he finds it necessary somehow to measure the value of these new forces. The search for a point of reference is what leads Adams to the study of the twelfth century. But rather than validating a medieval theology, Adams is led to see the value of his own human perspective, for the only common measure of the force of the Virgin and the force of the new rays enfigured in the dynamo is their effect upon the human subject—upon "Man," in short—and not upon some idealized abstraction, either, but upon a specific, concrete individual. The way to measure those forces, whether those of the Virgin or the dynamo, is by their "attraction on his own mind." "Here," he says, "opened another totally new education," one as dangerous to his being as any physical adventure. "The knife-edge along which he must crawl, like Sir Lancelot in the twelfth century, divided two kingdoms of force which had nothing in common but attraction. They were as different as a magnet is from gravitation, supposing one knew what a magnet was, or gravitation, or love. The force of the Virgin was still felt at Lourdes, and seemed to be as potent as X-rays; but in America neither Venus nor Virgin ever had value as force" (p. 383). Americans, Adams says, had always worshipped other symbols of force—the horse, as seen in equestrian statues, for example, or the railway train, the symbol Adams finds most appropriate for the phase of history he calls the "mechanical" and in which industrial America then found itself. But for Adams after 1895, the Virgin (and other female deities—Venus, Aphrodite, the goddesses of Indian mythology) has to be recognized as a powerful force, for she had been able to cause in a period of three centuries the erection of churches and cathedrals numbering in the thousands and valued in the billions of dollars.

The Virgin, unlike the railway train, is *only* a symbol, but she is nonetheless a symbol whose "energies acted as interchangeable forces on man" (p. 388). Her force may be as invisible as the rays of radium, but the effects upon humanity of her force are as measurable as the foot-pounds of work delivered by a steam engine. Regardless of whether the Virgin is seen as symbol or energy, however, Adams feels that by his new calibration she has been the greatest force ever let loose in the world. She had attracted "man's activities to herself more strongly than any other power, natural or supernatural," Adams believes, and it behooves him as a historian to track that energy—"to find where it came from and where it went to; its complex source and shifting channels; its values, equivalences, conversions" (pp. 388–89). He feels that the force of the Virgin could hardly be "more complex than radium" or "be deflected, diverted, polarized, absorbed more perplexingly than other radiant matter" (p. 389). He realizes that he knows little about any of these forces, but the important thing is his mind as a human being, for "by action on man all known force may be measured" (p. 388). As far as he is concerned, all energy, force, power might be occult, rather than mechanical, but "all reacted on his mind," he says, "and he rather inclined to think the Virgin easiest to handle" (p. 389). But his extended attempt to handle it occurs in *Mont-Saint-Michel and Chartres*, not in *The Education*, whose main task in the chapters that follow is to track not the twelfth century, but the nineteenth century as it moves into the twentieth. That task culminates in one more discovery about man, for Adams finally concludes that instead of *object* on which force reacts, man is the *subject* whose mind is the greatest—and perhaps only—source of unity available to the historical universe.

From Virgin to Dynamo to Man as Trope

> If the problem of knowledge is viewed not from the standpoint of the universe but from that of man himself . . . everything at once falls into perfect unity.
>
> —Ernst Cassirer, *The Problem of Knowledge*

> For the threshold of our modernity is situated not by the attempt to apply objective methods to the study of man, but rather by the constitution of an empirico-transcendental doublet which was called *man*.
>
> —Michel Foucault, *The Order of Things*

Adams enfigures history most effectively in such metaphors as the Virgin and the dynamo, but his favorite mode of historical explanation remains the narrative based upon metonymic analysis. In that respect, Adams never really escapes his eighteenth-century background. At times, contrary to the ordinary association of metonymy with tragic plots, he enfigures the plot of his narrative as a romance (which, White says, is usually affiliated with the trope of metaphor). He calls the "pursuit" of a new theory of historical knowledge, for example, "long and tortuous, leading at last into the vast forests of scholastic science." In the same vein, Adams says he must steel himself to enter "this old thicket of ignorance," filled with "labyrinths," in order to discover the secret he pursues, "the secret of education," which "still hid itself somewhere" in the "Abyss of Ignorance" (p. 389). But his dominant method remains that of metonymical analysis—the articulation of part to part, the reduction to principles of orderly, sequential progression. Thus it is the steps of analytic progress one sees in the final "adventure," rather than any jousting, figuratively, with rival knights or exterminating of demonic underworld foes. The tension between Adams's trope of adventure (suggesting the romantic quest) and the method of analysis (suggesting tragic schisms) contributes, therefore, to the sense of ironic failure that permeates *The Education*. For Adams, the discovery of either the Virgin or the dynamo might have given him his key to universal knowledge (and thus success in the terms of romance), but, in his way, he will not quit with the discovery implicit in the metaphor. Adams always has to take the next, the metonymical, step in order to specify the stages of his intellectual development, and then he always has to take one more, the synecdochic, step in order to show how all the parts fit in the larger scheme of the whole. But what he discovers in the larger scheme, alas, is the long decline from the "height of knowledge" he identified with the Virgin and her epoch to the "abyss of ignorance" of his own.

When Henry Adams braves the abyss, the major obstacle he has to overcome is the epistemology around which he had built his life for some sixty years. As a child of the eighteenth century, Adams had taken as a given that the universe was orderly, balanced, united in all its parts. He could accept change, did accept change, of course, for his career as a historian depended upon his explanations—his narrative accounts of causes and effects—of the changes in law, politics, the lives of statesmen. The fact of change, for him then, depended upon two things: first, a cause; second, a direction. He had seen that force caused change, but he did not see what caused the direction of change. Was there no teleological dimension to change, no goal or aim or end toward which the changes were drawn within the universe? Adams had felt that some "outside force" must exist to establish the direction, and he knew that religion and philosophy had always called this force God or the gods (p. 427). He could see that Darwin's evolutionary theory of natural selection, based upon a premise of survival of the fittest, could account for change in nature, but it could not, he had felt, account for the direction of evolutionary change.

Direction of change, he had thought, needed an "attractive force," "a shaping influence" (p. 427). For Adams—as generally for the mass of humanity for centuries—the answer provided by the Virgin, through the Schoolman St. Thomas Aquinas, was far preferable to any other answers previously given to the question of direction. Adams says St. Thomas would say: "Christ and the Mother are one Force—Love—simple, single, and sufficient for all human wants; but Love is a human interest which acts even on man so partially that you and I, as philosophers, need expect no share in it. Therefore, we turn to Christ and the Schools who represent all other Force. We deal with Multiplicity and call it God. After the Virgin has redeemed by her personal Force as Love all that is redeemable in man, the Schools embrace the rest, and give it Form, Unity, and Motive" (p. 428).

Such an answer, Adams begins to feel, is—had always been—enormously appealing, for it resolves all the perplexing issues of knowledge, being, cause, teleology, direction. Everything is abolished, he says, by "one flash of lightning," as all, in Aquinas's thought, is absorbed into God. "The student," says Adams, "felt warranted in doing what the Church threatened—abolishing his solar system altogether—in order to look at God as actual; continuous movement, universal cause, and the interchangeable force" (pp. 428–29). Adams can see that St. Thomas's answer "had merits," for it gives a way out of the problem of knowledge that science cannot. He concedes that "St. Thomas at least linked together the joints of his machine," whereas modern science does not even envisage a machine— only forces, for which it "offered not a vestige of proof, or a theory of connection between" them (p. 429).

But Adams cannot finally accept the answer St. Thomas, the Virgin, and the church provided. Like his friend Langley, Adams has come, if not to worship science, at least to believe that his theory of historical knowledge must fit into the paradigm of science. "Like most of his generation, Adams had taken the word of science that the new unit was as good as found" (pp. 431–32). Alas, "Modern science guaranteed no unity" (p. 429), and, worse, it seemed to drive any concept of traditional unity farther and farther from one's grasp. Adams had hoped, for example, that the new kinetic theory of gases would provide the unity he sought (p. 431), but that theory also reduces unity to multiplicity—and for Adams, still, knowledge depends upon a reversal of these: ever since the Greeks, multiplicity had had to be reduced to unity for knowledge to exist. Consequently, Adams asks what he considers the ultimate nihilistic question: Why not give up the notion of unity altogether?

Adams resolves to study once again the thought of scientists and diverse philosophers in an effort to find out why one "was to be forced to affirm" unity. Neither science nor philosophy helps. "Science," he concludes, "seemed content with its old phrase of 'larger synthesis,' which was well enough for science, but meant chaos for man" (p. 431). So Adams turns to European philosophers—Descartes, Hume, Berkeley, Kant, Hegel, Schopenhauer, and Hartmann—and "strayed gaily away with his Greeks—all merely to ask what Unity meant, and what happened when one denied it." To Adams's apparent surprise, he discovers that none of the philosophers ever denied unity. Even the bleakest pessimist, he says, turned "the universe of contradiction into the human thought as one Will." Even the most extreme subjectivism likewise claims that external reality can be known "as a motion of mind, and therefore as unity." Thus, metaphysics in general, Adams finds, treated the universe as either "one thought" or as "one universe" (p. 432).

But such naturalistic or nominalistic conclusions, Adams decides, reduce the unity sought to oneself, to the knowledge of one's own mind. Consequently, always inclined to seek larger wholes, he embarks upon a study of psychology, since, he says, he would rather avoid the study of only his own mind. In the end, however, psychology fails as much as science and mathematics to give him a source of ultimate unity, leaving Adams to conclude only that this "path of newest science" would not lead to unity either. One positive result comes from psychology, though, for from it Adams finds his "fixed point" to be used for "studying man as a force": "Any schoolboy could see that man as a force must be measured by motion, from a fixed point. Psychology helped here by suggesting a unit—the point of history when man held the highest idea of himself as a unit in a unified universe. Eight or ten years of study had led Adams to think he might use the century 1150–1250, expressed in Amiens Cathedral and the works of Thomas Aquinas, as the unit from which he might measure motion down to his own time, without assuming anything as true or untrue, except relation" (pp. 434–35).

Having at last reached a point of departure, Adams begins the study eventually published as *Mont-Saint-Michel and Chartres: A Study of Thirteenth Century Unity*, vestiges of which have shown up throughout *The Education* already.[12] Moreover, Adams indicates here that *Chartres* provided him with a fixed point for himself that would enable him to write its sequel: *The Education of Henry Adams: A Study of Twentieth-Century*

Multiplicity. "With the help of these two points of relation," he says, "he hoped to project lines forward and backward indefinitely, subject to correction from anyone who should know better" (p. 435). The one area from which correction must yet come is modern science and the functional "truth" of "relation"—relativity—that Adams has himself begun to adopt.

When Adams had descended into the "Abyss of Ignorance," he still needed to find a synecdochic image, like that of the Virgin for the age of religion, powerful enough to unify history, epistemology, and metaphysics, in an age of modern, post-Newtonian science. He had hoped for an affirmation of unity that would also affirm the eighteenth-century epistemology within which he had spent his life. But by the end of his study of the modern sciences he realizes that neither a defense of unity in the medieval way (the way of the historical phase Adams calls "religion") nor of the *âge classique* (the way of the phase of the "mechanical") would be forthcoming. Thus, when he resolves to study Karl Pearson's *The Grammar of Science* (1899), he hopes at least to discover therein the "larger synthesis," if not universal unity, that science has been promising for centuries—whenever, at any rate, it is forced to address epistemological problems beyond the merely local. Henry Adams's view is that awaiting a larger synthesis, the eighteenth-century uniformitarians of his "youth had wound about this universe a tangle of contradictions meant only for temporary support," but that they "had waited for the larger synthesis in silence and in vain." Worse yet, in the late nineteenth century "their universe had been wrecked by rays, and Karl Pearson undertook to cut the wreck loose with an axe, leaving science adrift on a sensual raft in the midst of a supersensual chaos" (p. 452). Adams says that Pearson is the first scientist to succeed in the "slaughter" of the "scientific lawgivers of unity" (p. 450). Denying the unity of force and matter, Pearson reduces the pursuits of science to the locality of the senses. "Briefly," says Pearson, "chaos is all that science can logically assert of the supersensuous." For his part, Adams concludes that his best hope for scientific unity—the kinetic theory of gas—was only "an assertion of ultimate chaos. In plain words, Chaos was the law of nature; Order was the dream of man" (p. 451). And, still worse, while Adams feels his opinion of all this as a historian is worthless, "he found himself on the raft" freed by Pearson's axe, "personally and economically concerned in its drift" (p. 453).

Pearson indeed provides a grammar for the objects occupying the universe of science, but he does not—nor does he believe it possible to—

provide a syntax, a synecdochic theory adequate to modern science's diversity. Since Adams has not given up yet on the search for larger synthesis, he "travels" first to Germany and then back to France, still hoping to find an adequate scientific defense of unity. In Germany, Ernst Haeckel gives Adams at least a faint hope, for in a study published in 1902 "Haeckel sank his voice almost to a religious whisper in avowing with evident effort, that the 'proper essence of substance appeared to him more and more marvellous and enigmatic as he penetrated further into knowledge of its attributes—matter and energy—and as he learned to know their innumerable phenomena and their evolution.'" But Haeckel's faint affirmation can hardly withstand Ernst Mach's vehement denial, for Mach "rejected matter altogether, and admitted but two processes in nature—change of place and interconversion of forms. Matter was Motion—Motion was Matter—the thing moved" (p. 453). Mach posits unity here, but it is a nonmaterial unity, and Adams is still too old-fashioned, too much the product of an eighteenth-century education, to find a universe of energy suitable to his desires.

In France, Adams turns to Henri Poincaré's *La Science et l'Hypothèse* (1902). Poincaré seems to Adams the one scientist who feels the same need of material unity in the universe the historian feels. But in the end Poincaré offers little more support than the Germans. His mathematics agrees with Adams's history in seeing an increase in multiplicity and complexity, and he suggests, too, that ever-improving means of investigation will continue to "discover the simple under the complex" (p. 455). But the "eternal bliss" that the mathematician might find in this "paradise of endless displacement" will horrify the historian. And Poincaré eventually denies continuity, pointing out that even our system of counting represents merely a man-made symbol system: "the mind has the faculty of creating symbols, and it is thus that it has constructed mathematical continuity which is only a particular system of symbols." Such symbol systems, Poincaré goes on to say, do not offer even a "relative truth." Mathematical systems—including Euclidian geometry, which long had been the touchstone of the absolutists, the unity seekers—are simply "the most convenient" of systems available to the scientist in doing work. If Poincaré is right, not even mathematics escapes the charge of relativity, multiplicity, facticity—even fictiveness. Adams concludes, somewhat ruefully, that "as it was in the Book of Genesis," so "chaos was a primary fact even in Paris" (pp. 455–56).

By such knowledge Adams has been cast back into the primal darkness of the beginning of creation. But there is no God after all to bring light to Adams. There is only Adams—that is, man—or, the same thing, man's mind. In man or mind, Adams finds his synecdochic trope, his all-encompassing figure of unification. Man and the mind comprise the force whose direction Adams must now discern: "The direction of mind, as a single force of nature, had been constant since history began. Its own unity had created a universe the essence of which was abstract Truth; the Absolute; God!" The human mind creates unity, and it exists in the names given it by the greatest philosophers: "To Thomas Aquinas, the universe was still a person; to Spinoza, a substance; to Kant, Truth was the essence of the 'I'; an innate conviction; a categorical imperative; to Poincaré, it was a convenience; and to Karl Pearson, a medium of exchange" (p. 456). From all these "truths," however, Adams seizes upon the name of just one for his "truth." Poincaré's "convenience" becomes the epithet Adams uses in order to stress the human origin for the larger synthesis brought to the multiplicity of the twentieth century. A human "convenience" is finally the site of origin for Adams's "Dynamic Theory of History" even more than the "truth" of force or the "law" of acceleration. If the term somehow suggests that our visions of universal unity are alimentary or even excremental, Adams would not shrink from that implication. For such is the vision inherent in what many consider Adams's very best enfiguration for the achievement of human thought—the pearl oyster: "As history unveiled itself in the new order, man's mind had behaved like a young pearl oyster, secreting its universe to suit its conditions until it had built up a shell of *nacre* that embodied all its notions of the perfect. Man knew it was true because he made it, and he loved it for the same reason" (p. 458). But above all, what this means is that Adams has reached the view of Giambattista Vico's *The New Science*, namely, that one can understand only that which one has made. And man has made history because, when it is articulated in writing and speech, it is a linguistic creation and therefore, finally, a tropological entity. For Adams, ironically, the greatest trope of all is man.

The way in which Adams enfigures man is crucial to his role as a modernist paradigm. Adams employs, in his preface to *The Education*, the metaphor of the manikin in order to suggest the artificiality of the figure inhabiting the pages of Adams's life. Adams's enfiguration, as Hayden White has pointed out, is consistent with such typical nineteenth-century figures as Thomas Carlyle's tailor's dummy in *Sartor Resartus*. The figure indicates a growing sophistication regarding the human sciences such as history, for it acknowledges the increasing awareness that their objects are human constructs, not irreducible objective existents, and that at their center sits yet another construct—man. The aptness of the manikin as an epistemological focus—in an age when the ego has been exploded—is indicated by White's remark that Adams's figure "signals the literal 'emptiness' of his text as a fit vehicle for representation of the emptiness of his own ego." White goes on to say that "what might be called a 'mannikin' theory of the literary work ... makes it not a product of a dialectic between form and content, but rather a relationship between two forms equally evanescent: the *clothes* in which the tailor's dummy is garbed and the *surface* of the dummy's body which feigns the form of a man but has no interior."[13]

If Carlyle's dummy sits next to Adams's manikin, the images of man defined in Cassirer and Foucault flank them both. As an epistemological locus, Cassirer's man is radically idealized, standing as the ultimate signifier for Cassirer; man is the dominant symbol in that whole philosophy of symbolic forms. If, says Cassirer, "the problem of knowledge is viewed not from the standpoint of the universe but from that of man himself," then "everything at once falls into perfect unity."[14] By contrast, Foucault's man is radically reductive, a "mere" construct, a verbal object come to be called "man," but fated to disappear into language itself in the passage from the nineteenth into the twentieth century. "Since man was constituted at a time when language was doomed to dispersion," says Foucault, "will he not be dispersed when language regains its unity,"[15] the dominant unity posited by structuralist and even poststructuralist thought? Adams can be situated between these two not because his manikin is qualitatively superior to Foucault's "homunculus," but because the Henry Adams created within the text of *The Education*, if less grand than the idealization enfigured by Cassirer, is a more powerful epistemological unity than Foucault's figure. Henry Adams may have used the trope of the manikin to represent the figure he had created in *The Education*, but readers can never take that manikin for the Adams created in the text. Man, as enfigured in Adams, remains an enlivening metaphor for managing our thought in ways that a mere manikin cannot.[16]

NOTES

1. See, for example, Wayne Lesser, "Criticism, Literary History, and the Paradigm: *The Education of Henry Adams*," *PMLA* 97.3 (May 1982): 378–94.

2. See "Foucault Decoded: Notes from Underground," in *Tropics of Discourse: Essays in Cultural Criticism* (Baltimore: Johns Hopkins University Press, 1978), pp. 230–60, and "Michel Foucault," in *Structuralism and Since: From Lévi-Strauss to Derrida*, ed. John Sturrock (Oxford: Oxford University Press, 1979), pp. 81–115; see also Michel Foucault, *The Order of Things: An Archaeology of the Human Sciences* (1971; New York: Vintage, 1973). It should be noted that White has written on Adams's *Education*, but his approach is not specifically tropological; he focuses instead on the problem of ideology and Adams's "code-switching," his creation of a text involving "a complex mediation between various codes by which 'reality' is to be assigned possible 'meanings' ": "Method and Ideology in Intellectual History: The Case of Henry Adams," in *Modern European Intellectual History: Reappraisals and New Perspectives*, ed. Dominick LaCapra and Steven L. Kaplan (Ithaca, N.Y.: Cornell University Press, 1982), pp. 280–310, 298. White would argue, I believe, that the dominant stylistic trope in *The Education* is irony; I agree that such is the case for Adams, the author, but for Adams, the character, the sequence of tropic moves must stop short of irony as a metatrope. White, in fact, provides a justification for this position, for Adams, he says, splits "himself into both the speaker who is hidden behind the anonymity of the narrative form and the referent or subject of the narrative, who occupies center stage" (p. 303). In this context, one should also see John Carlos Rowe, *Henry Adams and Henry James: The Emergence of a Modern Consciousness* (Ithaca, N.Y.: Cornell University Press, 1977).

3. For discussions of the structure of *The Education*, see, for example, R. P. Blackmur, *Henry Adams*, ed. Veronica A. Makowsky (New York: Harcourt, Brace, Jovanovich, 1980), a book that collects Blackmur's diverse writings on Adams; John A. Conder, *A Formula of His Own: Henry Adams's Literary Experiment* (New Haven: Yale University Press, 1970); and Melvin Lyons, *Symbol and Idea in Henry Adams* (Lincoln: University of Nebraska Press, 1970).

4. Henry Adams, *The Education of Henry Adams*, ed. Ernest Samuels (Boston: Houghton Mifflin, 1973; orig. pub. 1918), p. 19; further references to this work will be given parenthetically in my text.

5. James M. Edie, *Speaking and Meaning: The Phenomenology of Language* (Bloomington: Indiana University Press, 1976), p. 170.

6. See Conder, *A Formula of His Own*, p. 154, for the reference to Whitehead; see Whitehead's *Science and the Modern World* (New York: Macmillan, 1925), p. 71.

7. See Conder, *A Formula of His Own*, for a very thorough discussion of Adams's theme of the perfection of human society.

8. For those who are interested in a discussion of the current state of theory regarding evolution, see G. Ledyard Stebbins and Francisco J. Ayala, "The Evolution of Darwinism," *Scientific American* 253.1 (July 1985):72–82. Though Adams would be pleased to learn that the problems that plagued him regarding Darwinism have continued to present research problems, the general theory has continued to find confirmation in advances in molecular biology and in new syntheses of various theoretical models.

9. Adams's friend Clarence King was a geologist, and it was his profession, along with his personality and knowledge of art and poetry, among other things, that prompted Adams to regard him as the "ideal American," perfectly equipped for the epoch into which he was born. Unfortunately, the early bloom on King's life wore off, and he became at the end a paradigm for the American tragedy instead: see Lesser's article in *PMLA* on this theme in Adams.

10. See William Jordy, *Henry Adams: Scientific Historian* (New Haven: Yale University Press, 1952), for a discussion of Adams's career as a historian and his efforts to perfect a scientific history.

11. In *Metahistory: The Historical Imagination in Nineteenth-Century Europe* (Baltimore: Johns Hopkins University Press, 1973), Hayden White discusses the four major modalities of historical writing he perceives in the nineteenth century; these are the Romantic, the Idealist, the Positivist, and the Realist, the latter being represented by the great masters of nineteenth-century European historiography—Michelet, Ranke, Tocqueville, and Burckhardt. Adams's nine-volume history of the administrations of Thomas Jefferson and James Madison would, in all probability, fall into this last category. The entire cycle of history and historiography, moreover, eventuates in the essentially ironic authorial stance taken by Adams in *The Education*. White's summary statement in this regard is enlightening vis à vis Adams:

> As thus envisaged, the evolution of philosophy of history—from Hegel through Marx and Nietzsche, to Croce—represents the same development as that which can be seen in the evolution of historiography from Michelet, through Ranke and Tocqueville, to Burckhardt. The same basic modalities of conceptualization appear in both philosophy of history and historiography, though they appear in a different sequence in their fully articulated forms. The important point is that, taken as a whole, philosophy of history ends in the same Ironic condition that historiography had come to by the last third of the nineteenth century. This Ironic condition differed from its late Enlightenment counterpart only in the sophistication with which it was expounded in philosophy of history and the breadth of learning which attended its elaboration in the historiography of the time. (M, p. 42)

See also White's "Method and Ideology in Intellectual History" for his own assessment of Adams's view of history.

12. See, for example, Robert Mane, *Henry Adams on the Road to Chartres* (Cambridge, Mass.: The Belknap Press of the Harvard University Press, 1971), and R. P. Blackmur, *Henry Adams*, for a discussion of the relationship between *Mont-Saint-Michel and Chartres* and *The Education*.

13. "Method and Ideology in Intellectual History," p. 295.

14. *The Problem of Knowledge*, trans. William H. Woglom and Charles W. Hendel (New Haven: Yale University Press, 1950), p. 16.

15. *The Order of Things*, p. 386.

16. I have treated the trope of man as it occurs in Cassirer, Foucault, and Adams in somewhat greater detail in the following article: "The Problem of Knowledge in *The Education of Henry Adams*," *South-Central Review* 3.2 (Summer 1986):155–68. In addition, see my *The Exploded Form: The Modernist Novel in America* (Urbana: University of Illinois Press, 1980) for a consideration of other epistemological authorities assumed to underlie some of the modes of modernist fiction.

Chapter Four

The Tetrad and the Ironic Moment: Tropology and Emplotment in *Absalom, Absalom!*

Tropology, Emplotment, and Historical Understanding

> The plot structure of a historical narrative (*how* things turned out as they did) and the formal argument or explanation of *why* things happened or turned out as they did are *pre*figured by the original description (of the "facts" to be explained) in a given dominant modality of language use: metaphor, metonymy, synecdoche, or irony.
>
> —Hayden White, *Tropics of Discourse*

> Following the line indicated by Northrop Frye in his *Anatomy of Criticism*, I identify at least four different modes of emplotment: Romance, Tragedy, Comedy, and Satire.
>
> —Hayden White, *Metahistory*

Of Faulkner's novels, *Absalom, Absalom!* is the one that most directly confronts the epistemological problem of history at the same time that it raises narrative and tropological metaproblems regarding discourse in history and fiction. *Absalom, Absalom!* from the outset demands that any reading account for its historical contexts, but it is a novel more concerned with the problematics of historical knowledge than with the representation of history as history. David Levin summarizes this view when he says: "Faulkner's *Absalom, Absalom!* rewards the reader who is concerned with the writing of history, for in this modern masterpiece the search for historical knowledge dominates the central action and justifies—if it does not determine—the narrative method."[1] It is not only the fact that *Absalom, Absalom!* confronts the epistemological problem of history that makes it important to modernist fiction; the importance lies also in its particularly modernist approach to the problem. Faulkner rejects two of the most cherished shibboleths of traditional historians and novelists: that "facts," "data," and "documents" exist as objective givens, and that these objective givens are sanctified once they are rendered in chronological narration. In *Absalom*, virtually no fact, datum, or document is objectively given, brought forth without a mantle of interpretation; likewise, little in the different narrative accounts is presented in a straightforward, chronological way.

Failure to respect these two virtual doctrines has caused the novel to be decried vigorously by important traditionalist critics. A recent scholar reminds us that Yvor Winters, R. P. Blackmur, and Georg Lukacs—among others—have perceived what they consider unpardonable transgressions in *Absalom*. The narrative indeterminateness (in "facts" and chronology) does not impress Lukacs, for example; instead, he finds "a failure of intelligence" in Faulkner, "the lack of a consistent view of human nature. Man is reduced to a sequence of unrelated experiential fragments; he is inexplicable to others as to himself."[2] Lukacs's overt Marxist bias is not the cause for dismissing this particular novel; rather, it is his unwillingness to accept a truly modernist epistemology. Lukacs and like-minded critics would saddle every serious artist with nineteenth-century views of history and the novel. But the world of the modernist mind is not truly available to those models, and *Absalom, Absalom!* makes the traditionalist confront that fact.

One essential lesson of the "artifact" known as *Absalom, Absalom!*, therefore, has to do with the subjectivity, indeterminacy, and artificiality of historical knowledge, but the novel has a more fundamental lesson for readers than even that. Treating discourse in general, Hayden White (to repeat ideas outlined in my first chapter) has touched upon these features of historical knowing as aspects of the general nature of human thought. "When we seek to make sense of such problematical topics as human nature, culture, society, and history," says White in *Tropics of Discourse*, "we never say precisely what we wish to say or mean precisely what we say. Our discourse always tends to slip away from our data towards the structures of consciousness with which we are trying to grasp them; or, what amounts to the same thing, the data always resist the coherency of the image which we are trying to fashion of them." These remarks could have been directed specifically toward *Absalom*, and the sentence following seems almost to echo the anguished cries of traditionalist (and, early on, hard-put modernist) readers of Faulkner's great novel: "Moreover, in topics such as these, there are always legitimate grounds for differences of opinion as to *what* they are, *how* they should be spoken about, and the *kinds* of knowledge we can have of them" (p. 1). White is here opening the introduction to *Tropics of Discourse* to the study of the *what*, the *how*, and the *kinds* regarding the data that make up our discourse within what has come to be known as the human sciences. His subject, then, is tropes, tropology, the tropical or figurative element in every discourse, but White's "tropics of discourse" has a particular usefulness to the study of the accounts given by various characters of events ("real" and "imagined") in Faulkner's novel, for most of its critical and interpretative issues devolve to the problems of tropological elements in the major discourses comprising it.

Absalom, Absalom! is a novel whose main objective—pursued by several characters, not to mention any number of readers—is, simply, *understanding*, but how does that understanding develop within the text itself? In vastly important ways, the structure of presentation in *Absalom, Absalom!* is determined by the structure of the tropological process of understanding White has outlined. Understanding is made needful when one encounters the unfamiliar, the unknown, the uncanny. The process of understanding ordinarily begins with the displacement of the thing unknown toward something that is known, canny, familiar. The process of understanding thus begins with what White calls a "tropological shift." The domain of the unknown is shifted—by one trope or type of figuration—toward a domain or field presumably already mastered. According to White, there is a kind of "plot" involved in these shifts; both the plot and the stages at each shift are embraced by theorists varying from the speculative historian Vico and Renaissance and modern rhetoricians, to Freud and the genetic psychologist Jean Piaget. "The archetypal plot of discursive formation appears to require that the narrative 'I' of the discourse move from an original metaphorical characterization of a domain of experience, through metonymic deconstructions of its elements, to synecdochic representations of the relations between its superficial attributes and its presumed essence, to, finally, a representation of whatever contrasts or oppositions can legitimately be discerned in the totalities identified in the third phase of discursive representation." These moves, White suggests, following Vico, are fundamental to the efforts of consciousness to construct a world satisfactory to one's human needs, and, what is more, they reflect the "processes of consciousness" in general and "all efforts of human beings to endow their world with meaning." Basing his conclusions on Vico, Freud, Burke, Piaget, and others, White says that "discourse itself, as a product of consciousness's efforts to come to terms with problematical domains of experience, serves as a model of the metalogical operations by which consciousness, in general cultural praxis, effects such comings to terms with its milieux, social or natural as the case may be" (T, p. 5).

Understanding, to put White's ideas more simply, begins in the tropological move or shift known as metaphor. As a trope, metaphor is the basis of the other "master tropes" (metonymy, synecdoche, irony—as they are identified by Vico, Kenneth Burke, and White). White points out, in the essay on the *New Science* in *Tropics of Discourse*, that Vico regarded metaphor as "a kind of primal (generic) trope, so that synecdoche and metonymy are viewed as specific refinements of it, and irony is seen as its opposite" (T, p. 205). In discourse, metaphor seems to provide the energy that drives the mind's efforts to extend, clarify, comprehend. "Vico's most important contention," White says, "is that this primitive classification of phenomena by simple metaphorical identification of the unfamiliar sets up the tension between things and the words used to characterize them which makes further specification of the nature of things necessary and the further refinement of language possible by tropological variation" (T, p. 206). For White, as for Vico, a dialectical tension exists between the metaphorical pole of language and the ironical, with metonymy and synecdoche filling the space between. Further, the movement from the metaphorical toward the ironical represents, at the same time, an increase in the integration of knowledge or understanding and an increase in the awareness of the constructive or constitutive power of language. "Thus," says White of Vico's conception of tropes, "whereas metaphor constitutes the basis of every fable (or myth), the escape from metaphorical language and the transition into the use of a consciously figurative language (and thus into literal and denotative, or prose, discourse) are made possible by the emergence of an ironic sensibility. It is thus that the dialectic of figurative (tropological) speech itself becomes conceivable as the model by which the evolution of man from bestiality to humanity can be explained. Or to put it another way, the theory of metaphorical transformation serves as the model for a theory of the autotransformation of human consciousness in history" (T, p. 205).

There are, according to White, several other aspects to understanding as it relates to discursive narratives such as those found in history and fiction. The main ones associated with the sequencing of tropes are what White, in the introduction to *Metahistory*, calls modes of argument, modes of ideological implication, and modes of emplotment. Of particular interest to readers of fiction is the sequence of emplotments that White claims to grow out of the four major tropes. Using Northrop Frye's notions of archetypal narratives, White suggests that the trope of metaphor will find its expression in romance plots, the trope of metonymy in tragic plots, the trope of synecdoche in comedy plots, and the trope of irony in satiric (or, tautologically, "ironic") plots. In *Anatomy of Criticism*, Frye outlines the features he associates with each emplotment, and, like White, he suggests that there is a logical, if not chronological, relationship among the four archetypal "stories."[3] Frye imagines the plots as forming epicycles within a larger cycle that is (in Frye's term) "encyclopedic," recapitulating the entire mythic universe of narrative. In this globular universe, the emplotments Frye calls romance and irony-satire form epicycles above and below an "equator" that represents the division between "innocence" and "experience," respectively.

Romance emplotments come closest to reproducing the purely innocent heroes and heroines of mythology (where, unlike narratives set in "reality," characters have unlimited powers of action). Emplotments in the mode of irony-satire come closest to reproducing pure human experience, which, according to Frye, is characterized by powerless "protagonists," antiheroes, rather than heroes. Tragic and comic emplotments, according to Frye, represent descending and ascending narrative movements across the line dividing innocence and experience. Tragedy shows the fall of heroes from the imagined purity of the upper world into the all too human world of impotence, corruption, and nihilism. Comedy shows (or at least suggests in the story's last scene) the rise of humanly fallible but redeemable characters toward the imagined innocence of Frye's upper world, where, in the more romantic forms of the comic plot, the hero and heroine are presumed to live happily ever after.

These four emplotments, as Frye describes them, represent the total range of kinds of stories that might be told involving human figures, as opposed to gods or other superhumans, who provide the characters for actual myths. The exhaustiveness of these kinds (which, again, Frye calls narrative archetypes, modes, or forms) might better be understood if we envision them as forming quadrants in the logical square of opposition, which is also the basis for semiotics, schematized in A. J. Greimas's "semiotic square" forming the structure of signification.[4] The relations are shown here with attendant tropes, as White might display them:

ROMANCE	IRONY-SATIRE
(metaphor)	(irony as trope)
plus	minus
not minus	*not* plus
COMEDY	TRAGEDY
(synecdoche)	(metonymy)

Figure 1

In this schema, romance is regarded as the purely positive (plus) narrative choice, irony-satire as the purely negative (minus) or contrary of romance, comedy as the contradictory (*not* minus) to irony-satire (comedy is *not*-irony-satire, that is), and tragedy as the contradictory (*not* plus) to romance (tragedy, that is, is not-romance). This set of relationships may be rotated on its axis in either direction, but as long as the relations are maintained it will suggest the formal properties Frye associates with each emplotment: ironic or satiric plots are "anti-romances"; comic plots are "anti-tragedies." Thus, superposing Greimas's semiotic square over Frye's structuring of the archetypes, we can suggest in yet one more way that if one were going to exhaust the available kinds of stories (even in telling stories—or writing histories—about the same characters and events), these are the four possibilities one would have to employ. There are no other "pure" kinds of emplotments.

The presentation of the life and times of Thomas Sutpen in *Absalom, Absalom!* rather precisely mimes the progress of understanding as it moves tropologically from metaphor to irony and in emplotments from romance to irony-satire. Readers have long recognized that *Absalom* works through a number of narrative archetypes in the course of shifts among narrative points of view that include Rosa Coldfield, Quentin Compson, Quentin's father, Quentin's Harvard friend, Shreve McCannon, and his Grandfather Compson, who, it would appear, introduces the point of view of Thomas Sutpen himself. From the very earliest reviews, critics have noted every sort of plot in the book from Byronic romance to absurd tragicomedy to gothic melodrama. Recent criticism has begun to synthesize the earlier views (which tended to ascribe one narrative archetype to the entire novel). It is now a critical commonplace to assume that Rosa Coldfield's representation of Sutpen's "history" is in the mode of gothic mystery, Mr. Compson's in the mode of Greek tragedy, Quentin's (or, sometimes, Quentin's *and* Shreve's) in the mode of chivalric romance, and Shreve's (where his is separated from Quentin's) in the mode of the satiric tall tale, with the perspectives of Grandfather Compson and Thomas Sutpen generally left out of the sequence.[5] But there is much more to it than has been recognized. Thus, I want to show that Faulkner's overall effort reflects the tropological shifts underlying the growth of consciousness and knowledge itself, at the same time that it reveals the close relationship Hayden White has noted between narrative archetypes and specific tropological modes.

Metaphor and Romance

> The romance is fundamentally a drama of self-identification symbolized by the hero's transcendence of the world of experience, his victory over it, and his final liberation from it. . . . It is a drama of the triumph of good over evil, of virtue over vice, of light over darkness, and of the ultimate transcendence of man over the world in which he was imprisoned by the Fall.
>
> —Hayden White, *Metahistory*

Although the initial point of view in *Absalom, Absalom!* belongs to Quentin Compson (who, I shall show at the end, is the inclusive, synecdochic representation of all points of view), the first stage in the representation of the understanding of Thomas Sutpen belongs to Miss Rosa Coldfield. The mode of consciousness Rosa represents to us is distinctly metaphoric. Metaphoric consciousness serves primarily to name an object or field of discourse that otherwise exists as an undifferentiated chaos. The metaphor brings with it the sense that language and being actually correspond in some primal way. "The trope of metaphor, the explanation of the unknown in terms of the known is the naive man's way, the Adam's way of grappling with the world, when description of reality is only one remove away from the reality itself."[6] Metaphorical consciousness, therefore, seems to be "a primitive form of knowing in the ontogenesis of human consciousness in its passage from infancy to maturity," says White, but this is not to say that it is somehow inferior to other modes. Instead, "insofar as it is the fundamental mode of poetic apprehension in general, it is a mode of situating language with respect to the world every bit as authoritative as logic itself" (T, p. 10).

Faulkner uses Rosa's consciousness to bring the fact of Thomas Sutpen into view for readers—and for Quentin. The constitutive power of Rosa's language is clear from the outset. Faulkner refers to her "talking in that grim haggard amazed voice" out of which "the long-dead object of her impotent yet indomitable frustration would appear, as though by outraged recapitulation evoked, quiet inattentive and harmless, out of the biding and dreamy and victorious dust."[7] The partition between Rosa's language and the object it names disappears for Quentin as he is absorbed into the voice, as if he were a "ghost" haunting a voice "where a more fortunate one would have had a house" (p. 8). Amid this transformation of a voice into a haunted house, the novel's most vivid metaphorical presentation of Thomas Sutpen occurs:

> Out of quiet thunderclap he would abrupt (man-horse-demon) upon a scene peaceful and decorous as a schoolprize water color, faint sulphur-reek still in hair clothes and beard, with grouped behind him his band of wild niggers like beasts half tamed to walk upright like men, in attitudes wild and reposed, and manacled among them the French architect with his air grim, haggard, and tatter-ran. Immobile, bearded and hand palm-lifted the horseman sat; behind him the wild blacks and the captive architect huddled quietly, carrying in bloodless paradox the shovels and picks and axes of peaceful conquest. Then in the long unamaze Quentin seemed to watch them overrun suddenly the hundred square miles of tranquil and astonished earth and drag house and formal gardens violently out of the soundless Nothing and clap them down like cards upon a table beneath the up-palm immobile and pontific, creating the Sutpen's Hundred, the *Be Sutpen's Hundred* like the oldentime *Be Light*. (Pp. 8–9)

Clearly, the Thomas Sutpen figured forth in this passage (though he is not as yet named) is as much created by the language Quentin evokes of Rosa's telling as Sutpen's Hundred seems to be created out of the words *Be Sutpen's Hundred* "spoken" by Sutpen, as if in the very figure of the devil. Faulkner's entire effort here seems to be to create ex nihilo, to bring forth not only Thomas Sutpen, but all his domain from a "soundless Nothing," from "the long silence of notpeople, in notlanguage" (p. 9).

A tropological mode relying upon metaphor ordinarily brings with it, according to Hayden White, an emplotment in the mode of romance.

A metaphorical characterization of the field of life, experience, or history tends to be dualistic, White points out. For example, in the historian Jules Michelet, who works in a metaphoric mode of historical narrative, we see "the historical process conceived as a struggle of essential virtue against a virulent, but ultimately transitory, vice." In Michelet, "there was merely an interchange between the forces of vice and those of virtue—between tyranny and justice, hate and love, with occasional moments of conjunction, such as the first year of the French Revolution—to sustain his faith that a final unity of man with man, with nature, and with God is possible" (M, p. 150). Both the mode of metaphor and the emplotment as romance are seen in Michelet's "description of the spirit of France in the first year of the Revolution" as a "sequence of Metaphorical identifications that moves from its characterization as the emergence of light from darkness, to description of it as the triumph of the 'natural' impulse toward fraternity over the 'artificial' forces which had long opposed it, and ends, finally, in the contemplation of it as a symbol of pure symbolization" (M, p. 151). White's description of Michelet's treatment of the French Revolution could almost stand as a description of Rosa Coldfield's history of Thomas Sutpen's impact upon Yoknapatawpha County.

Like Michelet, Rosa Coldfield emplots her history as a drama "of disclosure, of the liberation of a spiritual power fighting to free itself from the forces of darkness, a redemption" (M, p. 152). Thomas Sutpen obviously represents the powers of darkness in Rosa's romantic myth. Sutpen is usually characterized as a figure of Satan, the devil, an ogre inhabiting an ogre-world (p. 21), articulated in an ogre-tale (p. 22). It is from the demonic power operating through Sutpen that Rosa's loved ones (indeed, her entire culture) must be saved. Thus, the mythos of salvation or redemption (along with such corollaries as exorcism, the removal of curses, or the elimination of possession) provides the structure of Rosa's narrative imagination. We see evidences of this romantic mythos everywhere:

> It was as though the sister whom I had never laid eyes on, who before I was born had vanished into the stronghold of an ogre or a djinn, was now to return through a dispensation of one day only, to the world which she had quitted, and I a child of three, waked early for the occasion, dressed and curled as if for Christmas, for an occasion more serious than Christmas even, since now and at last this ogre or djinn had agreed for the sake of the wife and the children to come to church, to permit them at least to approach the vicinity of salvation, to at least give Ellen one chance to struggle

with him for those children's souls on a battleground where she could be supported not only by Heaven but by her own family and people of her own kind; yes, even for the moment submitting himself to redemption, or lacking that, at least chivalrous for the instant even though still unregenerate. (P. 23)

But in Rosa's account, Ellen can never be the agency by which Sutpen will be defeated, or transformed, or redeemed. So Rosa concludes the passage by saying:

> That is what I expected. This is what I saw as I stood there before the church between papa and our aunt and waited for the carriage to arrive from the twelve-mile drive. And though I must have seen Ellen and the children before this, this is the vision of my first sight of them which I shall carry to my grave: a glimpse like the forefront of a tornado, of the carriage and Ellen's high white face within it and the two replicas of his face in miniature flanking her, and on the front seat the face and teeth of the wild negro who was driving, and he, his face exactly like the negro's save for the teeth (this because of his beard, doubtless)—all in a thunder and a fury of wildeyed horses and of galloping and of dust. (P. 23)

In Rosa's account, the only instrument of salvation capable of redeeming Sutpen is Rosa herself.

Rosa is a romantic. Despite her feeling that she has grown up in an absence of love, she believes nonetheless that love is the redemptive agent capable of saving those doomed by evil. She is specifically charged to save Judith from possession by evil, but she assumes a similar charge for everyone. Her sister Ellen on her deathbed had charged Rosa to protect Judith, even though Rosa is younger than her niece by some four years, so it is as the instrument of love that Rosa watches over Judith that "summer of wistaria" (p. 143) when Rosa's father had sent her out to Sutpen's Hundred, ostensibly herself to be watched over by Judith. In that "miscast summer" of Rosa's "barren youth" (p. 144), she did not compete with Judith for Charles Bon; instead, she watched over Judith, "spied" upon her, because she had become "all polymath love's androgynous advocate" (p. 146). Rosa's dream here is to bring Judith's love for Charles to the perfection it deserves. But this dream must fail. "Then my father returned," Rosa says, "and came for me and took me home and I became again that nondescript too long a child yet too short a woman" (pp. 148–49). Then, four years later, the war came, but for Rosa the dream, the ideal, of love remained: "The stable world we had been taught to know dissolved in fire and smoke until peace and security were gone, and pride and hope, and there was left only maimed honor's veterans, and love. Yes, there should, there must, be love and faith . . . else what do men fight for? what else worth dying for? Yes, dying not for honor's empty sake, nor pride nor even peace, but for that love and faith they left behind" (p. 150).

Rosa's dream of love's perfection through Judith and Charles is replaced by another dream of restoration after Charles is murdered by Henry at the gate of Sutpen's Hundred. The dream is displaced first toward Sutpen's domain. Rosa, Judith, and Clytie, "like nuns in a barren and poverty-stricken convent" (p. 155), wait for Thomas Sutpen to return, Rosa says, "because now he was all we had, all that gave us any reason for continuing to exist, to eat food and sleep and wake and rise again; knowing that he would need us, knowing as we did (who knew him) that he would begin at once to salvage what was left of Sutpen's Hundred and restore it" (p. 154). Until Sutpen returns, the women are caught in a state of suspended animation, an endless winter of despair, "that night which was four years long" (p. 169): "We now existed," Rosa says, "in an apathy which was almost peace, like that of the blind unsentient earth itself which dreams after no flower's stalk nor bud, envies not the airy musical solitude of the springing leaves it nourishes" (p. 155). The women await Sutpen's return, then, as the earth awaits the spring. And when Sutpen returns, he does indeed set out "to restore his house and plantation as near as possible to what it had been" (p. 160). He is their cynosure, and in this one respect he does not disappoint them.

Ultimately, the dream of restoration turns to Sutpen himself. Rosa will redeem him, at the same time that he will use her to restore his dream of Sutpen's Hundred. The moment at which Sutpen finally really *sees* Rosa as the potential salvation of his own dream is described by Rosa in the conventional language of romantic love. "He had seen me for twenty years," she says, "but now he was looking at me" (p. 162). It is as if "the path at the instant when he came in sight of me," she says, "had been a swamp out of which he had emerged without having been forewarned that he was about to enter light . . . it was not love . . . just a sudden over-burst of light, illumination" (p. 163). In that instant, the ogre of Rosa's childhood is transformed into a romantic hero (however aged) whose spirit will infuse "each ruined field and fallen fence and crumbling wall of cabin or cotton house or crib; himself diffused and in solution held by that electric furious immobile urgency and awareness of short time and the need for haste as if he had just drawn breath and looked about and realized that he was old (he was fifty-nine) and was concerned (not afraid: concerned) not that old age might have left him impotent to do what he intended to do, but that he might not have time to do it in before he would have to die" (p. 160). But Rosa herself is transformed, along with Sutpen. "You see," she tells Quentin, "I was that sun, or thought I was who did believe there was that spark, that crumb in madness which is divine, though madness knows no word itself for terror or for pity. There was an ogre of my childhood which before my birth removed my only sister to its grim ogre-bourne and produced two half phantom children . . . and I forgave it; there was a shape which rode away beneath a flag and (demon or no) courageously suffered—and I did more than just forgive: I slew it, because the body, the blood, the memory which that ogre had dwelt in returned five years later and held out its hand and said 'Come' as you might say it to a dog, and I came" (p. 167).

Rosa forgives Sutpen for his role as ogre in her child's imagination, but she insists that she also forgave him for the ultimate transgression against her ideals. When Sutpen reneges on the offer of marriage and turns it into a proposition (that is, if they should sleep together and she should bear him a son, he would then make the marriage legitimate), Rosa is so outraged she bolts Sutpen's Hundred, to make her life as a spinster eking out an existence on secret community handouts and her own petty "brigandage." She realizes that she has ample reason to damn Sutpen to hell forever, "not so much for the saying of it but for having thought it about her so that when she heard it she realized like thunderclap that it must have been in his mind for a day, a week, even a month maybe, he looking at her daily with that in his mind and she not even knowing it. But I forgave him. They will tell you different, but I did," she insists (p. 171). She does so, however, because Sutpen remains in a demonic world beyond hers. He seeks the very salvation Rosa had hoped to offer him, but she finally admits he is beyond her reach: "Because he was not articulated in this world. He was a walking shadow. He was the light-blinded bat-like image of his own torment cast by the fierce demoniac lantern up from beneath the earth's crust and hence in retrograde, reverse; from abysmal and chaotic dark to eternal and abysmal dark completing his descending (do you mark the gradation?) ellipsis, clinging, trying to cling with vain unsubstantial hands to what he hoped would hold him, save him, arrest him—Ellen (do you mark them?), myself, then last of all that fatherless daughter of Wash Jones' only child . . . —to find severence (even if not rest and peace) at last in the stroke of a rusty scythe" (pp. 171–72). It is clear that Rosa maintains her romantic dream of Sutpen's redemption to the end, even if she recognizes—with a certain vengeful satisfaction—that he remains beyond anyone's salvation, since "heaven cannot, and hell dare not, have" him (p. 172).

Metonymy and Tragedy

> In Tragedy, there are no festive occasions, except false or illusory ones; rather, there are intimations of states of division among men more terrible than that which incited the tragic agon at the beginning of the drama.
> —Hayden White, *Metahistory*

It seems plain enough that Rosa's first presentation (in chapter 1) of Thomas Sutpen provides *Absalom* with its "metaphorical characterization of a domain of experience" (T, p. 5) and that her second presentation (in chapter 5) extrapolates in the plot modality of romance associated with the trope of metaphor. It seems equally plain that when Mr. Compson takes over the narration, *Absalom* shifts toward the trope of metonymy, with its attendant emplotment in the mode of tragedy. In discourse of any sort (including novels), metonymy appears to introduce the features of logic, for metonymic development of the "domain" in question employs division (as in hierarchies or systems), reductive categorization into parts, and cause-effect entailments. An initial metaphorical characterization of the world through naming and resemblance gives way to a second phase in the course of understanding, "the metonymic apprehension," says Hans Kellner, "of the order of things as a grid-like system of representative order."[8] Metaphor constitutes the world in a name and as a whole, but metonymy divides the world into parts and shows the entailed relations among them. "Realities, in short, always have perceivable degrees," says Kellner; "to understand this is to constitute the existence of parts, which in turn make possible the reductions and ratios, the analyses and distinctions, characteristic of metonymy in general."[9] In its operations, metonymy seems to represent the rational, logical, even scientific consciousness. It would, as Hayden White says, "provide a model of that form of explanation which I have called mechanistic, inasmuch as the latter is characterized by an apprehension of the historical field as a complex of part-

part relationships and by the effort to comprehend that field in terms of the laws that bind one phenomenon to another as a cause to an effect" (T, p. 73).

Mr. Compson's account of the history surrounding Thomas Sutpen provides a metonymic extension of Rosa's metaphorical constitution of the field itself. The metonymic "deconstructions" of the historical domain named by Rosa result in a mechanistic explanation of causal relationships between or among parts in the system. The "system" Mr. Compson identifies is essentially social. Thus, the primary function of chapters 2, 3, and 4 is to represent social classes in their causally determined relations. In these chapters, Mr. Compson identifies the parts of the social system, suggests their vertical or hierarchical relationships, and argues that the outcome of these relationships (that is, the events in the plot he generates) is determined by "laws" of one sort or another (sociological or metaphysical).

The social space of Faulkner's Jefferson is first charted in *Absalom* through the account of Thomas Sutpen's arrival there, his construction of the mansion at the center of his hundred square miles of land, and his "assault upon respectability" through the agency of marriage into the community. All this is recounted in chapter 2, through a perspective that can be regarded as mainly communal, with details provided by a more or less omniscient narrator who seems situated in Quentin's mind, but whose knowledge of "facts" seems to come primarily from Quentin's grandfather and father. The major portion of narration cast in quotation marks comes from Mr. Compson, and criticism of *Absalom* generally ascribes this chapter to him. But it seems clear enough that Mr. Compson's objective is to recount the response of the community of Jefferson to Thomas Sutpen as a potential social phenomenon. In this construal of the historical field, Sutpen is almost entirely a social creature regarded by other social creatures who want to identify (or impose) the place within which he will be located on the social grid.

Metaphor is built upon similarity, but metonymy entails difference. If there is a single principle at work in chapters 2 and 3 it is the manifest difference between one set (Sutpen and his slaves) and another (the two levels of the community). The principle of difference is social, and is observed in strangeness, estrangement, foreignness. The power of the strange defines social relations. Since the language with which Rosa has "named" characters in chapter 1 persists into the descriptions provided by all subsequent narrative consciousnesses (except Sutpen's), we do not immediately notice the essential shift from a tropological mode of metaphor to one of metonymy. We may not notice, that is, that in chapter 2 we begin to see characters not in a heroic, but rather in a social, way. Thomas Sutpen is a demon or devil in Rosa's invocation, but in Mr. Compson's he is simply "the stranger" (p. 31), still mysterious, he and his horse "looking as though they had been created out of thin air" (p. 32), but nonetheless placed now in the social context necessary for definition of "the stranger." In Mr. Compson's account, Sutpen appears on a "Sunday morning in June with the bells ringing peaceful," the streets filled with "ladies and children," "house negroes," "and even a few men." He says that "when the other men sitting with their feet on the railing of the Holston House gallery looked up, ... there the stranger was" (p. 31). Thomas Sutpen remains the stranger throughout the social rituals by which he begins to claim a place for himself in the ruling hierarchy. His display of extraordinary prowess with his pistols, for example, is a ritual action aimed at social conquest, not criminal warfare; his "demonstration" (p. 33) is a further definition of his being as a separate, causal entity. It establishes a form of détente eventually leading (in a fashion) without bloodshed to acceptance of his presence by the community. Though Mr. Compson makes it plain that the deterrent to violence against Sutpen by a "vigilance committee" (p. 45) much later was their "thought about those two pistols" (p. 46), the vigilance committee, at the time it confronted Sutpen, did not realize that at the very moment of confrontation Sutpen was planning another step toward self-definition. He was riding into town to ask Mr. Coldfield for Ellen in marriage, thereby to gain actual admission into Jefferson's social hierarchy by taking a part of it to himself.

A mystery lies behind the goal of Sutpen's "assault" upon Jefferson, but that goal is nothing if not social. Sutpen's goal is marriage, not as a romantic liaison, but as a social bonding, a ceremonial assimilation of the stranger, who knows himself to be estranged, into the body politic of the community. Admittedly, the townspeople generally view it as having Sutpen stuffed down their throats: Mr. Compson refers to their unease as "an acute state of indigestion" (p. 46). And he refers to the actions of Ellen's aunt, once she sees that the townspeople are unlikely to attend the wedding, as "no longer ... merely thrusting Sutpen down the town's throat, but thrusting the wedding itself" (p. 54). Similarly, in the account of the reaction of the town to the wedding ceremony, Mr. Compson provides a description of a kind of public regurgitation, for when the wedding party departs the church and is set upon as they pass by a crowd hurling "dirt, filth, whatever it was . . . clods of dirt and vegetable refuse," the crowd is described as "a circle of faces with open mouths" (pp. 56–57). Significantly, as Mr. Compson notes, the men who had formed the vigilance committee and followed Sutpen "to Mr. Coldfield's gate . . . two months before" were the same who now formed the "mob" at the wedding. Those who had once regularly gone "out to Sutpen's Hundred . . . to hunt his game and eat his food . . . and on occasion gathering at night in his stable while he matched two of his wild negroes against one another" are now the ones who wish to purge him from their communal body (pp. 57–58).

While Mr. Compson extends the social space acted upon by Thomas Sutpen in Chapter 2 primarily by a metonymic process of renaming, classifying, or dividing, he does so in chapter 3 by extending Sutpen's familial relationships. These are also essentially social, for members of the family extend the same principles of class division as seen in the separation of Sutpen from the townspeople, or, analogously, but on a lower scale, the "wild" slaves from the white degenerates who comprise the "mob." As, at first, the very embodiment of the strange, Thomas Sutpen is the causal part in a syntax or syntagmatic chain that binds together disparate social strata. Others are defined, metonymically, against him. Mr. Coldfield comes into being *in the narrative* because Thomas Sutpen needs him and so, as Coldfield's antithesis, calls him up, and ever after in the narrative Mr. Coldfield exists because of the relationship he has had with Sutpen. He exists because he has been used by Sutpen. In the same way, Ellen Coldfield comes into narrative existence because she is needed for use by Sutpen. Her father legitimizes Sutpen's business dealings, and Ellen legitimizes him socially.

Rosa Coldfield is brought into being as the antagonist who can carry Sutpen into the twentieth century. We are told that Rosa saw herself defined against Sutpen. "Perhaps she saw in her father's death" (p. 61), Mr. Compson speculates, a "fate . . . supplying her with the opportunity to observe her sister's dying request" to "at least save Judith" (p. 22) from Sutpen's evil clutches. "Perhaps she even saw herself as an instrument of retribution: if not in herself an active instrument strong enough to cope with him, at least as a kind of passive symbol of inescapable reminding to rise bloodless and without dimension from the sacrificial stone of the marriage-bed" (p. 61). Finally, even Sutpen's progeny serve narrative existences just as dependent upon their father as those of the Coldfields have been. Charles Bon, Judith, and Henry become necessary as social extensions of Thomas Sutpen across a further space, one marked temporally. Sutpen's children carry into another generation the mark of the strange, the foreign, the very principle of difference. The mark is not in their faces, but in their fates, their destiny, their doom, and these are determined by Thomas Sutpen and perceived by the town in the same terms in which he had originally been defined.

The metonymical extensions of the social space of *Absalom*'s Jefferson continue in chapter 4, where Mr. Compson especially turns his attention to Sutpen's offspring. The focal point of metonymical differentiation undergoes an ironic shift from Sutpen to Charles Bon through the course of chapter 3 and dominates in chapter 4. But here, a principle of cultural knowledge, of "sophistication," rather than of mere "strangeness" or social hegemony, becomes the principle of difference. Such a shift means that the hierarchical relations are reversed, for those who were *up* (the Sutpens) are now *down* in some meaningful way. Bon's appearance in the community is clearly paralleled to Sutpen's: "He came into that isolated puritan country household almost like Sutpen himself came into Jefferson: apparently complete, without background or past or childhood." But where Sutpen socially had stood below Jefferson, Bon stands above the Sutpens, who are now seen as crude country folk: "He seems to hover, shadowy, almost substanceless, a little behind and above all the other . . . ultimatums and affirmations and defiances and challenges and repudiations, with an air . . . like that of a youthful Roman consul making the Grand Tour . . . among the barbarian hordes . . . , benighted in a brawling and childish and quite deadly mud-castle household in a miasmic and spirit-ridden forest." In comparison to Bon's "sophistication," "Henry and Sutpen were troglodytes" (p. 93). To Henry, Bon appears "a hero out of some adolescent Arabian Nights who had stumbled upon a talisman or touch-stone." By comparison, Henry himself is "the provincial, the clown almost" (p. 96), who goes off to the University "with his countrified clothes," barely "different from the negro slaves who supported" the Sutpens (pp. 96–97). And Judith, "this young countrybred girl" (p. 99), is "the bucolic maiden" to Bon's "metropolitan gallant" (p. 128). A major theme of Faulkner's characterization in this entire chapter, then, rests upon the ironic reversal of the principle of difference that Sutpen had introduced to Jefferson and Yoknapatawpha County.

The mythos or archetypal emplotment that structures the events represented in chapters 2, 3, and 4 is essentially social and depends upon the principle of hierarchization. While the tale told here partakes of the bifurcation of the world into good and evil that we see in Rosa's romance, Mr. Compson's account begins in chapter 2 to show the striving toward the unification of opposites one finds in comedy. His version of the first stage of Sutpen's story contrasts nature and culture in the ultimate hope of achieving a cultivated nature. Here, of course, we find Faulkner's "wilderness" theme, but as Mr. Compson presents it, the wilderness must be tamed, whether it is located in external nature or inside the human breast. The goal of Sutpen's "gaunt and tireless driving" (p. 36) is to subdue the wilderness by imposing the form of the plantation upon it, a vast cultivation, reigned over by the mansion. By dragging "house and gardens out of virgin swamp" (p. 40), Sutpen moves the lower order of nature toward the higher order of humanly cultivated community. Similarly, Sutpen moves a human community toward a higher form of socialization when he introduces his "wild negroes" (p. 36) to the "tame" ones of Jefferson. And, since it is clear that Sutpen, at least in the eyes of the town, is identified with the wild negroes, the process of his and their socialization tames the spirit or principle of wilderness within the human being. Such elements suggest, then, that we are in the midst of a romantic comedy. But it turns out, of course, that this is just the first of three acts in all. The apparent success of Sutpen's project is suggested by his rise in the community. In the passage of twenty years, he became the county's "biggest single landowner and cotton-planter." Moreover, he is "accepted" by the community, even if he is not liked. But at the height of his triumph he is unaware—as Mr. Compson puts it—that "behind him Fate, destiny, retribution, irony—the stage manager, call him what you will—was already striking the set and dragging on the synthetic and spurious shadows and shapes of the next one" (pp. 72–73).

The phase of the "drama" Mr. Compson is staging in chapter 3 involves two important metonymical transformations. The one involves Charles Bon, who would rename himself Sutpen in the syntax of events he generates. Indeed, as we have seen, Charles replaces Sutpen as the principal figure of difference. He is from a distant, "even foreign city," "a young man of worldly elegance and assurance beyond his years, handsome, apparently wealthy and with for background the shadowy figure of a legal guardian rather than any parents—a personage who in the remote Mississippi of that time must have appeared almost phoenix-like, fullsprung from no childhood, born of no woman and impervious to time" (p. 74). This shift, by which Bon replaces Sutpen, suggests that difference is a universal, perhaps inescapable, dimension of life. Once division is acknowledged, it can be seen as the primary determinant of any social existence. The effect of the shift, therefore, is to suggest that conflict, strife, and even warfare are inevitable.

The second metonymical transformation shifts the whole geographical space of Sutpen's social existence not merely toward Jefferson, but outward toward the entire South and the nation. At the moment Charles Bon becomes for the Sutpens a real presence, the Civil War, almost as an effect, also begins to loom. As Mr. Compson delineates the situation, "the time now approached" when the Sutpens must confront their destiny, "which for twenty years . . . had been like a lake welling from quiet springs into a quiet valley and spreading, rising almost imperceptibly and in which the four [family] members . . . floated in sunny suspension, [and] felt the first subterranean movement toward the outlet, the gorge which would be the land's catastrophe too" (p. 74). Since Charles Bon's role in the plot of chapter 3 is to focus the principle of difference that had previously resided in Sutpen, he thus becomes the "causal" principle dividing not only father from son and brother from sister, but also region from region—the North from the South. At the very moment we learn of "Lincoln's election and the fall of [Fort] Sumpter, . . . the knell and doom of . . . [Rosa's] native land," we also learn that "Henry had just vanished" as the result of a quarrel between him and his father (p. 78).

Henry's gesture of abjuration and renunciation, passively focused by Charles Bon, becomes the ultimate symbolic act of differentiation. The act brings about further divisions, separations, differentiations, as the plot of chapter 3 plummets toward chaos. Mrs. Thomas Sutpen—Ellen— "seemed to have retired to the darkened room which she was not to quit until she died two years later." Henry and Judith, "between [whom] there had been a relationship closer than the traditional loyalty of brother and sister even," are separated (p. 79). And, inevitably, mimicking Henry's gesture, the South renounces its father, a separation marked here in the secession of Mississippi from the Union. Finally, at the chapter's end we

109

do not find community. Instead, the roll call of characters, along with accounts of their actions during the war, is in every way a repetition of the modes of separation, division, and difference seen previously in this chapter. Thus, chapter 3 begins to turn the potentially comedic plot trajectory established in chapter 2 downward toward tragedy.

The mythos formed by chapters 2, 3, and 4—that is, the diegetic line formed by Mr. Compson's narration—culminates in 4. The shape Mr. Compson confers is tragedy's, and that shape is confirmed in the account of events given in chapter 4. The triumph achieved by Sutpen in the social arena (and the family's "innocence" of the costs, suggested in that metaphor of rising waters and unaware swimmers) disintegrates in the wake of the feuding within the family and the warfare that breaks out within the social macrostructure. The plot is tragic, rather than ironic, because the figures involved are heroic, not mere ciphers, and because they are caught up in a mechanistic system of causes and effects over which, ultimately, they have no control. Mr. Compson speaks of them as "people too as we are, and victims too as we are, but victims of a different circumstance, simpler and therefore, integer for integer, larger, more heroic and the figures therefore more heroic too" (p. 89). Their entrapment in a machine of destruction is frequently described as a form of fate, or destiny, or doom. Such terms occur throughout the three chapters, but they become markedly predominant in the fourth chapter. Mr. Compson sees Henry "doomed and destined to kill" Charles Bon (p. 91). With the Sutpen family destiny tied to that of the nation, Henry should have murdered Bon early on, Mr. Compson avers, but the event was delayed four years, "the four years, the interval, mere anti-climax: an attenuation and prolongation of a conclusion already ripe to happen, by the War by a stupid and bloody aberration in the high (and impossible) destiny of the United States, maybe instigated by that family fatality which possessed, along with all circumstances, that curious lack of economy between cause and effect which is always a characteristic of fate when reduced to using human beings for tools, material" (pp. 118–19).

All this, the entire tragic debacle of Sutpen destiny and the Civil War, is seen in the context of Mr. Compson's deterministic view of history itself. The ending of chapter 4, climaxing this particular tragic emplotment, follows hard upon one of the few direct contacts we have with "objective documents" in the novel. That document is the letter from Charles Bon to Judith Sutpen, with which we have been tantalized

since the very beginning of the fourth chapter. Like Quentin, we expect—
at least hope—that the letter will finally tell us something to explain
everything else. It does indeed tell us a lot, more than we have yet really
known about Charles, but it is quite—shall we say dead—wrong in its
one important prediction, "that you and I are . . . included among those
who are doomed to live" (p. 132). And it does not explain—for us or for
Mr. Compson or for Quentin—everything else. That, finally, is what
history is about:

> It's just incredible. It just does not explain. Or perhaps that's it: they don't
> explain and we are not supposed to know. We have a few old mouth-to-
> mouth tales; we exhume from old trunks and boxes and drawers letters
> without salutation or signature, . . . the people in whose living blood and
> seed we ourselves lay dormant and waiting, in this shadowy attenuation of
> time possessing now heroic proportions, performing their acts of simple
> passion and simple violence, impervious to time and inexplicable—Yes, Ju-
> dith, Bon, Henry, Sutpen: all of them. They are there, yet something is
> missing; they are like a chemical formula exhumed along with the letters
> from that forgotten chest . . . ; you bring them together in the proportions
> called for, but nothing happens; . . . you bring them together again and again
> nothing happens: just the words, the symbols, the shapes themselves, shad-
> owy inscrutable and serene, against that turgid background of a horrible
> and bloody mischancing of human affairs. (Pp. 100–1)

The end result of the "bloody mischancing of human affairs"—besides the
war itself—is the more intimate familial tragedy with which the fourth
chapter ends. That is the murder of Charles Bon by his half brother Henry.
The essence of the tragedy is captured in the distinctly material image
Wash Jones provides: "Henry has done shot that durn French feller. Kilt
him dead as a beef" (p. 133).

Synecdoche and Comedy

> In Comedy, hope is held out for the temporary triumph of man over his
> world by the prospect of occasional *reconciliations* of the forces at play
> in the social and natural worlds. Such reconciliations are symbolized in
> the festive occasions which the Comic writer traditionally uses to termi-
> nate his dramatic accounts of change and transformation.
>
> —Hayden White, *Metahistory*

Our sense of Rosa's account and of Mr. Compson's account of Sutpen's
life is distilled from what amounts to the first half of *Absalom, Absalom!*

The second half of the novel gives us two other rather distinctive perspectives on that life: Shreve McCannon's (which is usually attributed to both Quentin and Shreve) and Thomas Sutpen's as filtered through Grandfather Compson to Quentin (or, as Cleanth Brooks points out, first through Mr. Compson and then to Quentin, since Quentin would have been only about ten at his grandfather's death). These accounts are even more intermingled than those of Rosa and Mr. Compson. Shreve begins to "play" in the narrative game in chapter 6, and continues to play intermittently through chapters 7, 8, and 9. Sutpen's account is filtered through Grandfather and then to son and grandson in chapter 7. Readers of the novel may well feel that Sutpen's more or less direct account is the one most needful by the time it arrives, for it may provide a "factual" kernel to offset all the speculation and fabulation seen going on around Sutpen. Its status as "fact" is no more stable than that of the other accounts, but it at least does serve the tropological function one would expect in this place—the function of synecdoche. A synecdochic representation of Sutpen's life seems necessary in this narrative moment because of the "inherent movement" of the four tropes "through a fixed course: from metaphor, the preliminary naming operation, to metonymy, the process of reductive manipulation and formalization, to the integrative, macrocosm/microcosm relationships of synecdoche, to the final awareness within the series that all of its processes have been relativizing turns, the whole process ironic."[10] What we find in the novel's second half, that is to say, is an intensifying conflict between the functions of synecdoche observed in Sutpen's account and those of irony seen in Shreve's.

In *Absalom*, chapter 7 shifts the narrative toward Sutpen's whole life, rather than focusing on his impact upon the community of Jefferson. This shift provides a more organic causal relationship between the events as parts and the life as an integrated conceptual unity. Opposed to the metaphoric naming function of Rosa's account and the metonymic division into hierarchies of Mr. Compson's, this synecdochic turn begins to display the principles, the essences, the organic forces that will draw together Sutpen's life and, what is more, ally it with even greater wholes. According to Hayden White, synecdoche sanctions "a movement . . . towards integration of all apparently particular phenomena into a whole, the quality of which was such as to justify belief in the possibility of understanding the particular as a microcosm of a macrocosmic totality, which is precisely the aim of all organicist systems of explanation" (T, p. 73). Kenneth Burke, also speaking of the relation between microcosm and macrocosm, has suggested that "where the individual is treated as a replica of the universe, and vice versa, we have the ideal synecdoche, since microcosm is related to macrocosm as part to whole, and either the whole can represent the part or the part can represent the whole."[11] Burke illustrates the synecdochic principle through the conventional poetic conceit of "the remotest astronomical distances" representing the "truth within" (and vice versa), through the representation embodied in Leibniz's theory of monadology, and through the principle of political representation, "where some part of the social body (either traditionally established, or elected, or coming into authority by revolution) is held to be 'representative' of the society as a whole."[12]

There are two important synecdoches at work in the second half of *Absalom*. One is an abstract principle, the other a concrete object. The object, which becomes the dominant symbol in the novel, is the Sutpen mansion, the house Sutpen is at such expense of time, money, and integrity to build. Synecdoches develop into symbols out of a concrete context of local detail. "The symbol is the product of the organic growth of form," Paul de Man has said; "in the world of the symbol, life and form are identical. . . . Its structure is that of the synecdoche, for the symbol is always part of the totality that it represents."[13] The growth of Sutpen's mansion as a synecdoche/symbol is gradual within the novel, despite the fact Faulkner must have thought of it as a symbol from the very beginning, when he planned to call the book "Dark House."[14] True, it is mentioned early and often, from the first chapter on, but one cannot make an object into a symbol merely by proclaiming it symbolic. When Quentin thinks of it early, it is mainly an appendage to Sutpen, just an object exemplifying his heroic accomplishment: "Colonel Sutpen. Who came out of nowhere and without warning upon the land with a band of strange niggers and built a plantation" (p. 9). It remains an aspect of Sutpen's heroic stature in other early references: "He first rode into town out of no discernible past and acquired his land no one knew how and built his house, his mansion, apparently out of nothing" (p. 11), "a house the size of a court-house" (p. 16), a mansion that rose "plank by plank and brick by brick out of the swamp where the clay and timber waited" (p. 37).

By chapter 3, however, the house has become identified with Sutpen in a more organic way: it was "as though his presence alone compelled that house to accept and retain human life; as though houses actually possess a sentience, a personality and character acquired, not so much from the people who breathe or have breathed in them inherent in the wood and brick or begotten upon the wood and brick by the man or men who conceived and built them—in this house an incontrovertible affirmation for emptiness, desertion; an insurmountable resistance to occupancy save when sanctioned and protected by the ruthless and the strong" (p. 85). It has manifestly become a synecdochic object by the end of chapter 4, when Quentin imagines the confrontation of Henry Sutpen with Charles Bon at the mansion gate: "Inside the gate what was once a park now spread, unkempt, in shaggy desolation, with an air dreamy, remote and aghast like the unshaven face of a man just waking from ether, up to a huge house where a young girl waited in a wedding dress made from stolen scraps, the house partaking too of that air of scaling desolation, not having suffered from invasion but a shell marooned and forgotten in a backwater catastrophe—a skeleton giving of itself in slow driblets of furniture and carpet, linen and silver, to help to die torn and anguished men who knew, even while dying, that for months now the sacrifice and the anguish were in vain" (pp. 132–33).

And by chapter 5, whose major theme is Rosa's desire for the restoration of the domain, the conflation of Sutpen and house is entire. When Clytie speaks, Rosa thinks, "It was as though it had not been she who spoke but the house itself . . . the house which he had built, which some supperation of himself had created about him as the sweat of his body might have produced some . . . cocoon-like and complementary shell" (p. 138); later, not Clytie's but Judith's voice is displaced by the house, "the house itself speaking again" (p. 142); and again, later, Sutpen speaks to the house as if to himself, "talked . . . to the air, the waiting grim decaying presence, spirit, of the house itself, talking that which sounded like the bombast of a madman who creates within his very coffin walls his fabulous immeasurable Camelots and Carcassonnes." Finally, the synecdochic relation between Sutpen and house/domain is predicated as plainly as possible: "a part of him encompassing each ruined field and fallen fence and crumbling wall of cabin or cotton house or crib" (p. 160). When, at the chapter's end, Rosa tells Quentin that something is living in that house, readers primed by Rosa's synecdochic enfigurations can only imagine that that something is Sutpen's ghostly spirit. It turns out instead to be his son, another part of Sutpen who comes to represent the whole man, and who in that sense is indeed his spirit.

114

In chapter 6, the house suffers a comedown from the symbolic intensity emanating from it in Rosa's romantic account of Sutpen's doomed efforts to restore it. When Shreve first takes up the narration, it is simply "the house" (p. 176), "that rotting house" (p. 180), and even in Quentin's verbalizations here it is merely "the house" and "the house itself" (p. 183), while in a momentary authorial account, Faulkner refers to it as "the gray huge rotting deserted house" (p. 187) and Mr. Compson, given a shot at it, calls it "that decaying house" (p. 197). Only by chapter's end does it begin to resume some of its overdetermined significance out of the past. Now, in the novel's time-present (more or less), it is observed as "the old house," "the rotting shell of . . . house," and "that old house" (p. 213), before it finally becomes "the haunted house," haunted, we learn, by Clytie, who "must be more than seventy now" (p. 215), Jim Bond, and, it turns out, Henry Sutpen, almost as old as Clytie. These deflations of the synecdochic inflations seen earlier prepare for the overt revelation to Sutpen of the significance of the house, given us in chapter 7. His mansion shall stand in the place of the one from whose door he had been turned away as a youth. It will be his weapon to combat all those who can so lord it over him through his representatives: "To combat them you have got to have what they have that made them do what the man did. You got to have land and niggers and a fine house to combat them with" (p. 238). The "fine house" will become the centerpiece of Sutpen's design.

Sutpen's design is the synecdochic figure that gives the emplotment of his narration the shape of comedy. According to Northrop Frye, the goal of comedy is integration, usually the integration of the family, but it may also apply to other social levels as well. The principle underlying synecdoche, of course, is precisely integration, the interrelationship of parts to wholes, often envisioned through images of organic forces or essential spirits. Hayden White has outlined the relationship between synecdoche and the two forms of comic emplotment it entails: "the triumph of the protagonist over the society which blocks his progression to his goal, or the reassertion of the rights of the collectivity over the individual who has risen up to challenge it as the definitive form of community. The first kind of Comic emplotment may be called the Comedy of Desire, the second kind the Comedy of Duty and Obligation" (M, p. 190). Quite plainly, the emplotment of Sutpen's account of his early life in chapter 7 is of the first type. The fulfillment of Sutpen's desire is to be the end, goal, *telos* of his design.

Sutpen's desire is, quite simply, to achieve those objects in the world that would permit him to take his "proper" place among those who already possess them. His design is not so much an external structure of strategies and objectives as it is merely, synecdochically, the working out of his spirit or essence within society. His design is linked to his concept of destiny, or fate, which is quite different for him from Mr. Compson's concept (where the metonymic principle of cause-effect is dominant). Grandfather Compson makes this clear in his account of Sutpen's story of his West Indian adventure. According to Grandfather, Sutpen insisted that "there was something about a man's destiny (or about the man) that caused the destiny to shape itself to him like his clothes did . . . so that his . . . destiny had fitted itself to him, to his innocence, his pristine aptitude for platform drama and childlike heroic simplicity, just as the fine broadcloth uniform which you could have seen on ten thousand men during those four years [of the Civil War] . . . had fitted itself to the swaggering of all his gestures and . . . forensic verbiage" (pp. 245–46). For Sutpen, the design is to be so tightly interwoven with his life that he would not argue that one could be separated from the other—part and whole are integral. But for Sutpen the emphasis is on the larger whole, the principle of the design "to which he had dedicated himself" (p. 248). So when he tells Grandfather his story, "he was not bragging about something he had done; he was just telling a story about something a man named Thomas Sutpen had experienced, which would still have been the same story if the man had had no name at all, if it had been told about any man or no man over whiskey at night" (p. 247).

To his design Sutpen has the relation of a religious convert or disciple. It is something to which, in effect, he had consecrated his life, so that it became the force or power that energized him. We are told that he undertook to learn two new languages because of his design: "He had believed that courage and shrewdness would be enough but found that he was wrong. . . . He discovered that all people did not speak the same tongue and realized that he would not only need courage and skill, he would have to learn to speak a new language, else that design to which he had dedicated himself would die still-born." Like a religious convert, he even dedicates his sex life to the design. He tells Grandfather, "On this night I am speaking of (and until my first marriage, I might add) I was still a virgin . . . that too was a part of the design which I had in mind" (p. 248). And when Grandfather tells of Sutpen's triumph over the rebellious natives on that "little island set in a smiling and fury-lurked and incredible indigo sea, which was the halfway point between what we call the jungle and what we call civilization" (p. 250), he tells of it as if it were also an emanation from some spirit residing in Sutpen. When he "walked out into the darkness and subdued them," the natives perhaps turned and fled "from the white arms and legs shaped like theirs and from which blood could be made to spurt and flow as it could from theirs and containing an indomitable spirit which should have come from the same primary fire which theirs came from but which could not have, could not possibly have" (p. 254).

Again, like a religious devotee, Sutpen subordinates issues of morality and conscience to the design. Acts, decisions, choices, behavior all are subsumed to the design. The very first mention of his design occurs in his matter-of-fact remark to Grandfather that he had "put aside" the wife he had won when he subdued the natives because she "was not and could never be, through no fault of her own, adjunctive or incremental to the design which I had in mind, so I provided for her and put her aside" (p. 240); he had "repudiated that first wife and that child when he discovered that they would not be adjunctive to the forwarding of the design" (p. 262). And when that repudiated child, Charles Bon, shows up some thirty years later as the friend to the second, by-the-design legitimized son, Henry, and as the suitor to the daughter Judith, Sutpen can ask only what "mistake" he had made in fulfilling the design, as if he had sinned against the design. "Whether it was a good or a bad design is beside the point; the question is, Where did I make the mistake in it" (p. 263). Others, such as Rosa, might call it retribution or fatality or doom, but not Sutpen. It was "just an old mistake in fact which a man of courage and shrewdness . . . could still combat if he could only find out what the mistake had been" (pp. 267–68). And, according to Grandfather, Sutpen's further choices, decisions, acts had "all come from a mistake and until he discovered what that mistake had been he did not intend to risk making another one" (p. 268).

The emplotment of Sutpen's life is conceived through his devotion to the design in the structure of comedy. Each phase of his life, as Sutpen recounts it to Grandfather, contributes its part to the whole design. The first stage is that in which the structure of desire is created and the design becomes motivated. The second stage, which would have fulfilled both desire and design had it not been for the one "factor" of his wife's racial makeup, is that in which Sutpen achieves the substance of his desire, but not its idealized form. The third stage, then, is that in which he attempts again to join form and substance; the essential outline of this third stage provides the content of Mr. Compson's account of Sutpen's "assault" on Jefferson, but it is observed in chapter 7 largely through the account of the escaped architect, tracked down and returned to the construction of the mansion by Sutpen's wild slaves. Sutpen sees the West Indian phase and the next phase in terms of the "choices" he has to make in order to remain constant to the original design. When he sees that he will be unable "to preserve the status of his life's attainment and desire" (p. 272) once Charles Bon comes into the picture, he is once again faced with a choice in relation to his design. He explains his original choice to Grandfather: "I was faced with condoning a fact which had been foisted upon me without my knowledge during the process of building toward my design, which meant the absolute and irrevocable negation of the design; or in holding to my original plan for the design in pursuit of which I had incurred this negation. I chose, and I made to the fullest what atonement lay in my power for whatever injury I might have done in choosing, paying even more for the privilege of choosing as I chose than I might have been expected to, or even (by law) required" (p. 273).

He also explains the "second choice" to Grandfather. Like the first, this situation permits Sutpen to ignore the knowledge he has and thereby permit the appearance of his indeed having fulfilled his design. Once again he has to choose between substance and devotion to the idealized form. He tells Grandfather, "Either I destroy my design with my own hand, which will happen if I am forced to play my last trump card, or do nothing, let matters take the course which I know they will take and see my design complete itself quite normally and naturally and successfully to the public eye, yet to my own in such a fashion as to be a mockery and a betrayal" (p. 274). He chooses fidelity to the ideal design, and so commits himself to a "third time" (p. 278), a third attempt to fulfill the original desire, to have the son who will produce the "fine grandsons and great-grandsons springing as far as eye could reach" (p. 271). But if the first two attempts had been heroic, the third one can only be regarded as mock-heroic, and Sutpen, at the end, can do nothing but satirize his own life's design by his "proposition" to Rosa Coldfield and his "spotting-shot" (p. 279) court-ship of Milly Jones. These efforts to complete the design provide the material of the rhetorical and structural irony of Shreve McCannon's account of Sutpen's life. The form of comic emplotment Sutpen's design would entail shall not come to fruition.

Irony and Antiromance

> The archetypal theme of Satire is the precise opposite of [the] Romantic drama of redemption; it is, in fact, a drama of diremption, a drama dominated by the apprehension that man is ultimately a captive of the world rather than its master, and by the recognition that, in the final analysis, human consciousness and will are always inadequate to the task of overcoming definitively the dark force of death, which is man's unremitting enemy.
>
> —Hayden White, *Metahistory*

It is generally understood in criticism of *Absalom, Absalom!* that the presentation of Sutpen's story from Shreve McCannon's point of view is satiric. That means Shreve's account or interpretation is dominated by the trope of irony and emplotted as satire or antiromance. As a trope, irony can be regarded as the trope of tropes, the metatrope, the one that seems to embrace the other tropes in its operations. Hayden White says of irony: "Irony sanctions the ambiguous, and possibly even the ambivalent, statement. It is a kind of metaphor, but one that surreptitiously signals a denial of the assertion of similitude or difference contained in the literal sense of the proposition, or at least sets a crucial qualification on it" (T, p. 73). Ironic statements may also contain metonymy and synecdoche. White says that the statement, "He is all *heart*," contains a metonymy within a synecdoche, whereas the same statement delivered sarcastically, with the emphasis on *all*, "contains irony on top of a synecdoche." "What is involved here," White concludes, "is a kind of attitude towards knowledge itself which is implicitly critical of all forms of metaphorical identification, reduction, or integration of phenomena" (T, p. 73). Irony, therefore, is the trope that questions every enfiguration, every thought, every emplotment. Irony, in short, questions the very ability of language to represent truth.

There is much local irony running through the first five chapters of the novel, but a sustained modal irony begins with Shreve's active involvement in the accounts. The basic tactic of Shreve's irony is to deflate the language of the previous enfigurations. It starts with what amounts to a synecdochic inflation of Sutpen's tale, making it a part representing the whole South. Telling Shreve of Rosa's death, reported to him in a letter from his father, Quentin reveals an unusual affection for an old woman who is not even a relative. "You mean she was no kin to you," Shreve exclaims, "no kin to you at all, that there was actually one Southern Bayard or Guinevere who was no kin to you? then what did she die for?" In the epithets "Southern Bayard or Guinevere" Shreve's inflation of the part into the whole has already begun, at the same time the deflation of the irony is observable, too. Both the synecdoche and the attendant irony become clear in the generalized plaint of all Quentin's Cambridge friends: "Tell about the South. What's it like there. What do they do there. Why do they live there. Why do they live at all" (p. 174).

Shreve's basic rhetorical tactic is the ironic reversal, whether of deflation or inflation. The effect of Shreve's treatment here is to cast doubts on the tale told him. Hayden White says of such techniques, "The rhetorical figure of *aporia* (literally 'doubt'), in which the author signals in advance a real or feigned disbelief in the truth of his own statements, could be considered the favored stylistic device of Ironic language, in both fiction of the more 'realistic' sort and histories that are cast in a self-consciously skeptical tone or are 'relativizing' in their intention" (M, p. 37). In his initial recapitulation of "facts," Shreve deflates the tale told by Quentin by putting the actions of the Coldfield family in the least attractive terms. He asks Quentin, for example, if he means to say that "this old dame . . . grew up in a household like an overpopulated mausoleum, with no call or claim on her time but the hating of her father and aunt and her sister's husband in peace and comfort and waiting for the day when they would prove not only to themselves but to everybody else that she had been right?" Further, he asks, do you mean that then "one night the aunt slid down the rainpipe with a horse trader," and "then her father nailed himself up in the attic to keep from being drafted into the Rebel army and starved to death" (p. 176)? Readers can imagine Shreve shaking his head in puzzled disbelief. But then his irony takes another turn, from questions to apparent acceptance. He will take over the tale, but he radically inflates through an exaggerated mythopoesis. The "old dame" must have been right about Sutpen, he says, "because if he hadn't been a demon his children wouldn't have needed protection from him and she wouldn't have had to go out there and be betrayed by the old meat and find instead of a widowed Agamemnon to her Cassandra an ancient stiff-jointed Pyramus to her eager though untried Thisbe who could approach her in this

120

unbidden April's compounded demonry and suggest that they breed together for test and sample and if it was a boy they would marry" (p. 177).

Once he is absorbed into Quentin's quest for understanding, Shreve displays his ironic mode most outrageously in his enfigurations of Sutpen's life and career. His primary verbal flair is for catachresis. "The basic figurative tactic of Irony is catachresis (literally 'misuse')," according to Hayden White, "the manifestly absurd Metaphor designed to inspire Ironic second thoughts about the nature of the thing characterized or the inadequacy of the characterization itself" (M, p. 37). Shreve speaks of Sutpen as "this Faustus, this demon, this Beelzebub fled hiding from some momentary flashy glare of his Creditor's outraged face exasperated beyond all endurance, hiding, scuttling into respectability like a jackal into a rockpile." Again, he regards Sutpen as "this Faustus who appeared suddenly one Sunday with two pistols and twenty subsidiary demons and skulldugged a hundred miles of land out of a poor ignorant Indian and built the biggest house on it you ever saw" (p. 178). Sutpen, in Shreve's imagination, next becomes Satan, "who hid horns and tail beneath human raiment and a beaver hat and chose . . . a wife . . . not from one of the local ducal houses but from the lesser baronage whose principality was so far decayed that there would be no risk of his wife bringing him for dowry delusions of grandeur," "a wife who not only would consolidate the hiding but could would and did breed him two children to fend and shield both in themselves and in their progeny the brittle bones and tired flesh of an old man against the day when the Creditor would run him to earth for the last time and he couldn't get away" (pp. 178–79).

Next Shreve portrays Sutpen as a demon whose every action to get what he wants turns out to subvert it. The son provides the daughter with the fiancé, but then "the demon must turn square around and run not only the fiance out of the house and not only the son out of the house but so corrupt, seduce and mesmerize the son that he (the son) should do the office of the outraged father's pistol-hand when fornication threatened" (p. 179). And when everything else fails, this demon, in order to "get himself a new batch of children to bulwark him, . . . chose for this purpose the last woman on earth he might have hoped to prevail on, this Aunt R[osa] . . . proposed to her and was accepted." But then, with the possibility of a third try proceeding in legitimacy, the demon decides to hedge his bet, offering Rosa instead of marriage an opportunity to "breed" like "a couple of dogs together" (p. 180), saying that if the offspring is male they will get married. This "mortal affront" (p. 177) to Rosa can only "leave her irrevocably husbanded ... with the abstract carcass of outrage and revenge" (p. 180), and can only leave this demon to try once more, this last time with the fifteen-year-old granddaughter of a weevil-eaten sharecropper too shiftless to fight in the war.

Shreve's rhetoric has so influenced the story by now that even Quentin takes it up in the recounting of the episode of Sutpen with Milly Jones, though Quentin thinks of that rhetoric as sounding "just like father." Quentin's enfigurations of Sutpen's courtship of Milly Jones and death at the hands of the girl's grandfather bespeak the same reversal seen in Shreve's. Quentin depicts the aged Sutpen now as a "mad impotent old man" and an "old demon, the ancient varicose and despairing Faustus." He enfigures Sutpen's plight as "that of the show girl, the pony, who realizes that the principal tune she prances comes not from horn and fiddle and drum but from a clock and calendar." And he enfigures Sutpen's physical and sexual situation as that of "the old wornout cannon which realizes that it can deliver just one more fierce shot and crumble to dust in its own furious blast and recoil" (pp. 181–82).

Moreover, in the depiction of Sutpen's relationship to Wash Jones, the would-be surrogate father-in-law to Sutpen who instead will be his murderer, Quentin underlines very heavily the irony of the tawdry present against what might have been in the past. Jones is "this gangling malaria-ridden white man" whom Sutpen before the war had permitted to "squat in the abandoned fishing camp with the year old grandchild" (p. 183). Although a man of Sutpen's father's class, Jones is not permitted to approach the front of the mansion before war comes, and is permitted only as far as the kitchen door during it, but he regularly crosses the front threshold afterwards with a drunken, comatose Sutpen in tow and goes "on up the stairs and into the bedroom and [puts] him to bed like a baby and then [lies] down himself on the floor beside the bed." Jones's devotion to Sutpen apparently rests upon his vision of the man Sutpen had been— "blind Jones who apparently saw still in that furious lecherous wreck the old fine figure of the man who once galloped on the black thoroughbred about that domain two boundaries of which the eye could not see from any point" (p. 184). Jones's devotion is such that he will bring Sutpen with his own hands "the cheap ribbons and beads and the stale violently-colored candy with which an old man can seduce a fifteen-year-old country

122

girl" (pp. 182–83). But it is not such that he will not murder Sutpen with his own scythe when the old lech rejects mother and child (yet another daughter) as being less valuable than the mare Penelope and her new foal.

One of the features of Shreve's irony is its expression of a disbelief in the reality of Quentin's "South." For Shreve, the tale of the Sutpens is little more than a game, albeit a tremendously engrossing game, in which any number might play. At one point, Shreve implores Quentin to wait, "Let me play a while now" (p. 280). At other times, as well as in conjunction with the figure of game and play, Shreve sees the telling as theater, spectacle. He says to Quentin, "Jesus, the South is fine, isn't it. It's better than the theatre, isn't it. It's better than Ben Hur" (p. 217). Similarly, in the passage where Shreve asks to "play," he shifts the image to the theatrical play once he himself takes up the account, speaking of Wash Jones as "the faithful grave-digger who opened the play and would close it, coming out of the wings like Shakespeare's very self" (p. 280). Earlier, Mr. Compson had regularly employed figures of speech from theater, too, but in his case the figures suggest the presence of a power existing outside the characters that determines their actions against their wills. Shreve uses theater or play or game to suggest the make-believe element in his and Quentin's reconstruction of history. In a passage immediately following the one just quoted, Faulkner (as author) suggests that the "coloring of levity," "the flipness," and the "strained clowning" (p. 280) are the boys' efforts to suppress a youthful sentimentality. But in Shreve's case, these images are more than that, for they point to a basic ironic mode of tropological representation.

Shreve's essential irony surfaces once again when he almost totally takes over narration in chapter 8. Plot and style at times become difficult to untangle, for Shreve's verbal enfigurations develop from previous language and emplotments. Right away he shifts the subject of his narration from Sutpen and his relation to the children, to Charles Bon's mother and the figurative "father" who directs Bon's life in Sutpen's stead. Shreve imagines Bon's "creation" as a function of his relation not to Sutpen and Eulalia, but to Eulalia and her lawyer. He was "created between a lawyer and a woman," "created between this woman and a hired lawyer" (p. 306) who care for him not because of the child he is, but because of the man he will become. The tropic modality underlying Shreve's enfiguration here is the poetically just reversal or inversion. As Sutpen regarded everything and everyone as an instrument of his design, so in Shreve's narrative Eulalia and the lawyer regard their "son" as only an instrument. Shreve says, "It wasn't him at all she was washing and feeding the candy and the fun to but it was a man that hadn't even arrived yet, whom even she had never seen yet, who would be something else beside that boy when he did arrive like the dynamite which destroys the house and the family and maybe even the whole community" (p. 306). As for Sutpen, the mansion he desires is merely a weapon to beat the plantation owner with, so for Eulalia and the figurative father the son is just a weapon or, in another tropic turn, a domain to cultivate as much as Sutpen's Hundred. Shreve says Bon "saw that to her he would be little more than so much rich rotting dirt," at the same time the lawyer "had been plowing and planting and watering and manuring and harvesting him as if he already was" (p. 306), though the lawyer also regarded the mother as "his private mad female millionaire to farm" (p. 300). In Shreve's enfigurations, all seems a matter of, "as ye sow, so shall ye reap," as in style, so in emplotment.

The tropological strategy of Shreve's representation of Sutpen's story is irony, but so is the mode of emplotment. The plot structure of irony deals with what Northrop Frye calls "unidealized existence."[15] In general this treatment means that since the structures of romance are reversed or parodied, irony-satire is often most easily seen as antiromance. In *Absalom*, Shreve has an easy target for parody in the more heroic representations of Sutpen and his family given by Rosa, Mr. Compson, and Grandfather/Sutpen (himself). The most pervasive impact Shreve has on the Sutpen history occurs in chapter 8, in which he is the major narrator (though sometimes, we are told, melding indissolubly with Quentin). Shreve's sense of irony colors the entire account of what some critics have regarded as the chivalric romance emplotment embedded in the narrative. The chivalric romance (as discussed, for example, by Lynn G. Levins) focuses on the relationship among Charles Bon, Judith, and Henry, as seen from the putatively shared, symbiotic point of view of Quentin and Shreve. Levins gives to Quentin, however, most of the authority for the chivalric emplotment: "For the young narrator the doom that envelops a family is neither the result of demonic curse nor the hubris that destroyed the House of Atreus. Instead it becomes a 'glamorous fatality,' ennobling the participants who are condemned to suffer and sacrifice," Quentin conjecturing, moreover, "that the annihilation of the entire line of Sutpen does not necessarily have to be divorced from love and honor and may even have these eternal verities as its cause."[16] But it seems rather clear that in passages

Levins regards as crucial in this interpretation the voice is really Shreve's.[17] Thus, it substantiates the ironic perspective when Levins goes on to develop the thesis that Shreve's presentation comes from one "able to control his sympathies and his imagination's willing suspension of disbelief through cynicism and irony" (Levins, pp. 30–31).

Shreve's role as narrative voice is primarily to develop the reversals of romance one sees in ironic emplotments. Against Sutpen's "heroic design," Shreve plays, for example, the irony of those other "designs," the plans Eulalia and the lawyer draw up to get back at Sutpen. Most of what Shreve offers is only conjecture, but his conjectures expose the likelihood of shadowy congruences between events in Jefferson and New Orleans that bear on Sutpen's history. Shreve surmises that Eulalia, upon moving from Haiti to New Orleans, becomes associated with the lawyer almost exclusively to carry out her own plot (not yet called a design) in which young Charles, without his awareness, would be turned into a weapon for revenge, she "shaping and tempering him to be the instrument for whatever it was her hand was implacable for" (p. 299). But Shreve says that in order to carry out Eulalia's plot, her lawyer does now indeed have a "design," and that Charles may have realized so at one point, when "he believed he had fathomed the lawyer's design in sending him to that particular school [the University] to begin with" (p. 331). That complicated design (for which Charles does not yet know a motive) calls for Bon to meet Henry Sutpen and by this means for Judith Sutpen to fall in love with Bon, as she later does. But, eventually, a competing design arises to foil this one. Henry will become the agent or instrument of yet another of Thomas Sutpen's designs, this one to stop the marriage of Charles and Judith. Sutpen's aim becomes "Henry's dictum and design" (p. 335), but neither Henry nor Charles ever fully realizes the extent to which each is the instrument of real and surrogate parents fighting an unacknowledged, undeclared, but very tragic war.

The design Eulalia and the lawyer (presumably) have created does in fact have the result they plan. Charles becomes the instrument for revenge upon Sutpen, but there is an ironic effect of their design not anticipated: that was "love." It was not part of the (conjectured) design of either the mother or the lawyer for Charles Bon to fall in love with Judith, or for Henry to love both Judith and Charles so that he would believe it necessary to murder his half brother in order to save family honor. So, ironically, Shreve's speculations about Sutpen's three children do turn into something of a chivalric romance for a brief span, just as Shreve and Quentin themselves are wedded in the telling, by "some happy marriage of speaking and hearing wherein each before the demand, the requirement, forgave condoned and forgot the faulting of the other . . . in order to overpass to love" (p. 316). Henry first meets Charles at the University, to which the latter for that express purpose had been sent by the lawyer. Henry comes under Bon's spell, which soon "translated" him into "a fairy tale," a world in which nothing but Judith, Bon, and Henry existed (p. 318). As if following the design of Eulalia and the lawyer, Bon eventually journeys with Henry to meet Judith at Sutpen's Hundred. But while Henry was "still keeping distended and light and iridescent with steady breathing that fairy balloon-vacuum in which the three of them existed, lived, and moved . . . in attitudes without flesh—himself and the friend and the sister whom the friend had never seen" (p. 319), and at the same time that Judith might have seen the answer to her romantic "prayer," a "maiden meditative dream ridden up out of whatever fabulous land," "the silken and tragic Lancelot nearing thirty," Charles Bon comes "face to face" with "the man who might be his father" (p. 320), and Shreve's narration exchanges tropes of "design" for tropes of the "sign."

In the fable that Shreve makes up (in apparent complicity with Quentin), because Bon would give up everything for a "sign" from his father, the whole object of the narrative must change shape, from romantic comedy to tragic irony. Just as Eulalia and the lawyer could not foresee that the three Sutpen siblings would fall in love with each other, they apparently could not see (in Shreve's speculations) that Bon would give up love, fortune, and revenge for no more than a sign from Sutpen that they were father and son. Bon was to stay at Sutpen's Hundred for ten days that first visit, but "the day came to depart and no sign yet; he and Henry rode away and still no sign, no more sign at parting than when he had seen it [his paternity] first, in that face" (pp. 320–21). Shreve imagines that Bon would have accepted his father's "signal . . . in secret" (p. 321), but not even a secret sign is forthcoming. Instead, the signs that come to him are those promising Judith's love. Making Judith fall in love with him is as easy as getting a sign from his putative father is difficult. Judith's love is just one of those things—in Shreve's version of Rosa's words—"that just have to be whether they are or not." "He must have known," says Shreve, "it was going to happen" (p. 322). So, ironically, the sign Bon wants now more than anything does not come, and the sign he would rather not have comes regardless of his will: "Yes. Yes. I will renounce her; I will renounce love and all; that will be cheap, cheap, even though he say to me 'never look upon my face again; take my love and my acknowledgment in secret, and go' I will do that; I will not even demand to know of him what it was my mother did that justified his action toward her and me" (p. 327).

Shreve's sense of irony, finally, is responsible for the most damaging reversal affecting Sutpen's design. Sutpen had dreamed that his son would inherit the domain, but the "good" son turns out to be the murderer of the "bad" son (whose name—Bon—means "good") who would have married the daughter, committing both incest and miscegenation. Shreve is the narrator whose conjectures outline this story of the ironic dissolution of the Sutpen family. Though there are many indications that the tale has authorial validation, Shreve might well have made up the entire story (in complicity, again, with Quentin). Faulkner says of them, "It was Shreve speaking, though ... it might have been either of them and was in a sense both: both thinking as one, the voice which happened to be speaking the thought only the thinking become audible, vocal; the two of them creating between them, out of the rag-tag and bob-ends of old tales and talking, people who perhaps had never existed at all anywhere, who, shadows, were shadows not of flesh and blood which had lived and died but shadows in turn of what were (to one of them at least, to Shreve) shades too, quiet as the visible murmur of their vaporizing breath" (p. 303). It all grows in Shreve's imagination, apparently, because he wants to account for the wife who had been abandoned by Sutpen thirty years before.

Indeed, it is an ironic sense of accounting that marks Shreve's narrative extrapolations. He imagines Sutpen believing that he had paid off Eulalia and her father. Sutpen never had wondered, Shreve believes, what had happened after he had left, "had never once seemed to wonder what she might have been doing all that time, the thirty years since that day when he paid his bill with her and got it receipted, so he thought, and saw with his own eyes that it was (so he thought) destroyed, torn up and thrown to the wind" (p. 296). Similarly, he imagines Bon's recognition that Judith's love is "a fate, a doom on him, like what the old Aunt Rosa told you about some things that just have to be whether they are or not, just to balance the books, write *Paid* on the old sheet so that whoever keeps them can take it out of the ledger and burn it, get rid of it" (p. 325). Moreover, Shreve imagines that Bon believes he will have to pay for the sin of his father even if (at the particular moment) he does not yet know what that sin is: "Maybe he knew then that whatever the old man had done, . . . it wasn't going to be the old man who would have to pay the check; and now that the old man was bankrupt with the incompetence of age, who should do the paying if not his sons . . . ?" (p. 325). And even the vengeance that Eulalia seeks and for which she has turned her son into an instrument is reduced to an accounting. "Do you know that you are a very fortunate young man?" her lawyer says to Bon. "With most of us, even when we are lucky enough to get our revenge, we must pay for it, sometimes in actual dollars. While you are not only in a position to get your revenge, clear your mother's name, but the balm with which you will assuage her injury will have a collateral value which can be translated into the things which a young man needs, which are his due and which, whether we like it or not, may be had only in exchange for hard dollars" (pp. 337–38).

But Shreve's sense of irony is nothing if not touched with a fatal romance. And it is with the crassly mercantile comment of the lawyer that we begin to see the ironic denouements of the plot Shreve has imagined. The lawyer pushes too far with Bon and insults the honor of Judith Sutpen, whereupon Bon attacks him and challenges him to "either an apology or a bullet, as you prefer" (p. 338). In the telling, Shreve uses the vengeful lawyer now to polish off Eulalia, he imagining that "the lawyer had murdered her before he stole the money" and "departed for Texas or Mexico or somewhere" (p. 339). Then Shreve begins to imagine the bargaining that would have gone on between Henry and Bon during the war. To the end, Henry is concerned to stop the marriage of his brother to his sister, but Bon, for his part, is imagined never to want anything other than the sign from his father that he is recognized as a son. At first, Henry believes (according to Shreve's conjectures) that it is only incest he has to forestall: "Think how they must have talked, how Henry would say, 'But must you marry her? Do you have to do it?' and Bon would say, 'He should have told me. He should have told me, myself, himself. I was fair and honorable with him. I waited' " (p. 341). Henry (Shreve imagines) might even have begun to accept the incest (at least, Shreve thinks, he invokes historical precedent in Duke John of Lorraine to condone it). Therefore, to prevent Henry's wavering, Shreve imagines that Sutpen has to play his last trump card if he is to motivate Henry to block Charles's aim. Sutpen thus tells Henry (Shreve believes) of Bon's racial "flaw": "He must not marry her, Henry. His mother's father told me that her mother had been a Spanish woman. I believed him; it was not until after he was born that I found out that his mother was part negro" (pp. 354–55). But even after Henry has divulged this knowledge to Bon, the two refuse to go their separate ways in order to avoid the fatal confrontation that is inevitable otherwise. Even then Bon might have abandoned his plan and left Henry at the front. But "he never slipped away," Shreve said. "He could have, but he never even tried" (p. 358). And, tragically romantic to the end as Shreve imagines him, Bon dies at Henry's hand, his own hand clutching the talismanic locket with the telltale picture of his octoroon wife and child, a sign (Shreve conjectures) meant to say to Judith, "I was no good; do not grieve for me" (p. 359).

Metatropology and the Ironic Moment

[One's] ability [in a work] to fashion a tropological—that is, linguistically aware—picture of reality within the regulative discourse of [any *one* trope] demonstrates an awareness of the ability of *a moment within* the system to function as *the moment of* the system itself—as the Over-Trope.

—Hans Kellner, "A Bedrock of Order"

The one narrator's perspective not yet represented in this catalog of tropes and emplotments is Quentin Compson's. It is as necessary, I think, to separate Quentin from Shreve as it is to separate him from the other narrative perspectives that are not so symbiotically identified with him. In the reading of *Absalom, Absalom!* that tropology seems to entail, it becomes necessary to see each in relation to the others (distinguished metonymically, as it were), but it finally becomes necessary to determine whether each belongs as a part to some larger perspectival whole (synecdochically, let's say). Quentin's is that perspective of perspectives, and so will provide what Hans Kellner calls the "overtrope" and I would call the metatrope. Quentin, that is, synecdochically "contains" the enfigurations of Sutpen's history provided by Rosa, Mr. Compson, Grandfather Compson, and Shreve. Since Quentin's perspective therefore acts as a framing "moment" determining the overall shape of the novel, it stands in the relation to the "square" of tropes and emplotments (seen in figure 1 at the beginning of this chapter) as "signification" does in Greimas's quaternary structure:

$$
S = \frac{S_1 \quad | \quad S_2}{\text{not } S_2 \quad | \quad \text{not } S_1} \; :: \text{Quentin} =
\begin{array}{c|c}
\text{Rosa} & \text{Shreve} \\
\text{Romance} & \text{Irony-Satire} \\
\text{Metaphor} & \text{Irony as Trope} \\
\text{plus} & \text{minus} \\
\hline
\textit{not} \text{ minus} & \textit{not} \text{ plus} \\
\text{Synecdoche} & \text{Metonymy} \\
\text{Comedy} & \text{Tragedy} \\
\text{Grandfather} & \text{Mr. Compson}
\end{array}
$$

Figure 2

We can see that in *Absalom*, as in Greimas's structural casting of signification or understanding, meaning develops within a closed system of internal relations, embodying what Greimas calls "homologized contradictions" (*Game, Play, Literature*, p. 88). But we are left, because of the presence of that "S" outside the square, with serious questions: if he represents the "S" in the equation, then what is Quentin's tropic moment, and what is the mode of emplotment attendant upon that trope?

The way in which Quentin is employed in the novel as a locus for a consciousness with the power and motive to subsume all the other narrative perspectives is illustrated early in the first chapter. "Quentin had grown up with" tales of the Sutpen family and the South, Faulkner tells us. For him, "the mere names" of all those figures "were interchangeable and almost myriad. His childhood was full of them; his very body was an empty hall echoing with sonorous defeated names; he was not a being, an entity, he was a commonwealth. He was a barracks filled with stubborn back-looking ghosts" (p. 12). The interchangeability of the names, the virtual identity of the figures, suggests a metaphoric consciousness here, but metaphor gives way to synecdoche in the signification of Quentin as a "commonwealth," or "a barracks" filled with ghosts, a body containing the spirits of once living persons. Faulkner makes it clear, then, that Quentin both possesses and is possessed by these beings, names, ghosts, all of which seem to tell the tales of the Southern past to which they belong as parts, but in which unselfconsciously they play the active roles.

But while Quentin seems to locate the synecdochic force that holds these beings together, the motive power that drives him is his obsessive need to understand them. From the outset, my claim has been that *Absalom* is an expression of understanding working narratively through its tropologically entailed stages. Thus, though Quentin can be imagined to contain all those voices who speak to him of Thomas Sutpen, he cannot claim from the very start that he also understands their meanings. Quentin strives for understanding, but he never seems as certain of meanings as those—such as Rosa, Father, Grandfather, or even Shreve—who report their conclusive enfigurations to him. Their perspectives seem already bound by a single tropic determination, but Quentin seems to keep his options open—at least up to the text's end. Thus, his consciousness is essentially tropological in a broader sense, enough so to be regarded as metatropological. In one of the most important elucidations of White's tropology, Hans Kellner points out that any tropology *as such* is essentially ironic since tropologies study "the 'turns' by which linguistic structures create meaning."[18] Inasmuch as Quentin serves in this precise tropological role, the trope—the meta- or overtrope—that governs the entire novel as represented within the frame Quentin entails is not synecdoche, but irony. The ironic moment he represents is, finally, one that readers are left to ponder, one that has seemed to so many critics to be almost too bleak for words. "I just want to understand it," Shreve says of the South to Quentin. Quentin's reply captures the essence of irony: "You cant understand it. You would have to be born there" (p. 361).

The dominant narrative perspective in the first chapter of *Absalom* is Rosa's, but Quentin's nonetheless frames hers as it will frame the others in the novel. Thus, Rosa's metaphoric enfiguration of Sutpen in the plot mode of romance ("man-horse-demon," et cetera) becomes the first of the constitutive parts of Quentin's ironic vision. The relation of part to whole is at first suggested in the derivation of both from the tradition of stories within which each exists—within, that is, a synecdochic "voice." At first the voice is Rosa's, a "voice not ceasing but vanishing," to become for Quentin, metaphorically, "the voice which he haunted where a more fortunate one would have had a house" (p. 8). Then, synecdochically, Quentin absorbs both voices, as "hearing would reconcile and he would seem to listen to two separate Quentins now—the Quentin Compson . . . peopled with garrulous outraged baffled ghosts . . . ; and the Quentin Compson who was still too young to deserve yet to be a ghost, but nevertheless having to be one for all that, since he was born and bred in the deep South the same as she was." This sequence of enfigurations ends, finally, with the first of Quentin's schematic summaries of the tale told by Rosa, but once again, in order to suggest the incorporation of part into larger whole, the synopsis occurs—synecdochically or ironically?—in what Faulkner calls "the two separate Quentins now talking to one another in the long silence of notpeople, in notlanguage" (p. 9). Clearly, it helps to have been there.

But Sutpen's story can only be told in actual language, and Rosa has summoned Quentin to aid her because she imagines that he will become a man of letters.[19] She expects him never really to return to the South of his birth once he goes to Harvard, for "there is little left in the South for a young man," she tells him. "So maybe you will enter the literary profession as so many Southern gentlemen and gentlewomen too are doing now and maybe some day you will remember this and write about it" (pp. 9–10). She had, Quentin knows, "established herself as the town's and the county's poetess laureate," but since she must realize her own death is near, she knows another's literary voice will be necessary to carry on her mission—to explain "at last why God let us lose the War" (p. 11). Once again the passage leads to a brief summary of Sutpen's history, again with the suggestion that its metaphoric and romantic aspect forms a part of Quentin's physical being.

> It was a part of his twenty years' heritage of breathing the same air and hearing his father talk about the man Sutpen; a part of the town's—Jefferson's—eighty years' heritage of the same air which the man himself had breathed between this September afternoon in 1909 and that Sunday morning in 1833 when he first rode into town out of no discernible past and acquired his land no one knew how and built his house, his mansion, apparently out of nothing and married Ellen Coldfield and begot his two children—the son who widowed the daughter who had not yet been a bride—and so accomplished his allotted course to its violent (Miss Coldfield at least would have said, just) end. (P. 11)

But as Quentin's question of his father—"But why tell me about it?" (p. 12)—suggests, he does not yet know the meaning, the significance of the metaphoric "facts" he has absorbed—and been absorbed by—during his twenty years. All of it—the content of the stories, the telling of the stories—has the quality of a dream for Quentin, "the logic- and reason-flouting quality of a dream which the sleeper knows must have occurred, stillborn and complete, in a second, yet the very quality upon which it must depend to move the dreamer (verisimilitude) to credulity—horror or pleasure or amazement—depends as completely upon a formal recognition of and acceptance of elapsed and yet-elapsing time as music or a printed page" (p. 22). And readers of *Absalom*—in "horror or pleasure or amazement"—are no less captured by the "dream" than Quentin himself.

The first several versions of the "facts" of Sutpen's life are given in rather skeletal form, but each moves closer to the full-blown metaphoric enfiguration in a romantic archetypal emplotment. Rosa's relatively uninterrupted narration begins at the bottom of p. 14 and ends, with the chapter, at p. 30. Quentin's last effort to provide an account before Rosa takes over entirely comes just ahead of hers. By this stage in the emergence of Quentin's tropological consciousness, he himself has become aware of the way in which those figures who had been merely "figures," tropes, metaphors are now taking on embodiment—especially *that* figure, Thomas Sutpen. First, Quentin muses, "as though in inverse ratio to the vanishing voice, the invoked ghost of the man whom she could neither forgive nor revenge herself upon began to assume a quality almost of solidity, permanence." This figure, trope, enfiguration then takes over Quentin's function of thought, and takes Quentin reflexively back into itself. "Itself circumambient and enclosed by its effluvium of hell, its aura of unregeneration, it mused . . . with that quality peaceful and now harmless and not even very attentive." And then—once more in the originary mode of romance, gothic romance—this enfigured ghost, tropically, even hypertrophically, creates the rest of the cast of major characters in the tale Rosa will tell. That "ogre-shape," formed by Rosa Coldfield's voice, "resolved out of itself before Quentin's eyes the two half-ogre children, the three of them forming a shadowy background for [Ellen,] the fourth one" (p. 13). In this way, in the manner of a cinematic dissolve, Quentin's perspective is totally replaced by that engendered in Rosa's voice, her speaking presence.

Rosa Coldfield's metaphoric enfigurations and romantic emplotment provide Quentin his entrée to the narrativized world of Thomas Sutpen. For readers, as for Quentin, the first chapter serves as a compression chamber, as it were, that begins to move one by stages into the higher compressions of the various accounts—Mr. Compson's, Grandfather's, and Shreve's—that boil out of Rosa's as represented through Quentin as their medium, if not origin. The egress from the high compressions of the cumulative narratives is provided Quentin by Shreve. While it is not accurate to say that Shreve gives the entire novel its valence, it is accurate to say that his account radically determines the ironic tone, if not the events, of the last chapter, which, finally, belongs to Quentin (or, we might say, to Faulkner himself). Quentin has absorbed the accounts of Father, Grandfather, and "Aunt," but his body, it appears, has difficulty accepting the transplanted perspective Shreve gives him. The violent, uncontrollable jerking that overcomes Quentin, recounted at the beginning of the final chapter, may well be a sign of the resistance Quentin feels toward the puzzled irony Shreve injects. "Wait. Listen," Shreve says to Quentin: "I'm not trying to be funny, smart. I just want to understand it if I can and I don't know how to say it better. Because it's something my people haven't got. Or if we have got it, it all happened long ago across the water and so now there aint anything to look at every day to remind us of it. We dont live among defeated grandfathers and freed slaves (or have I got it backward and was it your folks that are free and the niggers that lost?) and bullets in the dining room table and such, to be always reminding us to never forget" (p. 361). And even Shreve picks up the synecdochic imagery of air, breathing, entailment, and genesis upon which Quentin had dwelt in the first chapter: "What is it? something you live and breathe in like air? a kind of vacuum filled with wraithlike and indomitable anger and pride and glory at and in happenings that occurred and ceased fifty years ago? a kind of entailed birthright father and son and father and son of never forgiving General Sherman, so that forevermore as long as your childrens' children produce children you wont be anything but a descendant of a long line of colonels killed in Pickett's charge at Manassas?" Quentin's reply is the laconic correction, "Gettysburg"—not Manassas, but Gettysburg—and the weary assent, "You cant understand it. You would have to be born there" (p. 361).

As Shreve picks up the imagery from chapter 1, moreover, the last chapter also projects what Quentin recognizes had been merely figures of speech into actual physical beings. Shreve tells Quentin that "the old dame, the Aunt Rosa," "refused at the last to be a ghost" (p. 362), only to go with Quentin out to the ruined shell of Sutpen's Hundred to discover a ghost in the form of Henry Sutpen, come at last to claim his birthright, where he hopes to die in peace. In the final chapter's account, for which Quentin serves as a focalizer, the emplotment of the journey with Rosa takes the form of the gothic quest, and all the tropic figures of speech from the first chapter take on flesh here. True, Quentin's hyperactive imagination conjures up the figure of Thomas Sutpen galloping across his domain atop his black stallion, imagined by Quentin through the eyes of Milly Jones as God himself (p. 363). That imagination, moreover, also pulls the figures of Henry and Bon from the past, evoked by the associations linked to the "two huge rotting gate posts in the starlight, between which no gates swung now," Quentin "wondering from what direction Bon and Henry had ridden up that day, wondering what had cast the shadow which Bon was not to pass alive." But there are "ghosts"—or ghostly people—who remain as defenders of the house, "the rotting shell," and who must be circumvented if Quentin and Rosa are to gain access to the last ghost of the Sutpens (p. 364).

One of these defenders is Clytie, whom Rosa "just knows," feels, is watching them as they make their parlous journey through the darkness to the ruined mansion, which "loomed, bulked, square and enormous, with jagged half-toppled chimneys" (p. 366) before them. They encounter Clytie only after they have broken into the house, where in the darkness a sound made by Clytie's striking a match hits Quentin "like an explosion, a pistol." But as a defender, Clytie is no more now than a "tiny gnomelike creature in headrag and voluminous skirts" (p. 368). In her manic quest for the final Sutpen ghost, Rosa thrusts her way past the frail spirit guarding the stairs, Rosa's "full-armed blow" leaving Clytie "a small, shapeless bundle of quiet clean rags" (p. 369). The second figure who guards the ruined mansion is one whom Quentin calls, ironically, "the scion, the heir, the apparent (though not obvious)" legatee of Thomas Sutpen. This heir "apparent" is not Henry Sutpen, but Jim Bond, grandson of Charles Bon and the octoroon mistress, this "scion" "a hulking young light-colored negro" with the "slack-mouthed" face of an idiot (p. 370). The object of their quest, Henry Sutpen, is the third and final ghost from the past. When Quentin, after Rosa had entered the room and gone, finally sees Henry, indeed, the old man lies on his sickbed, his "wasted hands crossed on the breast as if he were already a corpse" (p. 373).

Quentin's perspective upon the events recounted in the last chapter of *Absalom* operates within the trope of irony and the emplotment of satire because of the detached awareness Quentin has upon the entire set of enfigurations undertaken in the whole narration. If irony is marked by nothing else it is marked by a consciousness of the disparity between appearance and reality, between the illusion created by one's words and

the truth behind them. Quentin is shown to be well aware of the disparity
between the gothic machinery of his and Rosa's trip out to Sutpen's
Hundred and the mundane, not to say absurd, facts. The two form a truly
odd couple of ghost busters, he a nervous, self-conscious college boy, she
an aged, wizened, nearly demented spinster, the perhaps "helpless agent
of someone or something else who must know" what is going on at the
Domain. Rosa imagines that they will need weapons, but in the absence
of a pistol, an ancient hatchet "with a heavy worn handle and a heavy
gapped rust-dulled blade" she has stashed in her umbrella will have to
suffice (p. 365). When the hatchet is deployed against the shutters pro-
tecting the house, "they gave almost at once," "flimsy and sloven barri-
cading done either by an old feeble person—woman—or by a shiftless
man" (p. 367), and the window itself is a vacant frame they can simply
step through. When they are forced to do battle with the house's defenders—Clytie and "the hulking slack-faced negro" (p. 371), Jim Bond,
the one turns out to be "like picking up a handful of sticks concealed in
a rag bundle, so light she was" (p. 370), and the other simply too lacking
in "interest or curiosity" (p. 371) to care that the Domain is being invaded.

Above all disparities, however, is that between the expected reaction
Quentin should feel upon completion of the not so parlous journey and
the reaction he actually suffers. Quentin has begun to feel that the whole
experience has had the "logic- and reason-flouting quality of a dream" (p.
22) he had enfigured in the opening chapter. But what is worse, he has
himself moved into the dream, just as the ghosts of the first chapter have
taken on flesh and bones in the final one. In effect, he has lost his sense
of time and place as a result of the climactic event out at the Hundred,
his face-to-face confrontation with his alter ego, Henry Sutpen. Quentin
realizes, "He [Quentin] was twenty years old; he was not afraid, because
what he had seen out there could not harm him, yet he ran; even inside
the dark familiar house, his shoes in his hand, he still ran, up the stairs
into his room and began to undress, fast, sweating, breathing fast" (p.
372). Nonetheless, in thinking back over the experience, he can only say
to himself,

> 'I have been asleep' it was all the same, there was no difference: waking or
> sleeping he walked down that upper hall between the scaling walls and
> beneath the cracked ceiling, toward the faint light which fell outward from
> the last door and paused there, saying 'No. No.' and then 'Only I must. I
> have to' and went in, entered the bare, stale room whose shutters were

closed too, where a second lamp burned dimly on a crude table; waking or sleeping it was the same: the bed, the yellow sheets and pillow, the wasted yellow face with closed, almost transparent eyelids on the pillow, the wasted hands crossed on the breast as if he were already a corpse; waking or sleeping it was the same and would be the same forever as long as he lived. (Pp. 372–73)

The most evident way in which the emplotment of Quentin's perspective falls into an ironic mode is through its theme. Northrop Frye, in *Anatomy of Criticism*, points out that irony, the "mythos of winter," "attempts to give form to the shifting ambiguities and complexities of unidealized existence," often doing so, as we have seen both in Shreve's and, here, in Quentin's accounts, "as a parody of romance."[20] Quentin's perspective, especially in contrast to Shreve's, represents an "irony with little satire," "the non-heroic residue of tragedy, centering on a theme of puzzled defeat" (AC, p. 224), and illustrated in what Frye calls the sixth (and final) phase of the mythos of irony-satire, presenting "human life in terms of largely unrelieved bondage," in settings that "feature prisons, madhouses, lynching mobs, and places of execution," and differing from "a pure inferno mainly in the fact that in human experience suffering has an end in death" (AC, p. 238). Much of Frye's detail here seems almost a literal description of *Absalom, Absalom!*

Frye's enumeration of the characters of the most ironic phase of the mythos, moreover, fits the details of Faulkner's novel only too well. "The human figures of this phase," Frye says, are often "figures of misery or madness," female figures in the guise of witches, and frequently there appears a parody of the "helpful servant giant" of romance, as well as sinister figures representing the parents. Rosa, Clytie, and Henry all seem nothing if not figures of madness or obsession; at the same time, Rosa plays the role of the witch when it is not performed by Clytie, her surrogate, and Henry well represents for Quentin the sinister parent. The role of the helpful servant giant—parodied in *The Sound and the Fury* by the idiot Benjy, claims Frye—in *Absalom* is taken by the idiot Jim Bond, who assists Clytie in creating the roaring inferno that consumes Sutpen's mansion, which serves as the image of the prison, madhouse, and place of execution for Clytie and Henry, if not also for Rosa herself.

The end provided for the last remaining members of the Sutpen saga provides, therefore, the dual, contrapuntal images associated with what Frye defines as the bitterest of ironic emplotments and themes: death by

137

fire and burial in the iron cold of winter. Neither Henry's death nor the deaths of the others occur until some three months after the journey Rosa and Quentin make to the doomed estate. Having postponed, for whatever reasons, her efforts to deliver Henry from Clytie and into a hospital, Rosa makes a final trip out to the mansion, this time in an ambulance wagon and with two male attendants. But Clytie, seeing the black wagon careering up the frozen-rutted drive toward the house, sets fire to "the monstrous tinder-dry rotten shell" (p. 375), and perishes there with her half brother. She is last seen in an upper window of the burning mansion, her "tragic gnome's face beneath the clean headrag, against a red background of fire, seen for a moment between two swirls of smoke." And Rosa, with her mission finished and nothing to keep her alive, takes to her own bed, dying in the winter, when there was "nothing out there . . . but that idiot boy to lurk around those ashes and those four gutted chimneys and howl until someone came and drove him away" (p. 376). Rosa is buried soon after the destruction of the House of Sutpen: "The weather was beautiful," Quentin's father writes, "though cold and they had to use picks to break the earth for the grave yet in one of the deeper clods I saw a redworm doubtless alive when the clod was thrown up though by afternoon it was frozen again" (p. 377).

The "doomed house" (p. 375) of Sutpen *might* have brought Quentin and Shreve (to say nothing of readers) around to what Frye calls "the point of demonic epiphany," which he associates with images of "the dark tower and prison of endless pain, the city of dreadful night in the desert, or, with a more erudite irony, the *tour aboli*, the goal of the quest that isn't there" (AC, pp. 238–39). But neither of the two young men—or, certainly, not Quentin—suffers an epiphany of redemption (any more than that to-be-frozen redworm would represent a promise of renewal). Frye says that "on the other side of this blasted world of repulsiveness and idiocy, a world without pity and hope" (AC, p. 239), another world marked by positive human elements begins. There is no such world, however, opening up on the other side of Quentin's experience. As we know not from *Absalom*, but from *The Sound and the Fury*, what Quentin faces is whatever surcease there is in the grave. His epitaph (admittedly a long one) might well have been the words Father wrote him about Rosa: "Surely it can harm no one to believe that perhaps she has escaped not at all the privilege of being outraged and amazed and of not forgiving but on the contrary has herself gained that place or bourne where the objects of the outrage and of the commiseration also are no longer ghosts but are actual people to be actual recipients of the hatred and the pity" (p. 377).

Though I have not dwelt upon the ideological element in one's selection of tropes, it is plain that Faulkner's enfiguration *through* Quentin's irony participates in the irony characterizing the modern/postmodernist epoch. *Absalom* does not escape its "history," shall we say. True to personal form, Quentin himself, in his protestations to Shreve that he does not hate the South, desires the equipoise, the harmony, wholeness and integration represented in the synecdoche. But, also true to epochal, ideological form, he concludes by appearing to acquiesce to the force of Shreve's enfigurations of the denouement of the history of the Sutpens. That figure is shaped as an integrative metaphor—whose meaning is indeed "integration"—underlying a synecdoche: the whiteness valorized by the races in the South becomes intertwined with the Sutpen family, the family with the South, and both with the entire western hemisphere. "I think that in time the Jim Bonds are going to conquer the western hemisphere. . . . As they spread toward the poles they will bleach out again like the rabbits and the birds do, so they won't show up so sharp against the snow. But it will still be Jim Bond; and so in a few thousand years, I who regard you will also have sprung from the loins of African kings" (p. 378).

But the signification of the figure—whether metaphor or synecdoche—is bleakly ironic, in keeping with the social ideology of Faulkner's generation. The potentiality for a comedic ending exists in the words of Shreve's enfiguration, but the contexture provided here—and throughout the novel—makes it plain that the envisioned goal of the "integration" is not one Quentin or Shreve or the hemisphere would easily tolerate. It is with a double irony, then—intratextual, but also historical or epochal—that the message of love potentially present in the tale of Henry, Judith, and Charles concludes at best with an insistence not on integration, but disintegration, not on love, but on love's negation. The redworm thrown up in digging Rosa's grave might after all be just the right figure for the way in which *Absalom, Absalom!* ends. All those tales told might have, somehow, symbolized new life and hope, but they too end up frozen, shall we say, with Shreve and Quentin "in the iron New England dark" (p. 373).[21]

NOTES

1. David Levin, *In Defense of Historical Literature* (New York: Hill and Wang, 1967), p. 118.

2. Evan Watkins, *The Critical Act: Criticism and Community* (New Haven: Yale University Press, 1978), p. 188.

3. See Northrop Frye, *Anatomy of Criticism: Four Essays* (Princeton: Princeton University Press, 1957), pp. 158–239, where Frye discusses his theory of myths in relation to archetypal criticism.

4. See, for example, A.-J. Greimas and F. Rastier, "The Interaction of Semiotic Constraints," in *Game, Play, Literature*, ed. Jacques Ehrmann (Boston: Beacon Press, 1971), pp. 86–105; A.-J. Greimas, *Semiotics and Language: An Analytical Dictionary*, trans. Larry Crist et al. (Bloomington: Indiana University Press, 1982), and A.-J. Greimas, *Structural Semantics: An Attempt at a Method*, trans. Daniele McDowell, Ronald Schleifer, and Alan Velie (Lincoln: University of Nebraska Press, 1983). In these two books, Greimas reveals the insistent relation between the structure of the semiotic square and the tropic movement of thought toward semantics; moreover, his discussion of the microuniverse of Georges Bernanos in *Structural Semantics* (pp. 257–95) is highly tropological, without displaying a theory of tropology beyond a dyadic "figurativization" seen in metaphor and metonymy.

5. See, for example, the interpretation by Lynn Gartrell Levins, *Faulkner's Heroic Design: The Yoknapatawpha Novels* (Athens: University of Georgia Press, 1976), pp. 7–54.

6. Andrew Ezergailis, Review of *Metahistory: The Historical Imagination in Nineteenth-Century Europe* by Hayden V. White, *Clio* 5.2 (Winter 1976):238.

7. William Faulkner, *Absalom, Absalom!* (New York: Modern Library, 1951), pp. 7–8. Quotations from this novel will be identified by page numbers within parentheses in my text hereafter, and Faulkner's italics will be eliminated whenever practicable.

8. Hans Kellner, "The Inflatable Trope as Narrative Theory: Structure or Allegory?" *Diacritics* 11 (Mar. 1981):20–21.

9. Ibid., 24.

10. Ibid., 16–17.

11. Kenneth Burke, "Appendix D: Four Master Tropes," in his *A Grammar of Motives* (Berkeley: University of California Press, 1969), p. 508.

12. Ibid., p. 508.

13. Paul de Man, "The Rhetoric of Temporality," in *Interpretation: Theory and Practice*, ed. Charles Singleton (Baltimore: Johns Hopkins University Press, 1969), p. 176, quoted from Kellner, "The Inflatable Trope," 23.

14. David Minter, in *William Faulkner: His Life and Work* (Baltimore: Johns Hopkins University Press, 1980), says that in one sense Sutpen "creates the action of the novel; it takes him, as one of the narrators puts it, 'to make' all the rest" (p. 154).

15. Frye, *Anatomy of Criticism*, p. 223.

16. Levins, *Faulkner's Heroic Design*, p. 30.

17. See the notes section in Cleanth Brooks, *William Faulkner: The Yoknapatawpha Country* (New Haven: Yale University Press, 1963), pp. 429–36, for a clear delineation of the voices as they appear in the course of the novel, as well as determinations of "facts" as opposed to "conjectures" regarding Sutpen and his family.

18. Hans Kellner, "A Bedrock of Order: Hayden White's Linguistic Humanism," *History and Theory* 19: *Beiheft* 19 (1980):25 (the entire *Beiheft*, it is worth noting again, is devoted to White's *Metahistory*).

19. The irony residing in Quentin's becoming a "man of letters" will be appreciated by those familiar with the psychoanalytic theories of Jacques Lacan: see, for example, Lacan's "The Agency of the Letter in the Unconscious or Reason Since Freud," in his *Écrits: A Selection*, trans. Alan Sheridan (New York: Norton, 1977), pp. 146–78.

20. Frye, *Anatomy of Criticism*, p. 223; in order to avoid confusion with quotations from *Absalom*, subsequent quotations from this text will include the abbreviation AC along with page numbers.

21. Since it is my view that *Absalom, Absalom!* has elicited some of the best criticism ever written on Faulkner, I ought to mention at least some of the essays besides ones already mentioned that I have found significant for my thinking on the novel: Melvin Backman, "Sutpen and the South: A Study of *Absalom, Absalom!*," *PMLA* 80.5 (Dec. 1965):596–604; Cleanth Brooks, "History, Tragedy, and the Imagination in *Absalom, Absalom!*," *Yale Review* 52 (Mar. 1963):340–51; James H. Justus, "The Epic Design of *Absalom, Absalom!*," *Texas Studies in Literature and Language* 4.2 (Summer 1962):157–76; Ilse Dusoir Lind, "The Design and Meaning of *Absalom, Absalom!*," *PMLA* 70 (Dec. 1955):278–304; John T. Matthews, *The Play of Faulkner's Language* (Ithaca, N.Y.: Cornell University Press, 1982), pp. 115–61; David L. Minter, *The Interpreted Design as Structural Principle* (New Haven: Yale University Press, 1969), pp. 191–219; Noel Polk, "The Manuscript of *Absalom, Absalom!*," *Mississippi Quarterly* 25.3 (Summer 1972):359–67; Walter Sullivan, "The Tragic Design of *Absalom, Absalom!*," *South Atlantic Quarterly* 50 (Oct. 1950):552–66; Patricia Tobin, "The Time of Myth and History in *Absalom, Absalom!*," *American Literature* 45.2 (May 1973):252–70; Edgar Whan, "*Absalom, Absalom!* as Gothic Myth," *Perspective* 3 (Autumn 1950):192–201; and Robert H. Zoellner, "Faulkner's Prose Style in *Absalom, Absalom!*," *American Literature* 30 (January 1959):488–502. A more complete, unannotated bibliography on the novel may be found in Beatrice Ricks, *William Faulkner: A Bibliography of Secondary Works* (Metuchen, N.J.: Scarecrow Press, 1981), pp. 17–44, listing just over 400 items.

Conclusion

Return to Metaphor:
The Phenomenology of Language
in *The Centaur*

Language, Myth, and Metaphor

> In the light of this basic principle of mythic metaphor we can grasp and
> understand, somewhat more clearly, what is commonly called the meta-
> phorical function of language.
>
> —Ernst Cassirer, *Language and Myth*

> We shall see that metaphors are the things that reanimate this original
> power of words. They are the veritable Fountain of Youth from which
> language derives a new vigor.
>
> —Mikel Dufrenne, *Language and Philosophy*

In my introduction, as well as in chapter 1 (on White's tropics), I suggested
that if one were to explain tropology in terms other than its own, it would
be necessary to place tropology within a larger philosophical framework.
I there suggested that the most appropriate framework is phenomenology,
particularly the attitude toward language formulated by phenomenologists
beginning with Husserl, Merleau-Ponty, Ricoeur, Gusdorf, Dufrenne, and
others. For the post-Saussurean linguist, language may be regarded in its
aspects of both *la langue* and *la parole*, but the phenomenologist mainly
regards it in its function as *la parole*—speech or speech acts or language
as an event in time, rather than as language in the abstract. Georges Gusdorf, for example, says that "man is the speaking animal," that "this
definition, after so many others, is perhaps the most decisive one. It over-
laps and absorbs such traditional definitions of man as the animal who
laughs, or the social animal."[1] The use of language that speaking entails
is crucial in a phenomenological definition because, Gusdorf says, "speech
isn't involved simply to facilitate these [political or social] relations; it

142

constitutes them. The universe of discourse has covered over and transfigured the material environment" (p. 4). This is not to claim, of course, that language creates the world—only that "the power of language" constitutes "a universe to the measure of man" at or beyond the point where "incoherent sensations leave off" (p. 9). Thus, for Gusdorf, language and the world become intertwined, the value of the one not to be distinguished, "when all is said and done," from the value of the other (p. 10).

Versions of tropology, whether of Vico or Burke or Hayden White, have depended on the idea of a return. Tropologists have had the notion that as consciousness moves through the tropic moments it becomes exhausted, but there exists the potential for reinvigoration in the *ricorso*, the cyclic return to the source of energy provided by metaphor. Tropologies link themselves in this way to aesthetic theories that involve concepts entailing formal progression and cyclic return. Roman Jakobson suggests that the two broadly defined types of discourse are keyed to particular tropes; while prose is metonymic, according to Jakobson, poetry is metaphorical (though neither discourse will include only one trope or the other). Hayden White suggests that specific tropological strategies are linked to specific types of plot. And Northrop Frye, whose theories are recruited by White to his network of tropological modalities, propounds an aesthetic theory that implies a progressive movement among the literary modes.[2] All of these, to some degree, are inclined to suggest that lyrical or expressive forms of art reveal the origins of the creative act. And that act, when it is bound up in language, seems always to be identified primarily with metaphor. As a consequence, the return to metaphor and metaphorical thinking is almost universally regarded as the most effective means of renewing creativity, language, and consciousness. In a work of fiction that is essentially lyrical (as opposed to mimetic), therefore, the valorized tropological moment is most likely to be the metaphorical. In the lyric expressiveness of *The Centaur* one can see John Updike's effort somehow to transcend a postmodern world of exhausted possibilities through the return to a world "resonant with metaphor."[3]

Where Updike's *The Centaur* is concerned, the symbolic philosophy of Ernst Cassirer—though he is not primarily regarded as a phenomenologist—is a good place to start in order to assess the relationships among language, the world, and Updike's characters. Because of the scope and quality of his *The Philosophy of Symbolic Forms*, Cassirer is often recruited for use by the phenomenologists. Implicit in Cassirer's philosophy of language, moreover, is the same cyclical pattern of tropic development one finds in the great tetradic tropologies of Vico, Burke, and White. Cassirer's "story" of language, most succinctly argued in *Language and Myth*, like White's cyclic "story" of tropic consciousness, involves an organic cycle of birth, growth, death, and renewal. The language cycle begins in metaphor, Cassirer argues, where myth also resides in the "primitive" mind. Like the phenomenologists, Cassirer says that language is also rooted in the experiential world from which myth arises. The two, language and myth, are "diverse shoots from the same parent stem, the same impulse of symbolic formulation, springing from the same basic mental activity, a concentration and heightening of simple sensory experience" (p. 88). The "stem" for both these symbolic forms—language and myth— is *"metaphorical thinking,"* says Cassirer; "the nature and meaning of metaphor is what we must start with if we want to find, on the one hand, the unity of the verbal and the mythical worlds and, on the other, their difference" (p. 84).

But for Cassirer, metaphorical thinking of the sort exemplified in originary language and in myth gives way to the sort of thinking associated with logical, or discursive, or theoretical and abstract functions of language—those functions tropologists (such as White) identify with metonymy, part-part relations, cause-and-effect entailments, and the like. Such a shift, for Cassirer, is clearly a fall from grace. He represents the turn here as a disintegration, a dissolution, a reduction of words "to the status of mere conceptual signs" (p. 97). Cassirer's cyclical pattern, however, permits a return, in other forms, of the qualities associated with metaphorical thinking. These new integrative forms (which White would label synecdochic) are the symbolic expressions seen in art. Art reasserts, "upon a higher level," "the spiritual unity" of language and myth. Artistic expression, for Cassirer, rejoins human thinking to its existential roots in sensory experience, such expression undergoing "a sort of constant palingenesis, at once a sensuous and a spiritual reincarnation. This regeneration is achieved as language becomes an avenue of artistic expression. Here it recovers the fullness of life; but it is no longer a life mythically bound and fettered, but an aesthetically liberated life" (p. 98). Finally, for Cassirer, the lyrical form of verbal art is the one that most fully conjoins language, myth, and phenomenological life. In the lyric expressiveness of *The Centaur*, therefore, one may see the ways in which questions of speaking, styles of enfiguration, the generation and regeneration of myths, and the

144

eschatological (perhaps transcendent) quality of art might be answered in one highly experimental novel.

The Tropological Perspective

> The advent of the word manifests the sovereignty of man. Man inter-
> poses a network of words between the world and himself and thereby
> becomes the master of the world.
>
> —Georges Gusdorf, *Speaking*

Several critics have alluded to what is a most crucial matter in resolving issues of theme and form in *The Centaur*.[4] That matter is an answer, phenomenological in nature, to the question, Who is speaking? But it remained for Edward P. Vargo, a decade after *The Centaur*'s publication, to answer the question bluntly: "The entire novel is presented to us as the experience of Peter, reliving three days in his life with his father, while he lies beside his black mistress in varying states of wakefulness or sleep." Thus, Vargo concludes, "the entire novel is a fusion of the dreams and reveries and actual narration of Peter."[5] While I agree with the contention that Peter Caldwell establishes the location of the narration, I must dis-agree with Vargo's further argument that "the experience takes on the character of a rite for Peter" (p. 453). For Vargo to call the novel a rite or ritual not only is to contradict his claim regarding "dreams and reveries," it also is to suggest that Peter plays a more public and ceremonial, even priestly, role than in fact he does. The central issue may be nothing but a problem of definition. One suspects it is much more, however, for it seems instead one of generic or modal perception. In literary analysis, rite or ritual is more properly associated with the genre of drama or the dramatic mode in fiction, but *The Centaur* is neither. Rather, its art is essentially lyrical, the phenomenological representation and the expressive symbol of Peter's elegiac feelings for his father. Peter's relation to the novel, therefore, is primarily that of the lyric poet to the poem in which every detail ultimately comes out of the creative center of the poet's sensory and emotional experience. For that reason, *The Centaur* is a very effective illustration of the process by which consciousness and language join together to create an expressive artifact close to the mythic and metaphoric sources of human understanding.

The phenomenological consciousness Updike represents in Peter Caldwell gives the novel its lyrical, elegiac shape. Such a consciousness

145

accounts for the novel's constant intertwining of thought, speech, and concrete experiences. Typically, Updike's emphasis is placed on the speaking presence of his people, and his handling of points of view seems closer to forms of poetry than of fiction. The role Peter plays as narrator, for example, is much like that of Hart Crane's poetic persona in *The Bridge*, the one embedded in "The Harbor Dawn," located in "Powhatan's Daughter," the second section of the poem. As in Crane's long poem, Updike's narrator does not appear as a narrative persona until a portion of the story has been presented. In *The Bridge* one first sees both the "Proem" and "Ave Maria"; in *The Centaur* one sees the long chapter devoted to George Caldwell's receiving his arrow wound, visiting the blacksmith Hummel to have it removed, and later resuming his classroom teaching duties. When Peter does appear in his role as narrator it is precisely in the situation of Crane's persona, who is lying abed with his lover-mistress:

> And you beside me, blessèd now while sirens
> Sing to us, stealthily weave us into day—
> Serenely now, before day claims our eyes
> Your cool arms murmurously about me lay.[6]

Peter overtly appears in *The Centaur* having just "dreamed," as he sleeps beside his lover, the account of the day in the life of his father given in chapter 1. That day from Peter's adolescence is long in the past, but it lives in memory because of the vitality of speech. "I wake now," he says, "often to silence, beside you, with a pang of fear. ... But in those days I always awoke to the sound of my parents talking, voices which even in agreement were contentious and full of life" (pp. 46–47).

Another means by which Updike valorizes speech and foregrounds the speaking consciousness is recurrently to show Peter and his lover in the relationship of storyteller to listening audience. In chapter 4 Peter asks, "Why is it, love, that faces we love look upon each remeeting so fresh, as if our hearts have in this instant again minted them?" (p. 117). In chapter 8, which is especially rhapsodic in celebration of the lover, he says, "My love, listen. Or are you asleep? It doesn't matter" (p. 265). Shortly after this, he says, "My story is coming to its close" (p. 268), and just a bit later he says, "The weariness I felt [after spending the night at the home of the Hummels] overtakes me in the telling" (p. 282). But these brief notations serve best not so much to identify Peter in the role of a storyteller as to highlight his role as the lyric persona from whose experiences and emotions the novel grows. His role as mythic "poet," analogous, perhaps, to his vocation as an abstract expressionist painter, may give Peter an audience, but it is not an audience for which a rite could be performed such as Vargo proposes. As Peter realizes, an external audience "doesn't matter," since the lyrical expression, whatever form it takes, is mainly personal and private. The poet is his own best audience.

The lyrical persona in fiction and poetry, because of the highly charged phenomenological consciousness, will often play a tropic or metamorphic role. The very being of the lyrical persona, expressing itself through varied performances of speech, becomes a trope as it assumes different voices. In his role as a lyrical persona, Peter thus accounts for what one critic calls the "mixture of genres," the different "modes of narration" in *The Centaur*.[7] But rather than "nominal and ineffective," as he claims, Peter's performance really exists phenomenologically in the various modes and voices and is effective at many points in the narrative in direct proportion to the extent to which Peter's own personal voice is changed. The lyric poet's effectiveness comes in the achieved tropic and metamorphic virtuosity of the poem. If Crane can "speak" through dream, meditation, and ecstasis in *The Bridge*, or William Carlos Williams can "speak" through meditation, narrative, newspaper extracts, geological tables, and virtually every other form of human expression in *Paterson*, surely Updike's Peter Caldwell can speak through the objective omniscience of chapter 1, the first-person subjectivity of chapters 2, 4, and 8, the formally decorous pastoral myth of chapters 3 and 9, the newspaper obituary of chapter 5, the first-person stream of consciousness of chapter 6, and the third-person objectivity of chapter 7. In *The Centaur*, as in the long yet essentially lyric poem (such as *The Waste Land*, *The Bridge*, and *Paterson*), the main principle of narrative is tropic, emphasizing change, variation, discontinuity. But as there is always at the center of such poems a single figure (Eliot's Tiresias, Crane's "Hart Crane," Williams's Noah F. Paterson) through whom the poet projects his voices, so at the center of *The Centaur* is the tropic figure of Peter Caldwell.[8]

The tropic role of the persona in lyrical art also has considerable importance in other ways. Of primary significance in *The Centaur* is the way in which the phenomenological consciousness Updike creates determines the shape-shifting, tropological style. Essentially, what Updike has done is put one in touch with the origins of language in metaphor and metaphorical thinking. The technique of metaphor is to say that this *is* that, that A *is* B. In *The Centaur*, the world of metaphor takes over entirely in those chapters, such as 1, 3, 6, and 9, in which Caldwell *is* Chiron and, as in 6, where Peter *is* Prometheus. In these chapters there is no projected distance between the realistic characters in the narrative and the metaphorical beings of myth. Speaking to his love about his life with his family, Peter says in one place, "We moved, somehow, on a firm stage, resonant with metaphor" (p. 70). Peter's expressive, dreamlike, imaginative recreation of that world is itself "resonant with metaphor," and much of the texture of narrative comes from the metaphorical habit of language Updike gives Peter's narrative voices.

But not even in chapters 1, 3, 6, and 9 is there any simple relation between the two tropic realms, the "real" and the "mythic." The multiple tropic perspectives of the novel's style, for example, permit an irony of sorts to emerge, and it emerges, of all places, from the lowly pun. Puns arise when a word in one context suddenly turns toward another meaning when its place within another context is recognized. Updike's puns occur as a result of his characters' human roles being subjected to metonymical associations evoked by the novel's mythic contexts. Possessed of no self-consciousness, Updike's creatures do not know that they are not simply "people," but are "centaurs" and "gods" and the like living in what, from our perspective, appears as a *locus amoenus*. Thus the centaur—half man, half horse—can say to Hummel (who doubles as the mythic Hephaestus), "I got to *high-tail* it." And when the mechanic (and god of fire and forge) will not take any money for having removed the arrow from the creature's ankle, George (as man, not centaur) can think, "And this was the way with all these Olinger aristocrats. They wouldn't take any money but they did take an authoritative tone. They forced a favor on you and *that made them gods*." Finally, when Hummel tells George that the days are bad, George can reply, "It's no *Golden Age*, that's for sure" (pp. 16–7). These highlighted words—*high-tail*, *gods*, *Golden Age*—become puns because of the double contexture, but that contexture exists only for us and for the one who dreams the dream.[9] Because readers share Peter's multiple perspective, one combining both metaphoric naming and metonymic associations, readers share with him also the binocular ability to encompass the mythic past and the nonmythic present. Such a vision is required if one is to see the tropic play of language in the instances cited, as well as dozens of others one might cite from the novel, many of which are located readily by use of the mythological index Updike appends.

Peter's expression does not always move in that world of total metaphor, which in Jakobson's view is one pole of the dialectic of language, nor does it always move in the world of total metonymic realism, Jakobson's other pole of language. The one is illustrated in the metaphoric characterization of figures such as George Caldwell as Chiron the Centaur, and Peter Caldwell as Prometheus (and so on); the other is identified by Peter as that "patch of Pennsylvania in 1947" (p. 293), the contemporary world emphasized by those critics like Mizener who value Updike's realism more than his mythopoesis. There is, besides, a middle ground discernible in the tropology of Peter's style. When the projected distance between the metaphoric or mythic and the metonymic or realistic worlds increases, Peter's verbal technique shifts to the simile. As Peter uses them, the similes make direct connections between the two polar realms of metaphor and metonymy by using *like* and *as* and *seems*. When, for instance, George Caldwell speaks of Peter's psoriatic skin condition to the hitchhiker, Peter (who, again, is metaphorically the rock-bound Prometheus) reports to us: "*In effect* my father had torn off my clothes and displayed my prickling scabs. In the glare of my anger his profile *seemed* that of a *blind raw rock*" (p. 89). Though obviously figurative, the similes mediate between the metaphoric and the metonymic, but they work because of the metonymic contexts we must recognize. For further instance, Peter says this about the hitchhiker, who metaphorically is Hermes (or the winged Mercury): "Through the dusty rear window I watched our guest, looking *like a messenger* with his undisclosed bundle, dwindle. The hitchhiker became a brown wisp at the mouth of the bridge, *flew upwards, vanished*" (pp. 90–91). Such simile—playing upon the metonymic details implicit in the originating metaphors—performs a very important role in Peter's style when he relates details about himself. Of his skin problem, for example, he says: "Had the world been watching, it would have been startled, for my belly, *as if pecked by a great bird*, was dotted with red scabs the size of coins" (p. 52). Of his bright red shirt (behind which, metaphorically, stands the image of Prometheus's gift of fire to humanity), Peter remarks: "I would carry to my classmates on this bitter day a *gift of scarlet, a giant spark*, a two-pocketed *emblem of heat*" (p. 55). In other places, both as first and third persons, he speaks similarly about that garment: "I unbuttoned my pea jacket so the devil-may-care *flame* of my shirt showed" (p. 117); "My shirt was eating my skin with *fire*" (p. 176); "*On fire*," we read, "he turns his *red* back on the crowd" (p. 240).

Peter also speaks of other characters, such as Doc Appleton, Minor Kretz, and Zimmerman, in terms of simile, and again the metaphoric is played off against the metonymic. Doc Appleton's mythic identity is Apollo, so Peter uses similes to draw into the texture of narrative two of Apollo's main roles, as the sun who brings light and as the slayer of the serpent, Python, at Delphi. When Doc Appleton (Apollo was also a healer) speaks his name, Peter says, "*Like a ray of sunlight* the old man's kindness and competence pierced the morbid atmosphere of his house" (pp. 125–26). And when the doctor puts down his stethoscope, Peter says, "It *writhed* and then subsided *like a slain rubber serpent*" (p. 128). Similarly, Minor Kretz, who runs the luncheonette where all the school kids hang out, is offered as a parallel to Minos, King of Crete, whose erotic interest is Pasiphae (Mrs. Passify in the novel). Of the man who runs the luncheonette and the woman who runs the post office next door, Peter says, "The symmetry [between the two establishments], carried right down to the worn spots of the two floors and the heating pipes running along the opposing walls, was so perfect that as a child I had imagined that Mrs. Passify and Minor Kretz were secretly married" (p. 115). But Minor is also the Minotaur (*borne* of Queen Pasiphae), so that at one point Peter speaks of Minor's place as "a maze" (p. 116); he says also, "Minor *charged* over to our booth. Anger flashed from his bald dome and *steamed* through his *flared nostrils*. 'Here, hyaar,' he *snorted*" (p. 183); and later Peter says, "The luncheonette . . . is all but empty, like a stage. . . . Within, Minor is a cauldron of rage; his *hairy nostrils seem seething vents*" (p. 202). And Zimmerman, the school principal, doubles in the mythic world as Zeus. The narrator and other characters thus refer to him several times in figures that suggest his role as an Olympian god. George Caldwell, for example, moans, "I could feel Zimmerman sitting in there *like a big heavy rain-cloud*" (pp. 208–9). Later the narrator says, "Zimmerman sees *as if through a rift in clouds* that Caldwell's glimpse of Mrs. Herzog is at the bottom of his fear and his mind exults" (p. 248). At another time, finally, Peter thinks of Zimmerman's finger (like that of Michelangelo's God) as "dense with existence" (p. 243).

Peter's father, of course, is the most important character who comes in for the ironic enfigurations posed by similes in those chapters, especially, where metonymic realism dominates metaphoric myth. The main referent for Peter's images is the equine portion of the mythic centaur's body. Thus, for example, once when Peter and his father are walking together, we are told: "We seemed from our shadow to be a prancing one-headed creature with four legs" (p. 113). At another time, when George has felt Zimmerman (Zeus) as "a dark cloud" around him, we read: "*Lifting his head and sniffing,* Caldwell experiences a vivid urge to walk on faster, *to canter* right past Hummel's, *to romp neighing* through the front door and out the back door of any house in Olinger that stood in his way, *to gallop* up the brushy winter-burned flank of Shale Hill and on, on, over hills that grow smoother and bluer with distance, on and on" (p. 201). And near the end of the novel, Peter sees his father walking toward home: "His shape before me was made less human by the bag of groceries he was carrying and it seemed, my legs having ceased to convey the sensations of walking, that *his was the shape of the neck and head of a horse I was riding*" (p. 285).

Figurative language such as this suggests one extra dimension Updike gives *The Centaur*. There is a very real sense in which Peter's search through his memory and imagination, in the process of "dreaming" this narrative, is ultimately for that original, innocent, prelapsarian world "resonant with metaphor." He searches for a world in which identities exist between reality and myth, existence and dream, earth and heaven, but the very necessity to speak, for example, of Appleton, Minor Kretz, Zimmerman, or his father in the largely metonymic terms of simile—of *as, like, seems*—reveals the distance the youth has fallen from his golden age. Consequently, Updike's epigraph for the book, from Karl Barth, creates an appropriate context for the uses Peter makes of language, for Peter, as much as his father, is that creature Barth describes, "the creature on the boundary between heaven and earth," between the "creation inconceivable to man" and the "creation conceivable to him." The novel thus represents Peter's effort to recapture through the lyricist's powers of language an image made resonant by his father of the most felicitous time in his life.

A Tropology of Furthest Things

The words that [first] name the great images—the abyss, night, sky, earth—are at the same time names of gods, all inextricably mixed and mingled in cosmogonies and theogonies. . . . Next there appear names of different powers—death, passion, war—which still designate something divine. . . . Finally, there emerge the concepts of ontology and physics, as a result of a sort of secularizing of the names of powers.
—Mikel Dufrenne, *Language and Philosophy*

A phenomenology of language, because it rests upon a relationship between words and concrete human experience, might at first glance seem unavailable to the larger philosophical questions of metaphysics, eschatology, transcendence. On the contrary, because of the indissoluble interrelationship of human consciousness and the physical world, language in its phenomenological intensity works at the highest levels of expressive symbolism—represented, according to philosophers such as Cassirer, Husserl, Heidegger, and Merleau-Ponty, in the great forms of art and literary expression. These forms—Cassirer's "symbolic forms," we may say—are readily identified in such literary genres as the epic, tragic drama, and lyrical poetry. It is lyrical poetry, according to Cassirer, that most vividly constitutes the relationship between human being and human existence. Consequently, the modality of lyrical expressiveness in *The Centaur* puts one in touch with those transcendent themes that raise art to the level of metaphysics.

As a result of Peter's role in it and the attitude he brings, *The Centaur* belongs to that genre of lyrical expression known as the elegiac. Larry E. Taylor has detailed many of the formal ways in which Updike has created a pastoral elegy. To begin with, Taylor suggests that the four interspersed short chapters—chapters 3, 5, 8, and 9—help to generate the pastoral elegiac structure because each is a variation of a basic convention of the traditional form, both in its subject matter and in its language and imagery. "The language of these touchstone chapters," Taylor writes, "provides the lyricism and formality required to keep the novel from being ironic, satiric, and comic. Seen as a highly personal expression of both Updike's and Peter's sense of loss (Updike has left Shillington to become a writer for the *New Yorker*, and Peter is painting abstractions in a New York loft), *The Centaur* appeals to the impersonality of stock pastoral conventions as a vehicle for transforming life into art—the personal into the universal."[10] Drawing upon effects achieved by Milton in the spirit of the pastoral in an elegy such as *Lycidas*, Taylor outlines the parallels between the novel and the poem in subject matter.[11] But the limitations Taylor sets for himself will not allow him to get into the detailed analysis of those narrative and thematic patterns in the novel that relate directly to the more conventional elegiac elements. The most important such patterns are those associated with the elegy's concern with matters of eschatology, the "furthest things"—time, death, man's goal, or end, or *telos*.

One of the major concerns in *The Centaur* is with time. It is manifested in Peter's interest in the knowable historical past and the unknowable future. To know the past, Peter believes, is to know more about the present, so he is always fascinated by details of the lives of people he knows, whether the details concern the more intimate relationships of a woman like Vera Hummel to various men or just the public triumph of someone like Zimmerman on the Olinger track team. But even more than with the past or the present Peter is concerned with and believes in the future. It is in the future that he believes his desires can be fulfilled. He knows, for example, that in the normal course of things, he will outlive Zimmerman, his father's viciously petty supervisor, so the future holds his dream: "Triumphantly, Peter feels descend upon him, his father's avenger, this advantage over the antagonist: he has more years to live. Ignorant and impotent here and now, in the dimension of the future he is mighty" (p. 242). For Peter the future becomes his dimension, its airy spaces his natural element, as water is Deifendorf's: "The world of water was closed to me," he thinks, "so I had fallen in love with the air, which I was able to seize in great thrilling condensations within me that I labelled the Future: it was in this realm that I hoped to reward my father for his suffering" (p. 105).

What, no doubt, Peter wishes to reward his father with is a reply to the question his father asks: it is a simple, but ultimate, question, "What's the answer?" (p. 223). Once he has inhabited his imagined future, however, Peter must admit that he is as impotent there as he was in the past to find "the answer." Neither his chosen form of artistic expression nor erotic attachment has given him answers to his eschatological questions. *Inside* his future, looking back over his past, he says:

> I glance around at the nest we have made, at the floorboards polished by our bare feet, at the *continents* of stain on the ceiling like an old and all-wrong *discoverer's map*, at the earnestly bloated canvases I conscientiously cover with great streaks *straining to say what even I am beginning to suspect is the unsayable thing*, and I grow frightened. I consider the life we have made together, with its days spent without relation to the days the sun keeps and its baroque arabesques of increasingly attenuated emotion and its furnishings like a scattering of worn-out Braques and its rather wistful half-Freudian half-Oriental sex-mysticism, and I wonder, *Was it for this that my father gave up his life?* (P. 270)

There are no empirical truths in eschatology, however, and while abstract expressionism and erotic mysticism may allow one to pursue his own personal answers, they will permit one only to say the thing to oneself, not to say the unsayable to another. The truths Peter may discover empirically and may relate concretely, rather than abstractly, lie in his experience. Experience itself can lead him to an appropriate art and a transcendent love, and the center of that experience is his relationship to his father.

Death is the furthest thing in human experience, for it is the last final thing empirically humanity knows will happen to it. As most readers of *The Centaur* know, death is the primary concern of the novel, as it is the primary concern of most of Updike's work. The general theme is itself teleological, involving as it does humanity's end, its place in the universal scheme of things. This particular aspect of the eschatological, elegiac theme is exhaustively presented in the various cosmological systems the novel invokes. These systems are really "myths" of one sort or another, symbolic forms whose unity has the integrative force of single metaphors. They appear in two groups, one broadly scientific, the other broadly humanistic. Among the scientific are the myth of biological evolution, the myth suggested by modern cosmological astronomy, and the oxygen cycle in chemical nature given the form of a mythic narrative; among the humanistic are the pastoral myths of the Greeks and the Christians.[12] Each of these myths represents human attempts to explain and/or to come to terms with the question of one's own predestined end. In the elegiac form of the narrative we can see Peter review and discard the various "answers" until he discovers his own adequate answer in his myth of art.

According to Hayden White, the trope of metaphor has a very close affinity to the mode of thinking we call narrative: metaphor's tendency is to generate stories. Thus, it comes almost as a consequence of the return to expressive, metaphoric thinking in *The Centaur* that those great abstractions from astronomy, biology, and chemistry should be turned into stories, myths, mythoi. A mythos is a traditional story, and it is as a traditional story that George Caldwell tells to his class the history of biological evolution. He does it in terms of the "creation clock" all of us have seen in one place or another. He begins with the estimated age of the universe, five billion years, speaks of various stars—the sun, Venus, Alpha Centauri, the Milky Way, the constellation Sagittarius—and of the hundred billion galaxies, each containing a hundred billion stars, numbers, in their unfathomableness, that remind Caldwell of death (p. 37). Consequently, he says to his class, "Let's try to reduce five billion years to our size. Let's say the universe is three days old. Today is Thursday. . . . Last Monday at noon there was the greatest explosion there ever was. We're still riding on it" (p. 38). This explosion, he tells his class, came five billion years ago from a "primeval egg," one cubic centimeter of which weighed two hundred and fifty tons. After a period of darkness and "the expanding flux of universal substance" (p. 39), stars begin to shine, the Earth begins to form, and "for a whole day . . . , between Tuesday and Wednesday noon, the earth is barren. There is no life on it. Just ugly rocks, stale water, vomiting volcanoes, everything slithering and sliding and maybe freezing now and then as the sun like a dirty old light bulb flickered up there in the sky. By yesterday noon, a little life showed up. Nothing spectacular; just a little bit of slime. All yesterday afternoon, and most of the night, life remained microscopic" (p. 40). With the advent of microscopic life, the evolutionary process accelerates rapidly. But Caldwell's concern, like humanity's, lies in the relation of life to death. Thus, "the volvox, of these early citizens in the kingdom of life, interests us because he invented death . . .[;] by pioneering this new idea of *cooperation*, [the volvox] rolled life into the kingdom of certain—as opposed to accidental—death. . . . It dies sacrificially, for the good of the whole, . . . the first altruists. The first do-gooders. If I had a hat on, I'd take it off to 'em" (p. 42). The story of life goes very quickly now, from trilobites to the first vertebrate fishes, the first plants, the insects, the reptiles, and the mammals. Finally, at a point when Caldwell's "very blood loathed the story he had told," "One minute ago, flint-chipping, fire-kindling, death-foreseeing, a tragic animal appeared . . . called Man" (p. 46).

In this now traditional story, mankind knows it is at the apex of a process that explains the fact of death. But knowledge cannot reconcile this tragic animal to the death it foresees. Neither can the "humanistic values implicit in the physical sciences" that Zimmerman speaks of in his report on Caldwell's lecture on the mythos of biological evolution. (Caldwell's thought upon seeing the phrase is, "Maybe down deep in the atom there's a little man sitting in a rocking chair reading the evening paper" [p.111].) Nor can the mythos of astronomy, the theory of the "big bang" according to Hoyle. We discover astronomy's limitations when Peter imagines a universe falling through space as he watches snowflakes falling beneath a tall light:

Directly under the light, the wavering fall of the particles is projected as an erratic oscillation, but away from the center, where the light rays strike obliquely, the projection parabolically magnifies the speed of the shadow as it hastens forward to meet its flake. The shadows stream out of infinity, slow, and, each darkly sharp in its last instant, vanish as their originals kiss the white plane. . . . He turns scientist and dispassionately tries to locate in the cosmography his father has taught him an analogy between the phenomenon he has observed and the "red shift" whereby the stars appear to be retreating at a speed proportional to their distance from us. Perhaps this is a kindred illusion, perhaps—he struggles to picture it—the stars are in fact falling gently through a cone of observation of which our earthly telescopes are the apex. (Pp. 255–56)

Peter can find a place from which to observe the relative motions of this snowflake galaxy, but that place in his imagined universe, "pinned, stretched, crucified like a butterfly upon a frame of unvarying geometrical truth," gives him little security. Walking away from the light he seems "to arrive at a kind of edge where the speed of the shadows is infinite and a small universe both ends and does not end." Thus the vision he has here of the universe as it is enfigured by modern astronomy gives Peter little consolation. Only by returning his gaze to the concrete reality of the town can Peter overcome what he thinks of as the "sickly" nature of his "cosmic thoughts" (p. 256).

The mythos of astronomy suggests to Peter a one-way process of humanity and human life disappearing into a nebulous "center," a cosmic black hole such as those only recently discovered by astronomers. Consequently, the mythos of the oxygen cycle as it is seen in the formula (p. 187):

$$C_6H_{12}O_6 + 6O_2 = 6CO_2 + 6H_2O + E$$

may be somewhat more appealing to one's imagination. The formula represents the creation of energy and, thus, of life. As Caldwell explains to his class, " 'When this process stops'—he Xed through the equation—'*this* stops'—he double-Xed out the E—'and you become what they call dead. You become a worthless log of old chemicals" (pp. 187–88). But at least this process can be reversed. The equation can also be read backwards in order to represent the process of photosynthesis that occurs in plants: "That's the way the world goes round. . . . Round and round, and where it stops, nobody knows" (p. 188). The formula thus offers human beings

156

an objective symbol for the cyclic process of death and renewal in nature. It *may* offer the illusion of death and renewal for humanity itself.

The mythoi of the Greeks and the Christians suggest that man as an individual can achieve the immortality once foresaken by the altruistic volvox. Moreover, these myths already exist as stories and are more personal than the chemical symbols for the organic process. They return human consciousness to the equations that science has formulated, and, at least potentially, they can express and contain the emotional impact of death. But for Peter, the Greek myths seem more germane than the Christian. Many critics read the novel as if it were a paean to the traditional church, yet Christianity in *The Centaur* offers little more than those myths of science. There really is not much to cling to in the doctrines expressed by its representative, the Reverend March. George comes to him troubled in mind and seeking "the answer" he has sought from others. "I can't make it add up," he says to March, "and I'd be grateful for your viewpoint." George's own view, for example, of the difference between Lutherans and Calvinists is, "the Lutherans say Jesus Christ is the only answer and the Calvinists say whatever happens to you, happens to you, is the answer." The son of a minister, George also has a certain conception of Presbyterian doctrine: "There are the elect and the non-elect, the ones that have it and the ones that don't, and the ones that don't have it are never going to get it. What I could never ram through my thick skull was why the ones that don't have it were created in the first place." March's reply to these ideas is ministerial jargon about orthodoxy, Christocentrism, substantive Eucharistic transformation, and understanding the doctrine of predestination "as counterbalanced by the doctrine of God's infinite mercy" (pp. 252–53).

None of the Reverend March's answers is concrete enough for George to grasp. To George God's mercy itself is one of the furthest things, for it is "infinite at an infinite distance" from him as he lives his life. There is nothing either in the substance or the tone of what the reverend says that will reconcile George to the death he lately has come to face. And there is nothing any more affirmative in the Christian cosmology the novel offers elsewhere, in a passage occurring just before the dialogue between Caldwell and the reverend. The same snowstorm that gives Peter his cosmic thoughts enters into Updike's elaborate metaphor of Olinger as "yet one more Bethlehem. Behind a glowing window the infant God squalls. Out of zero all has come to birth. The panes, tinted by the straw of the crib within, hush its cries. The world goes on unhearing. The town of white roofs seems a colony of deserted temples; they feather together with distance and go gray, melt" (p. 239). Whether it is only because the town does not listen or whether the infant is just one more rough beast, shuffling toward Bethlehem, such a vision can offer no consolation to one who has the thoughts besetting George Caldwell. Since they cannot reconcile George, neither can they offer reconciliation to Peter Caldwell.

The Greek myths one sees concretely enfigured in those interchapters offer much more to *The Centaur*. Their substance can be no more meaningful than the mythoi of evolution, astronomy, the oxygen cycle, or even Christianity. But the affective significance they bring to the novel gives them priority over all those others, for it is finally the emotional response to the fact of death that Peter's lyrical expression must contain. The Greek myths, more than the other mythoi, seem to express the archetypes that create the concrete patterns Updike favors and that Peter must eventually accept in his vision of art. Echoing Vico and the phenomenologists, Carl Jung says that primitive man does not create his myths, he experiences them. In *The Centaur* it is the experiencing of Greek myth that we see, for these chapters (3, 9) more than any others are ones in which the world "resonant with metaphor" is achieved. Because Caldwell *is* Chiron, *is* the centaur, in these chapters, there is no distance between the mythic world of human desires and the real world in which humanity resides. Consequently, when Chiron speaks to his students on "the Genesis of all things," there seems little in the story to make his blood sicken as Caldwell's does when he relates the mythos of evolution: "In the beginning," Chiron says, "blackwinged Night was courted by the wind, and laid a silver egg in the womb of Darkness. From this egg hatched Eros. . . . And Love set the Universe in motion. . . . Men lived without cares or labor. . . . Death, to them, was no more terrible than sleep" (p. 99).

Such a story, idyllic in both content and tone, can offer to Peter not only a symbolic narrative archetype that expresses in human terms the abstract meaning of the oxygen cycle; it also offers a figure, a trope, a symbol to contain his feelings of love and goodwill toward his father. This archetype is connected to the themes of the pastoral elegy, but it also relates directly to the enfiguration of George Caldwell as the scapegoat-dying god. It thus balances the wasteland against Arcadia, and, in the formal pattern of the elegy, it joins nature and human nature. Both father and son participate in the pattern because of their identifications with nature itself. Each is related to the seasonal rhythm in some way: Peter's psoriasis, for instance, is a "rhythmic curse that breathed in and out with [God's] seasons" (p. 53); George's whole life—identified as it is with his birth date near the winter solstice (just before Christmas; see p. 54)—and his role as the constellation Sagittarius seem interconnected with natural patterns. George himself, in relation to his son, becomes not just the "old man" Peter must replace or "trade in for" (p. 89); he becomes "Old Man Winter's belly" (pp. 278, 281), that archetypal figure of the wasteland who holds life in bondage. But whether as the old man or as Winter's belly, George can offer Peter hope. Although the "emasculate" Sky might leave "his progeny to parch upon a white waste," George can think: "Yet even in the dead of winter the sere twigs prepare their small dull buds. In the pit of the year a king was born. Not a leaf falls but leaves an amber root, a dainty hoof, a fleck of baggage to be unpacked in future time" (p. 295). The hope George can leave Peter seems finally to be found in nature itself.

Art and the Phenomenology of Expressiveness

> The spirit lives in the word of language and in the mythical image without falling under the control of either. What poetry expresses is neither the mythic word-picture of gods and demons, nor the logical truth of abstract determinations and relations. The world of poetry stands apart from both, as a world of illusion and fantasy—but it is just in this mode of illusion that the realm of pure feeling can find utterance, and can therewith attain its full and concrete actualization.
> —Ernst Cassirer, *Language and Myth*

The Greek myths allow Peter to discover the one mode of human expression that is appropriate for him. That mode is *art* as an eschatological trope, as a symbolic unifying form, as a means both of expressing and containing those furthest things that have always troubled humanity. Peter's grandfather Caldwell had religion, his father had science, and Peter—the end of the classic decline (p. 269) from priest, to teacher, to artist—has art. To Peter, art, "however clumsy and quaint and mistaken," can radiate "the innocence and hope, the hope of seizing something and holding it fast, that enters whenever a brush touches canvas" (p. 267). The paintings of Vermeer enfigure for him manifestations of that hope. They become, he says, "the Holy Ghost" of his adolescence: "That these paintings, which I had worshipped in reproduction, had a simple physical existence seemed a profound mystery to me: to come within touching distance of their surfaces, to see with my own eyes the truth of their color, the tracery of the cracks whereby time had inserted itself like a mystery within a mystery, would have been for me to enter a Real Presence so ultimate I would not be surprised to die in the encounter" (p. 85).

It becomes Peter's dream to be able to create in the profound way of a Vermeer. Eventually, Peter has a revelation as to how he too can create art's mystery within a mystery. He says, "I must go to Nature disarmed of perspective and stretch myself like a large transparent canvas upon her in the hope that, my submission being perfect, the imprint of a beautiful and useful truth would be taken" (p. 293). It is a recognition that bears out Vargo's explanation of the connection of Updike's novel to Karl Barth's philosophy: "Man exists not on the boundary between God and creation, but on a boundary within creation itself: between the *visibilia et invisibilia*, the conceivable and inconceivable, the humanly attainable and the humanly transcendent" (p. 454). The impact of *The Centaur* suggests that, in effect, Peter Caldwell has submitted himself to the attainable facts of his father's human life. The son may have been in his vocation only a second-rate abstract expressionist painter, but in his avocation he has become a first-rate representational artist, who, in the verbal contours of Greek pastoral elegiac myth, has sketched a beautiful and useful and transcendent truth.

Peter creates a beautiful and transcendent truth, but it is useful because it is also experiential. It is on this point that one must finally take issue with Vargo's fine essay on *The Centaur*. The problem is simply that he stresses too much the form of the novel as rite or ritual. To the extent that it is formalized as a thing done, the novel may constitute a ritual action, but in that case every work, every poem, becomes a rite, since all can be defined as symbolic actions. Consequently, in this case *rite* is clearly less useful a term than *myth*, for myth suggests better than rite the verbal, the expressive, dreamlike quality of the work and its locus in a mind, a phenomenological consciousness. The hermeneutic superiority of myth becomes clear when Vargo states that "the chief function of ritual in this novel ... is to serve as an action against death" (p. 458). But the novel, instead, is no imagining of an action; it is an imagining of an imagining, an introjection, an emotional assimilation of the fact of death. The novel seems far less a rite than a speech act, an utterance, an expression of love, grief, and consolation. Vargo is much more to the point when he writes, "By its transformation of a particular situation into a paradigm, myth

160

makes rite dynamic and meaningful. Without it, ritual is an empty shell" (p. 459).

The movement of the novel, in other words, suggests that the basic, meaningful focus lies on neither rite nor myth, but on the phenomenological conjoining of their structures in experience, existence. Rite alone cannot give meaning to existential experience, nor, alone, can myth, but joined in experience, they are infused with substance, as speech gives body to the ideal structures of language. To make structure primary is to discount the phenomenon of George Caldwell in Peter's experiences—indeed, to leave a form that would be "an empty shell." For Peter, as, apparently, for Updike, existence precedes essence, the flesh precedes the word, but they need each other for either to have significance. Thus, it is Peter's speaking of his father's life and possible death that makes concrete the sacral universe of which Vargo speaks and through which humanity can make contact with God or the Transcendent. Art is finally the ultimate answer to the eschatological questions Peter raises. Art permits phenomenological expression to the question of eschatology. It is finally the art of Peter's expression that transmutes experience and creates—as perhaps by definition every new work of art must—a new enfiguration for his time.

The Centaur is an elegy, not upon the death of a friend, a leader, or a god, but upon the death, real or imagined, of a man's father. As a lyrical expression of grief and love, this novel comes close to the spirit of a poem like e. e. cummings's "my father moved through dooms of love."[13] Like cummings's poem, Peter's is a celebration of a father's life, an act of atonement for the suffering that the father endures in his life. Cummings's poem says his father has moved through conformity ("sames of am"), selfishness ("haves of give"), indifference ("dooms of feel"), and alienation ("theys of we"); Peter's says his father has moved through "waste, rot, hollowness, noise, stench, death," "the many visages which this central thing wears" (p. 251). But cummings's poem concludes with the kind of affirmation that seems possible to a man in the face of that furthest thing known as death.

> because my father lived his soul
> love is the whole and more than all

Peter's elegiac expression comes to a similar affirmative conclusion. It comes, moreover, directly out of his own and his father's life experience. Knowing now he is not going to die momentarily from the cancer he had feared, George Caldwell feels at the end "that in giving his life to others he entered a total freedom" (p. 296). As if this revelation also allows him to regain the innocent world of total, resonant metaphor, George is then cast as a mediator, as a place wherein the forces of life can meet and regenerate themselves: "Mt. Ide and Mt. Dikte from opposite blue distances rushed toward him like clapping waves and in the upright of his body Sky and Gaia mated again" (pp. 296–97). In his body, that grotesque medium formed from man and beast, the wasteland he might have bequeathed to his son is revivified. And the beautiful, useful, transcendent truth of Peter's art is revealed: "Only goodness lives. But it does live" (p. 297). The most satisfying of the beauties of this truth, coming as it does from a celebration of a son's love for his father, is the fact that it is the *father's* father, George's father, who evokes it in the first place. The novel suggests not the biblical notion that the sins of the fathers are visited upon the sons, but the more benevolent idea that the wisdom of the fathers is passed along. The novel's form thus contradicts George Caldwell's repeated mutterings about his inheritance only of "a Bible and a deskful of debts." It clearly contradicts his feeling that he will pass on to Peter only a message of despair. The elegiac form Peter creates finally expresses more than a son's personal feeling; it expresses reverence for life and faith in the continuity of the human spirit.

A phenomenology of language seems finally a way of placing tropology—and the use of tropology to analyze works of fictional narrative such as *The Centaur*—because it draws together the disparate aspects of life and philosophy. Phenomenology is, paradoxically, a metaphor (or, in White's way of thinking, a synecdoche) that stands on a higher plane of abstraction than tropology, and, if we invoke a sort of Gödel's Theorem for systems besides those from mathematics, such a higher level is necessary if one is to explain or justify tropology—whether White's or Burke's or Vico's. But a phenomenology of language is particularly appropriate for the literary or other artistic product because it provides a basis for the very fact of the artistic enterprise. James M. Edie has indicated both the metaphoric (or synecdochic) unity of humans with their world and that feature of human identity (the faculty of speech) that most distinguishes us from other creatures. On the one hand, says Edie, phenomenology regards language "as one aspect of a total, contextual, human activity of 'expressing' which cannot be studied in isolation from man's existential insertion in his life-world." On the other, a phenomenological analysis

162

does not permit of division of "human reality into 'pure' disembodied consciousness" on one side and "a body as its corporeal 'instrument' on the other." Edie's epigrammatic summary of the two doctrines of phenomenology turns us back toward the linkage between lyric or poetic art and the springs of language—the expressive, creative, regenerative domain of metaphor: "Human reality as a unitary whole is intentional of the world." For Edie, the crucial point here is the sense—in the phenomenologist's term *intentional*—that through language humans reach out to the world as it reaches toward them. Language thus, in intentionality, speaks both humanity and the world. "Another way of saying the same thing is to say that man is essentially *expressive*," Edie concludes, and man's expressive nature reaches its highest form in linguistic utterance.[14]

Therefore, since for Edie the essence of language is its figurative power, it would appear that the aims of tropology and of phenomenology, which are to see human reality as a unitary whole, are both essentialized in metaphor and its integrative forms such as synecdoche. Although the narrative curriculum of White's tetradic tropology foreshadows the death of unity in irony, after irony's dark night, metaphor will once again rise to cast its illumination over all tropic space. The epilogue to *The Centaur* expresses this double—heroic and ironic—vision as well as any other words one might select: "Zeus had loved his old friend, and lifted him up, and set him among the stars as the constellation Sagittarius. Here, in the Zodiac, now above, now below the horizon, he assists in the regulation of our destinies, though in this latter time few living mortals cast their eyes respectfully toward Heaven, and fewer still sit as students to the stars" (p. 299). The lesson, finally, that Updike's novel teaches us is that the "grand images" of the world (as Dufrenne calls them) are out there in the phenomenological universe, but only our language, our figures, our tropes, can capture them for human use. A sense of tropology infused with the spirit of the phenomenological is, perhaps, the very instrument by which we might, for our use, capture the stars, the constellations of significance in human life.

NOTES

1. Georges Gusdorf, *Speaking*, trans. Paul T. Brockelman (Evanston, Ill.: Northwestern University Press, 1965), p. 4. Subsequent quotations will be cited by page numbers within parentheses in my text. Other significant studies related

to the phenomenology of language include Edmund Husserl, *Formal and Transcendental Logic*, trans. Dorion Cairns (The Hague: Martinus Nijhoff, 1969), Maurice Merleau-Ponty, *The Prose of the World*, trans. John O'Neill (Evanston, Ill.: Northwestern University Press, 1973), and Jacques Derrida, *Speech and Phenomena and Other Essays on Husserl's Theory of Signs*, trans. David B. Allison (Evanston, Ill.: Northwestern University Press, 1973).

2. See Northrop Frye, *Anatomy of Criticism: Four Essays* (Princeton: Princeton University Press, 1957), pp. 158–239, for Frye's discussion of the cycle of narrative archetypes; see Hayden V. White, *Metahistory: The Historical Imagination in Nineteenth-Century Europe* (Baltimore: Johns Hopkins University Press, 1973), for discussions of the interrelations of narrative archetypes and tropes.

3. John Updike, *The Centaur* (New York: Knopf, 1963), p. 70. Further references to the novel will be cited by page numbers within parentheses in the text.

4. See, for example, Arthur Mizener, "The American Hero as High-School Boy: Peter Caldwell," in *The Sense of Life in the Modern Novel* (Boston: Houghton Mifflin, 1964), pp. 265–66; Bryant Wyatt, "John Updike: The Psychological Novel in Search of Structure," *Twentieth Century Literature* 13 (July 1967):93–94; and David Myers, "The Questing Fear: Christian Allegory in John Updike's *The Centaur*," *Twentieth Century Literature* 17.2 (Apr. 1971):73–82.

5. "The Necessity of Myth in Updike's *The Centaur*," *PMLA* 83.3 (May 1973):453. Vargo's essay is included in his *Rainstorms and Fire: Ritual in the Novels of John Updike* (Port Washington, N.Y.: Kennikat Press, 1973). Two other excellent studies of *The Centaur* are contained in Joyce B. Markle's *Fighters and Lovers: Theme in the Novels of John Updike* (New York: New York University Press, 1973), and John B. Vickery's "*The Centaur*: Myth, History, and Narrative," *Modern Fiction Studies* 20.1 (Spring 1974):29–43.

6. Hart Crane, *The Bridge* (Garden City, N.Y.: Doubleday and Co., 1958), p. 11.

7. Mizener, "The American Hero," pp. 266, 262.

8. Hayden White somewhere points out that the Greek word *tropos* means "turn," or "swerve," and that the archetypal figure of the hero, Odysseus, is called also by the epithet *polytropos*, meaning "man of many turns, changes, shapes."

9. I would point out, in this context, that Jacques Lacan bases his reinterpretation of Freudian theories of dreams upon the working of the tropes of metaphor and metonymy. One might want to refer to my chapter 2, which employs a Lacanian tropics in the interpretation of Joseph Heller's novel *Something Happened*.

10. Larry E. Taylor, *Pastoral and Anti-Pastoral Patterns in John Updike's Fiction* (Carbondale: Southern Illinois University Press, 1971), p. 90.

11. Here is Taylor's sketch of the parallels:

1) Chapter 1, only five pages long, shows the pastoral hero Chiron involved in his daily tasks of teaching the children of the gods in Arcadian groves. Idyllic in the strictest sense, the passage includes a conventional catalogue of flowers and herbs and celebrates the tranquility and beauty of the hero as he was in life. Roughly, it corresponds to lines 25–36 of *Lycidas*.

2) Chapter 5, four pages long, is a newspaper obituary, giving a coldly factual account of Caldwell's life. It suggests the conventional expression of communal grief. It is the elegiac announcement of death, roughly comparable to the flat shock value of the fact, "For Lycidas is dead, dead ere his prime," lines 10 and following of *Lycidas*.

3) Chapter 8 (the first four pages), is the expression of Peter's personal grief for the loss of the pastoral hero. Here Peter-Prometheus sings his lament to his Negro mistress. He questions the meaning of his father's death in a version of the elegiac interrogation of the universe, roughly analogous to lines 50–85 of *Lycidas*.

4) Chapter 9, four pages long, is a consolation and reconciliation, an account of the Centaur's acceptance of death, and his son's reconciliation to it. The short epilogue is an account of the Centaur's apotheosis as a star. Roughly, it corresponds to lines 165–93 of *Lycidas*. (Pp. 89–90)

12. Vargo speaks (p. 456) of two other myths—one of "the City" and one of "the Future" (of which I have already spoken), but neither myth has quite the dynamic, etiological quality these other myths possess. Indeed, for Peter, the city and the future are parts of the problem, not the answer, as Peter realizes.

13. *e. e. cummings: A Selection of Poems* (New York: Harcourt, Brace & World, 1965), p. 119–21.

14. James M. Edie, *Speaking and Meaning: The Phenomenology of Language* (Bloomington and London: Indiana University Press, 1976), p. 152. Edie, I might add, is the general editor of the series published by the Northwestern University Press entitled Studies in Phenomenology and Existential Philosophy.

Selected Bibliography

Barthes, Roland. "The Imagination of the Sign." In *A Barthes Reader*. Edited, with an introduction, by Susan Sontag. New York: Hill and Wang, 1982, 211–17.

Bohn, Willard. "Roman Jakobson's Theory of Metaphor and Metonymy: An Annotated Bibliography." *Style* 18.4 (Fall 1984):534–50.

Brooke-Rose, Christine. *A Grammar of Metaphor*. London: Secker & Warburg, 1958.

Burke, Kenneth. "Appendix D: Four Master Tropes." In his *A Grammar of Motives*. Berkeley: University of California Press, 1969, 503–17.

Carroll, David. "On Tropology: The Forms of History." *Diacritics* 6 (Fall 1976): 58–64.

———. *The Subject in Question: The Languages of Theory and the Strategies of Fiction*. Chicago: University of Chicago Press, 1983.

Cassirer, Ernst. *An Essay on Man*. New Haven: Yale University Press, 1944.

———. *Language and Myth*. Translated by Susanne K. Langer. New York: Dover, 1953.

———. *The Philosophy of Symbolic Forms*. Translated by Ralph Manheim. 3 vols. New Haven: Yale University Press, 1953, 1955, 1957.

———. *The Problem of Knowledge: Philosophy, Science, and History Since Hegel*. Translated by William H. Woglom and Charles W. Hendel. New Haven: Yale University Press, 1950.

Culler, Jonathan. *The Pursuit of Signs: Semiotics, Literature, Deconstruction*. Ithaca, N.Y.: Cornell University Press, 1981.

Derrida, Jacques. *Speech and Phenomena and Other Essays on Husserl's Theory of Signs*. Translated by David B. Allison. Evanston, Ill.: Northwestern University Press, 1973.

———. "Structure, Sign, and Play in the Discourse of the Human Sciences." In *The Structuralist Controversy: The Languages of Criticism and the Sciences of Man*, edited by Richard Macksey and Eugenio Donato. Baltimore: Johns Hopkins University Press, 1970, 247–70.

Dufrenne, Mikel. *Language and Philosophy.* Translated by Henry B. Veatch. Bloomington: Indiana University Press, 1963.

Du Marsais, César, and Pierre Fontanier. *Les tropes.* Edited by Gérard Genette. 2 vols. Geneva: Slatkine Reprints, 1967.

Eco, Umberto. *A Theory of Semiotics.* Bloomington: Indiana University Press, 1976.

Edie, James M. *Speaking and Meaning: The Phenomenology of Language.* Bloomington: Indiana University Press, 1976.

Ezergailis, Andrew. Rev. of *Metahistory: The Historical Imagination in Nineteenth-Century Europe* by Hayden V. White. *Clio* 5 (Winter 1976):235–45.

Fontanier, Pierre. *Les figures du discours.* Paris: Editions Flammarion, 1968.

Foucault, Michel. *The Archaeology of Knowledge.* New York: Pantheon, 1972.

———. *The Order of Things: An Archaeology of the Human Sciences.* 1971. New York: Vintage, 1973.

Frye, Northrop. *The Great Code: The Bible and Literature.* New York: Harcourt, Brace, Jovanovich, 1982.

Genette, Gérard. *Figures III.* Paris: Seuil, 1972.

Greimas, A.-J. *Semiotics and Language: An Analytical Dictionary.* Translated by Larry Crist et al. Bloomington: Indiana University Press, 1982.

———. *Structural Semantics: An Attempt at a Method.* Translated by Daniele McDowell, Ronald Schleifer, and Alan Velie. Lincoln: University of Nebraska Press, 1983.

———, and F. Rastier. "The Interaction of Semiotic Constraints." In *Game, Play, Literature*, edited by Jacques Ehrmann. Boston: Beacon, 1971, 86–105.

Gusdorf, Georges. *Speaking.* Translated by Paul T. Brockelman. Evanston, Ill.: Northwestern University Press, 1965.

Jakobson, Roman. "Closing Statement: Linguistics and Poetics." In *Style in Language*, edited by Thomas A. Sebeok. Cambridge: M.I.T. Press, 1960, 350–77.

———. "Two Aspects of Language and Two Types of Aphasic Disturbances." In Roman Jakobson and Morris Halle, *Fundamentals of Language*. The Hague: Mouton, 1956, 53–82.

Jameson, Fredric. "Figural Relativism, or the Poetics of Historiography." *Diacritics* 6 (Spring 1976):2–9.

———. *The Political Unconscious: Narrative as a Socially Symbolic Act.* Ithaca, N.Y.: Cornell University Press, 1981.

———. *The Prison-House of Language: A Critical Account of Stucturalism and Russian Formalism.* Princeton: Princeton University Press, 1972.

Kellner, Hans. "A Bedrock of Order: Hayden White's Linguistic Humanism." *History and Theory* 19: *Beiheft* 19 (1980):1–29.

———. "The Inflatable Trope as Narrative Theory: Structure or Allegory?" *Diacritics* 11 (March 1981):14–28.

———. "The Issue in the Bullrushes: A Reply to Wallace Martin." *Diacritics* 12 (Spring 1982):84–88.

Lacan, Jacques. *Écrits: A Selection*. Translated by Alan Sheridan. New York: Norton, 1977.

———. *The Four Fundamental Concepts of Psycho-Analysis*. Edited by Jacques-Alain Miller, and translated by Alan Sheridan. New York: Norton, 1978.

———. *Speech and Language in Psychoanalysis*. Translated, with notes and commentary, by Anthony Wilden. Baltimore: Johns Hopkins University Press, 1981.

Laplanche, J., and J.-B. Pontalis. *The Language of Psycho-Analysis*. Translated by Donald Nicholson-Smith. New York: Norton, 1973.

Lévi-Strauss, Claude. *The Savage Mind*. Chicago: University of Chicago Press, 1966.

Lodge, David. *The Modes of Modern Writing: Metaphor, Metonymy, and the Typology of Modern Literature*. Ithaca, N.Y.: Cornell University Press, 1977.

Man, Paul de. *Allegories of Reading*. New Haven: Yale University Press, 1979.

———. "Semiology and Rhetoric." *Diacritics* 3 (1973):27–33.

Martin, Wallace. "Floating an Issue of Tropes." *Diacritics* 12 (Spring 1982):75–83.

Mellard, James M. *The Exploded Form: The Modernist Novel in America*. Urbana: University of Illinois Press, 1980.

———. "Lacan and Faulkner: A Post-Freudian Analysis of Humor in the Fiction." In *Faulkner and Humor*, edited by Doreen Fowler and Ann J. Abadie. Jackson: University Presses of Mississippi, 1986, 198–220.

Merrell, Floyd. "Metaphor and Metonymy: A Key to Narrative Structure." *Language and Style* 11 (1978):146–63.

———. "Of Metaphor and Metonymy." *Semiotica* 31 (1980):289–307.

Metz, Christian. *The Imaginary Signifier: Psychoanalysis and the Cinema*. Translated by Celia Britton. Bloomington: Indiana University Press, 1982.

Miller, J. Hillis. "The Fiction of Realism: *Sketches by Boz, Oliver Twist,* and Cruikshank's Illustrations." In *Charles Dickens and George Cruikshank*, edited by J. Hillis Miller and David Borowitz. Los Angeles: Clark Memorial Library, 1971, 1–69.

Nelson, John S. Rev. of *Metahistory: The Historical Imagination in Nineteenth-Century Europe* by Hayden V. White. *History and Theory* 14 (1975):74–91.

Norrick, Neal R. *How Proverbs Mean: Semantic Studies in English Proverbs.* Trends in Linguistics: Studies and Monographs, 27. New York: Mouton, 1985.

———. *Semiotic Principles in Semantic Theory.* Amsterdam Studies in the Theory and History of Linguistic Science, series 4: Current Issues in Linguistic Theory, 20. Amsterdam: John Benjamins B.V., 1981.

Ragland-Sullivan, Ellie. *Jacques Lacan and the Philosophy of Psychoanalysis.* Urbana: University of Illinois Press, 1985.

———. "The Magnetism between Reader and Text: Prolegomena to a Lacanian Poetics." *Poetics* 13 (1984):381–406.

Rice, Donald, and Peter Schofer. *Rhetorical Poetics: Theory and Practice of Figural and Symbolic Reading in Modern French Literature.* Madison: University of Wisconsin Press, 1983.

Sallis, John C. "Phenomenology and Language." *The Personalist* 48.4 (Autumn 1967):490–508.

Schofer, Peter. "The Rhetoric of Displacement and Condensation." *Pre/Text* 3 (1982):9–29.

———, and Donald Rice. "Metaphor, Metonymy, and Synecdoche Revis(it)ed." *Semiotica* 20 (1977):121–49.

Shapiro, Michael, and Marianne Shapiro. *Hierarchy and Structure of Tropes.* Bloomington: Indiana University Press, 1976.

Silverman, Kaja. *The Subject of Semiotics.* New York: Oxford University Press, 1983.

Todorov, Tzvetan. *The Poetics of Prose.* Translated by Richard Howard. Ithaca, N.Y.: Cornell University Press, 1977.

———. *Theories of the Symbol.* Translated by Catherine Porter. Ithaca, N.Y.: Cornell University Press, 1982.

Vico, Giambattista. *The New Science.* Translated by Thomas G. Bergin and Max H. Fisch. Ithaca, N.Y.: Cornell University Press, 1968.

White, Hayden V. *Metahistory: The Historical Imagination in Nineteenth-Century Europe.* Baltimore: Johns Hopkins University Press, 1973.

———. "Method and Ideology in Intellectual History: The Case of Henry Adams." In *Modern European Intellectual History: Reappraisals and New Perspectives,* edited by Dominick LaCapra and Steven L. Kaplan. Ithaca, N.Y.: Cornell University Press, 1982, 280–310.

———. "Michel Foucault." In *Structuralism and Since: From Lévi-Strauss to Derrida,* edited by John Sturrock. Oxford: Oxford University Press, 1979, 81–115.

———. *Tropics of Discourse: Essays in Cultural Criticism.* Baltimore: Johns Hopkins University Press, 1978.

Williams, Linda. *Figures of Desire: A Theory and Analysis of Surrealist Film.* Urbana: University of Illinois Press, 1981.

Index

Adams, Henry: and *Mont-Saint-Michel and Chartes*, 80, 83; and other works, 75; as historian, 74–80; his eighteenth-century mode of thought, 65, 76–77; mentioned, vii, 60–88 *passim*, 90
Adams, John, 62
Adams, John Quincy, 62
Allison, David B., 11, 164
Aporia (doubt): and irony, 120
Aquinas, St. Thomas, 62, 82, 83
Archetypes, narrative (or emplotment), 96, 97–139
Art: and eschatology, 161
Ayala, Francisco J., 89

Backman, Melvin, 141
Barth, Karl, 151, 160
Barthes, Roland: and the symbol, 4; mentioned, 6, 11
Beauzée, N., 3
Bergin, Thomas G., 11, 34
Berkeley, George, 83
Bernanos, Georges, 140
Blackmur, R. P., 88, 90, 92
Bloom, Harold, viii
Bohn, Willard, 11
Borowitz, David, 11
Boston: as a trope for Adams, 63, 66, 67
Brockelman, Paul T., 36, 164
Brooks, Cleanth, 141
Burckhardt, Jacob, 23
Burke, Kenneth, vii, viii, x, 2, 10n, 13, 93, 94, 112–13, 140, 143, 144, 162

Cairns, Dorion, 164

Canaday, Nicholas, 59
Carlyle, Thomas: and tailor's dummy as trope, 87
Carroll, David, 30–32, 35
Cassirer, Ernst: and Man-as-trope, 87; mentioned, 2, 8, 36, 80, 90, 142, 143, 152, 159
Castration: and Oedipal theme, 54; complex, 45; in Lacan, 38, 43
Catachresis: as ironic technique, 121
Civil War: for Adams, 67–68
Comedy, 95–97, 115; as emplotment, 91; romantic, and tragic irony, 126; structure of, 117
Conder, John, 63, 76, 88, 89
Condillac, E. B. de, 3
Consciousness, 145, 147
Crane, Hart, 146, 147, 164
Croce, Benedetto, 23
Cummings, E. E., 165

Darwin, Charles: and evolution and natural selection, 81; his law of natural selection, 68
Darwinism: in *The Education of Henry Adams*, 69–73
Davis, Robert Con, 58
Deconstruction: theory of, in tropes, 7
Deism, 70
Derrida, Jacques: and metaphysics of origin, 4; mentioned, 4, 6, 7, 11, 164
Descartes, René, 83
Desire, structure of: in language, 38; metonymic linkages in, 50, 53; neurotic, and displacements, 45

171

Note on the Author

James M. Mellard is a professor of English at Northern Illinois University, DeKalb, where he has taught since 1967. A Ph.D. from the University of Texas, Mr. Mellard specializes in twentieth-century American literature, prose fiction, and the rhetoric of fiction. He is the author of numerous articles in such journals as *Journal of English and Germanic Philology*, *Modern Fiction Studies*, *Mississippi Quarterly*, and *PMLA*, and author, co-author, or editor of four books: *The Exploded Form: The Modernist Novel in America*; *Quaternion: Stories, Poems, Plays, Essays*; *The Authentic Writer: English Rhetoric and Composition*; and *Four Modes: A Rhetoric of Modern Fiction*. Continuing his interests in tropology, he is currently working on a book applying the psychoanalytic theories of Jacques Lacan to a variety of narrative texts.